Music in Elementary Education

Music in Elementary Education

Enjoy, Experience, and Learn

Marylee McMurray Lament

CLEVELAND STATE UNIVERSITY

Macmillan Publishing Co., Inc.
New York
Collier Macmillan Publishing
London

Copyright © 1976, Marylee McMurray Lament
Printed in the United States of America

Macmillan Publishing Co., Inc.
866 Third Avenue, New York, New York 10022

Collier Macmillan Canada, Ltd.

Library of Congress Cataloging in Publication Data

Lament, Marylee McMurray.
  Music in elementary education.

  Bibliography: p.
  1. School music—Instruction and study—United
States. 2. Music—Instruction and study—Juvenile.
I. Title.
MT3.U5L313   372.8'7   74-24365
ISBN 0-02-367340-0

Printing: 1 2 3 4 5 6 7 8   Year: 6 7 8 9 0 1 2

To my daughter, Claudia,
and my mother and father
with gratitude and affection for their
understanding and encouragement
throughout this endeavor.

Credits

Grateful acknowledgment is given to the following publishers for permission to use and adapt copyrighted material.

Alfred A. Knopf, Inc., from *The Treasure Bag*, Lean Barksdale, ed., 1947:

> "Counting-Out Rhyme"

Allyn and Bacon, Inc., from the *This Is Music* textbook series, copyright 1961:

> "Are You Sleeping?" from Book 2
> "Navajo Happy Song" from Book 3
> "This Old Man" from Book 2 of *This Is Music for Today*

American Book Company, from the ABC *Music Series*, from *Music for Young Americans* (Kindergarten), 1963:

> "Roll That Red Ball"

Cooperative Recreation Service, Inc., Delaware, Ohio:

from Kit V, *Joyful Singing*

> "Zum Gali" (no date)

from *Song Sampler No. 1*, January, 1956

> "Kum Ba Ya"
> "Music Alone Shall Live" (Himmel Und Erde)
> "Shalom Chavereim"

from *Work and Sing*, an International Songbook, 1948

> "Ma Bella Bimba"
> "She'll Be Comin' Round the Mountain"

from *Joyful Singing* (no date)

    "Round of Thanks" (For Health and Strength)

from *Manitowoc Sings* (no date)

    "Weggis Song"

from *Pocket Songs* (no date)

    "My Hat"

from *Aloha Sings*, 1948

    "Aloha Oe"

from *Song Sampler No. 3*, July 1956 (Folk Songs of Asia)

    "Cherry Blossoms" (Sakura)

from *East–West Songs*, 1960

    "El Coqui"
    "Saturday Night"

from *English Country Dances of Today*, 1948

    "Irish Washerwoman"

G. Schirmer, Inc., from *36 South Carolina Spirituals* by Carl Diton, copyright 1930, 1957 by G. Schirmer, Inc. Used by permission:

    "The Angel Band"

Ginn and Company, from *Singing on Our Way*, from *Our Singing World* series, © Copyright, 1959, 1957, 1949, by Ginn and Company. Used with permission:

    "The Bus"

M. Baron Company, from the *Collection of Original Calypso Songs of the West Indies*, 1943:

    "Tinga Layo"

McGraw-Hill, Inc., from *Singing Fun*, by Lucille F. Wood and Louise B. Scott © 1954:

    "My Hands"

National 4–H Service Committee, Chicago, Illinois, 1968. Assigned to National 4–H Service Committee and © 1933:

    "Sing for the Wide, Wide Fields"

Plymouth Music Co., Inc.

    "African Noel"

Prentice-Hall, Inc., from *Growing with Music*, Related Arts Edition Book 7 by Harry R. Wilson, Walter Ehret, Alice M. Knuth, Edward J. Hermann, and

Acknowledgments

A project of this scope can be completed only with the generous cooperation of many people. I would, therefore, like to thank Dr. Charles Walton of Columbia University for his valued counseling in the compilation of the theoretical aspects in this book; Mrs. Kathleen F. Fassig for evaluating the manuscript with reference to the responsibility of the elementary classroom teacher in guiding children through exploratory experiences in music; the students and teachers in my methods classes at Central Michigan University, Mount Pleasant, during the 1971–1972 academic year; the first-year art students of Professor Swanstrom at Central Michigan; and Mrs. Mary Lou Jones and her pupils at the Pike Central Elementary School, Indianapolis, Indiana.

Mr. Dale Lucas cooperated in promoting a pilot project with me for all pupils in grade 3 in a Classroom Keyboard Experience Program, and Mr. Joseph Carter provided materials and facilities for recording research and experimental data.

I also extend appreciation to Rhythm Band, Inc., Fort Worth, Texas, for counsel and permission to use illustrations and catalogue descriptions of classroom instruments; to the staff at the School of Music, Ball State University, Muncie, Indiana, for welcoming me to audit an advanced seminar in theoretical study and to a demonstration adapting the Carl Orff approach to music education in the American public school; and to the College of Education, Ohio State University, Columbus, Ohio, for the use of facilities, research data, and texts pertaining to all areas of music education.

Marylee McMurray Lament

Contents

Chapter 1

Introduction: Music Education for Today's Children

Teaching music is a craft. It can be as exciting for you as you want it to be, whether you are an experienced classroom teacher, music specialist, novice teacher, or teacher in training. If you, with your children, will become totally involved in the musical experiences presented in this text, significant personal satisfaction will follow.

Education for today's youth requires a new spectrum of ideas of leadership and guidance, an essential part of which is the teacher's enthusiasm to motivate the children to explore concepts and make discoveries for themselves. Therefore, it can be stated that teaching is a creative challenge—it is working with people to achieve a specific objective. In music education that objective is a simple one: to understand how music is made.

A gradual accumulation of knowledge of music can be achieved best through the *developmental* approach (moving from the simple to the complex). Samples of procedures and lessons are offered throughout this text to emphasize the value of *reinforcement* of a learned concept. Ways in which children can become involved actively in exploring music through the activities of listening, singing, free movement, creating, playing, and reading are presented.

ORGANIZATION OF THE TEXT

The repertoire of songs selected for this study is a generally familiar one. It displays a variety that illustrates the concepts to be explored. This conceptual growth pattern is structured as a simple-to-complex procedure most applicable and beneficial to children of primary school age. The procedure is consistent within each presentation. However, the material in its entirety does not necessarily move consistently from the simple to the complex. Each of the elements of music is discussed (MELODY, RHYTHM, HARMONY, FORM, DYNAMICS, TEMPO, and TONE COLOR).

Suggestions for exploring the same concepts on the intermediate level are included as examples of how to implement the developmental procedure. These suggestions are not presented necessarily in structured exploratory procedures as they are on the primary level. As a result, discovery techniques are left to the discretion of the individual teacher within his or her unique situation, including that of special education.

The suggested listening activities that appear at the end of each section are based on the RCA Adventures in Music record series.* Reference to recordings in the text are based on elementary concepts a child can be expected to learn after listening a minimal number of times. Therefore, the exploratory devices and questioning techniques leading to discovery are broad and objective in scope. The teacher can refer to the RCA Teacher's Guides that accompany each volume of the series for a more thorough and complete analysis of each musical composition. In addition, the Appendix at the end of this text furnishes the names and addresses of publishers of music education textbooks and choral music. An Index of Musical Terms is also included.

The developmental approach emphasized in this book fosters a spirit of sharing between teacher and student: together we enjoy, together we experience, together we learn. Thus, music education can emerge as an exciting, satisfying, and inspirational area in the school curriculum. For these reasons, suggestions for integrating a music education program into the school curriculum are an essential part of this text.

---

*Individual recordings of these compositions also are available from record dealers.

Chapter 2

The Role of Music in Early Childhood

There is an emphasis in general education today on studying and understanding early childhood development that is the result of the increasing demand for, and appearance of, nursery schools, Head Start programs, and day-care centers for preschool children. Educators are striving to consider all of the physical and mental characteristics of the young child of two to four years of age to serve subsequently as a basis for establishing and justifying strategies and guidance techniques in educating the very young.

It is the purpose in this chapter to do that exactly: to consider the characteristics of early childhood to determine how such activities as singing and dancing (free movement), and listening to, playing, and creating music can contribute to the over-all development of the young child.

Chronological age is not the sole determinant of whether a specific activity will be appropriate for a child. Sarah H. Leeper, in *Good Schools for Young Children*, states:

> Because the child is not ready to participate in one activity (such as clapping in time to music) the teacher may decide that he should not be forced and leave him alone. . . . [however] the teacher can arrange many worthwhile experiences. There should be opportunities to climb, run, and jump which can help the child gain control of the large muscles. As he experiments with body movement he will set his own tempo.[1]

---

[1] Sarah Hammond Leeper et al., *Good Schools for Young Children,* 3rd ed. (New York: Macmillan, 1974), p. 375.

Also, A. Theodore Tellstrom notes that:

> Music, as other subjects, must be presented within a cognitive framework, so that the child can discover the structure that leads to meaning and understanding. Verbal symbols must give way to the young child's nonsymbolic way of knowing. A multiple sensory approach must be used to include not only the visual and tactile but the auditory and kinesthetic as well. . . .
>
> Music can be of particular assistance in helping children learn how to learn because so much of that training can take place initially through sensorymotor experiences.[2]

The attempt to plan for musical experiences in the growth process, keeping the statements of these authorities in mind, will benefit from a compilation of a list of the prominent general characteristics of growth and development of the two year old child. One should then proceed chronologically to the four year old, relating suggestions for incorporating the aforementioned musical activities into a developmental program of learning. In that way, the emphasis will be on general patterns of growth and not on the specific achievements of individual children.

"Norms developed through years of child study serve only as a relative guide, indicating what may generally be true of many children in each group."[3] Thus, even though nursery schools usually cater to three and four year olds, an understanding of the two year old will be helpful in planning and building a music program for three and four year old children.

The values of implementing a music education program into early childhood development are numerous. An example of a long-term objective might be that musical experiences offer a readiness program for the very young child encouraging total involvement in such music activities as listening, singing, creating, playing instruments, and dancing (free movement).

In an article appearing in *Early Childhood*, Ethelouise Carpenter maintains that:

> Readiness evolves from practice with the environment, people, and materials which promote the desire to look beyond the commonplace, beyond self-interest: to reach a level of physical maturity, of social competence, of emotional control, and of mental alertness. Readiness for reading, as for anything else, is built on such experiences over a long period of time. In nursery school and kindergarten the child is helped to listen to others, to wait his turn, to do critical thinking, to take responsibility to the degree that he needs these competencies right now in order to be a contributing member of his present group. . . . The plan of living in preschool groups makes possible a comfortable evolvement of self and readiness for what is and what will be. It is an environment of exploration, not of heated preparation.[4]

---

[2] A. Theodore Tellstrom, *Music in American Education* (New York: Holt, 1971), pp. 281–282.

[3] Adeline McCall, *This Is Music for Kindergarten and Nursery School* (Boston: Allyn, 1966), p. 8.

[4] Ethelouise Carpenter, "Readiness Is Being," in *Early Childhood—Crucial Years for Learning*, ed. by Margaret Rasmussen (Washington, D. C.: Association for Childhood Education International, 1966), pp. 57–58.

Also, because concept formation is of major importance in early childhood development, another long-term objective might be that musical experiences contribute to the thought processes from which the formation of concepts evolves.

Similarly, relating early childhood development to intellectual growth, Rose Murkerji states:

> These are the years when curiosity impels a child to reach out into his environment . . . to try to know. His primary strategy for intellectual growth is active, manipulative, and sensory. He utilizes material and active intercourse to build his conceptual scheme of the world.[5]

Furthermore, Emma Louise Widner insists that:

> Concepts are the nucleus of a child's thinking process. They represent his attempts to organize his own personal environmental experiences into relationships invested with meaning for him. Concepts can be formed, clarified, and extended by provision for direct experiences, multisensory impressions, motor manipulation, problem solving, creating, and questioning. Through involvement in the following types of activities, young children's early beginnings of concept formation will grow in fertile ground. Included in activities are:
>
> > Music, recordings, dances, games, and rhythms.
> > Audiovisual materials—films, filmstrips, tapes, television, photographs.
> > Puppets, dramatization, role playing, and play activities.[6]

Therefore, in planning musical activities for young children, remember to fit the song into their environment by substituting words with which the children will be most familiar.

Example:

THE MUFFIN MAN*

English

Oh, do you know the Muf - fin Man, The
Muf - fin Man, the Muf - fin Man; Oh, do you know the
Muf - fin Man, That lives in Dru - ry Lane?

*Public domain.

[5] Rose Mukerji, "Roots in Early Childhood for Continuous Learning," in Rasmussen, op. cit., p. 18.

[6] Emma Louise Widner, *The Critical Years: Early Childhood at the Crossroads* (Scranton, Pa.: International Textbook Company, 1970), pp. 33–34.

When singing this song in a class in New York City or any other large metropolis, it might be more appropriate to substitute another name for the "Muffin Man." The children might relate more logically to the pretzel man, the hot dog man, or the balloon man. In a suburban area or a small residential locality, children might be more familiar with the ice cream man, the grocery man, or the bakery man.

The teacher who has initiative and imagination will strive to make the songs meaningful to the children. There is great flexibility possible in music and time spent with music in the classroom can be an exciting experience when the maturational needs of the children are being met by the level and content of the music.

As Evangeline Burgess states:

> New experiences are more readily assimilated when built on the familiar. ... Accelerated learning of abstract concepts without sufficient related direct experience may result in symbols without meaning.[7]

Thus, a picture of a dog

reminds the children that dogs make sounds: bow-wow, wooo-ooooof, eyiiipppppppp, grrr-rrrr-rr. This may simultaneously remind them of a song about a puppy dog, such as "Oh Where, Oh Where Has My Little Dog Gone?"

EARLY CHILDHOOD—THE TWO YEAR OLD

General Characteristics of Early Growth

1. Single words are used: "single words are also used to indicate a state of things."[8] For example, "raining" means "cannot go outdoors to play" or "hot" means "the cereal is too hot to eat now."
2. Two year olds can walk and push and pull toys quite competently.
3. The urge to explore and discover individually may end in the child having a temper tantrum if limitations are placed upon the extent to which he is allowed to explore for himself.[9]

---

[7]Evangeline Burgess, *Values in Early Childhood Education* (Washington, D.C.: NEA 1965), p. 35.
[8]John Gabriel, *Children Growing Up*, 3rd Ed.; (London: University of London Press Ltd., 1969), p. 198.
[9]Ibid., pp. 198–202.

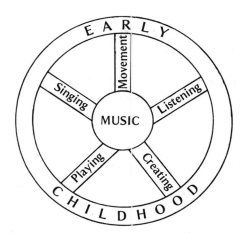

The Two Year Old

4. "They laugh with others; they are tender with a baby and will touch and stroke it; they show a sturdy independence and resist too much restriction of their movements."[10]

5. "In parallel play each child pursues his own activity, even though children are together in the same room. This is typical of a group of two year olds. On observing such a group you will see, for example, that one is pulling a little trolley; another is attempting simple manoeuvres with a toy car; a third is pounding clay . . . ."[11]

6. The two year old tends to show imitation and an awareness of others.

7. The two year old displays imitation in movement: running, jumping, and swinging to music.

8. The two year old will walk with arms outstretched and will identify "up, down, and 'round" using arm movements.

9. The language of the two year old is spontaneous and rhythmical in its repetitiveness.

10. The two year old is ritualistic; he likes to hear the same song or story over and over again.[12]

[10] Ibid., p. 202.
[11] Ibid., p. 218.
[12] Hope M. Heimann et al., "Profile, the Child 3–5," mimeographed (Atlanta, Ga.: Music in Early Childhood Study, MENC National Commission on Instruction, pp. 1–2.

Characteristics of Music for the Two Year Old[13]

1. The music should have a strong pulse and a definite pattern.
2. The different tonal sounds of instruments, as well as vocal intonation, should be experimented with in the classroom.
3. Instruments should be introduced within the context of a musical activity.
4. The daily repetition of very simple familiar songs is advisable. Avoid introducing new material too soon.
5. Music that encourages spontaneous body movements (bouncing, jumping, running, rocking, swaying) should be selected for the classroom.

Note:

The musical activities that follow are suggested as most appropriate for the two year old. The general characteristics of the growth pattern of this age child should have been previously recorded by the class teacher to serve as a basis for initiating these musical experiences.

The songs included here are illustrated in directional word patterns to guide the teacher in the up-and-down movement of the melody and to motivate the teacher to create his or her own melody for the descriptive words of the song. Composing original melodies is another example of implementing flexibility in presenting music in the classroom. However, for easy reference, a definite melody for each song is notated on the staff beneath the symbolic illustration. The songs are arranged in developmental sequence.

I Title of Song: Up, Down, and 'Round

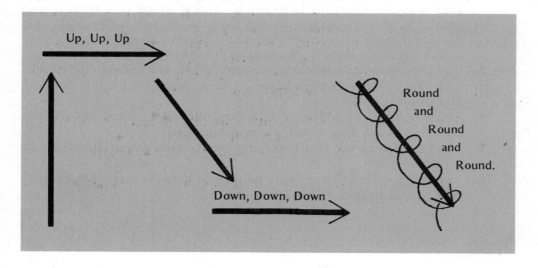

[13] McCall, op. cit., p. 9.

UP, DOWN, AND 'ROUND*

M. Lament

Up, Up, Up;   Down, down, down; Round and round and   round.

*Original.

■ *Suggested Musical Class Activities for "Up, Down, and 'Round"*

Singing: Sing the repeated words to discover when the MELODY is high (up), and low (down).

Playing: Place bells on wrists or ankles so they jingle when reaching up, bending low, and running 'round and 'round.

Dancing (free movement): Bounce or jump (up), squat or bend (down), and run freely on the words "'round and 'round."

Creating: Dramatize the words by reaching (for up) and sitting (for down). Run in circles or roll over for " 'round and 'round and 'round."

Listening: Shake bells or tap a drum while others sing the song. Listen and react to the words as they are sung through expressive body movement. (See Dancing.)

II Title of Song: Touch Your Head

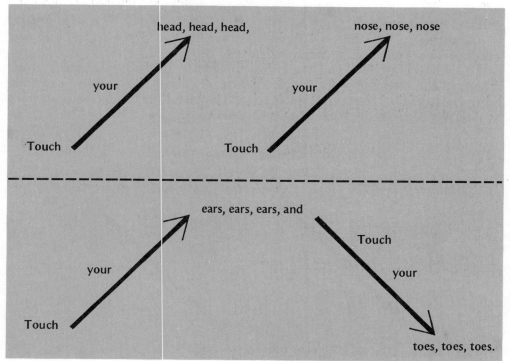

TOUCH YOUR HEAD*

M. Lament

Touch your   head,   head,   head; Touch your   nose, nose, nose;

Touch your ears,   ears,   ears; And   touch   your   toes, toes,   toes.

*Original.

■ *Suggested Musical Class Activities for "Touch Your Head"*

Singing: Discover the repeated melody patterns by singing, discover the repeated word pattern through dramatization, and discover the direction of the MELODY by singing and dramatizing the rise and fall of the melody line.

Playing: Tonal sounds can be discriminated by having one child (or leader) play on a wood block throughout the song while the rest of the class sings the song. On the repeat, second child can play a drum or bells throughout the song.

Dancing (free movement): Touch and point to parts of the body mentioned in the song. One child, acting as leader, could have his body movements imitated by the class.

Creating: Dramatize the words of the song and make up and add new words, such as eyes, mouth, arms, legs, and so on.

Listening: Choose percussion instruments to play after listening to the sounds of the bells and wood block together; or choose any available combination of instruments to play. Respond to the words of the song as they are sung by pointing to the head, eyes, and ears. (See Dancing.)

III Title of Song: Bounce the Ball

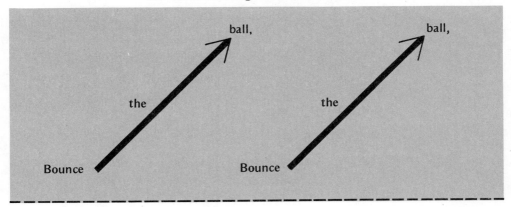

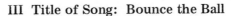

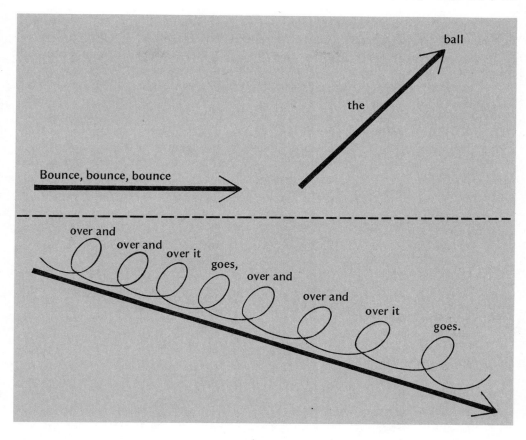

BOUNCE THE BALL*

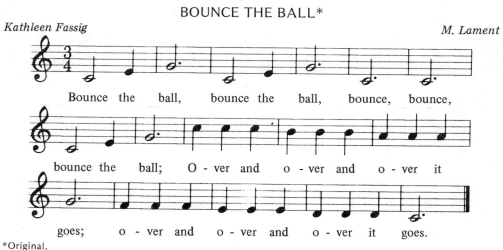

Kathleen Fassig

M. Lament

Bounce the ball, bounce the ball, bounce, bounce,

bounce the ball; O - ver and o - ver and o - ver it

goes; o - ver and o - ver and o - ver it goes.

*Original.

■ *Suggested Musical Class Activities for "Bounce the Ball"*

Singing: Sing the repeated words and melody patterns.
Playing: Tap a drum or tone block whenever the word *bounce* is sung.

Dancing (free movement): Pretend to be bouncing a large ball in a standing position on the word "bounce"; or pretend to be rolling a ball or tapping a balloon. Substitute these pretend motions by using a real ball or balloon and making it "roll over" just as a ball rolls "over and over and over" in the song.

Creating: Make up new words after the song is known well, such as, "roll the ball" or "tap the balloon."

Listening: Listen for the specific words "bounce" and "ball" and respond to them rhythmically by pretending to see the motion of bouncing a ball. Listen for a change in MELODY for "over and over and over it goes," and react by rolling the body or the ball or balloon over and over until the end of the MELODY. (See Dancing.)

IV Title of Song: Rockety-Roo

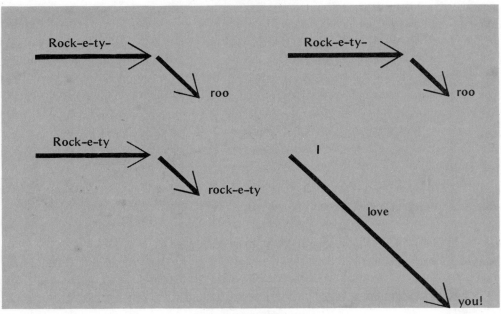

ROCKETY-ROO*

Kathleen Fassig   *M. Lament*

Rock - e - ty roo,   rock - e - ty roo,

rock - e - ty rock - e - ty   I   love you!

*Original.

■ *Suggested Musical Class Activities for "Rockety-Roo"*

Singing: Discover the repetition of "rockety-roo" on the natural intonation of the childhood chant (the descending minor third interval), as illustrated here on the musical staff:

Playing: Pretend to be riding rocking horses. Tapping coconut shells together or tapping a tone block with a mallet will simulate the sound of horses' hooves.

Dancing (free movement): Pretend to be riding rocking horses, moving in time with the music, or, have the children sing while actually riding rocking horses.

Creating: Make up new words, such as

Listening: Quietly listen and then respond to the rhythmic flow of the MELODY by rocking to and fro. (See Dancing.)

V Title of Song: "Sleepy Time"

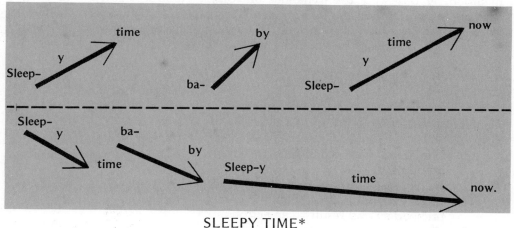

SLEEPY TIME*

M. Lament

Sleep - y time ba - by, sleep - y time now;

Sleep - y time ba - by, sleep - y time now.

*Original.

■ *Suggested Musical Class Activities for "Sleepy Time"*

Singing: Sing the words softly to discover how this lullaby rocking song is different from the rocking horse song. *The rocking horse song is sung vigorously which is in contrast to the quiet serenity of "Sleepy Time."* Discover the repetition of the easy words. (The teacher can point out that the direction of the MELODY is up and down mostly by step, see p. 127.)

Playing: Choose a triangle or large drum to tap lightly during the song. (The teacher can guide the child in his or her choice of an instrument through questioning techniques: Why would you choose the sound of a triangle rather than a drum for this rocking song? Is this rocking song a "sleepy" song? When it's sleepy time, does mother ever rock you? When it's sleepy time would you like to hear the "boom, boom" of a drum?)

Dancing (free movement): Pretend you are "sleepy babies" rocking yourselves to sleep while singing this song.

Creating: Pretend you are riding your hobby horses while rocking and singing; then, pretend that you are sleepy from riding and sway or rock while you sing "Sleepy Time." (Is your rocking motion different now? Is it as fast as when you were "riding" your horses?)

Listening: Listen for the differences in the rocking songs "Rockety-Roo" and "Sleepy Time." (Guide the children to have them identify the differences in mood by observing the dynamics of volume (loud and soft) while singing first one song and then the other immediately after. Also guide the children to listen for the beginning of each song: hold your arms high or low when starting to sing—"Rockety-Roo" begins high (up) and "Sleepy Time" begins low (down).

THE THREE YEAR OLD

General Characteristics of Early Growth

1. The three year old begins to enjoy group play.
2. He or she likes to plan ahead—the three year old is already able to comprehend an end result to an action.
3. There is a vocabulary increase.[14] "Children of this age chatter a lot: they chatter away to mother or to any available adult."[15]
4. The three year old enjoys fantasy and imaginative play.
5. In this age group there is an increase in the span of attention, but repetition remains necessary.

The Three Year Old

6. The three year old looks at picture and story books and can react to verbal cues.

---

[14] McCall, loc. cit.
[15] Gabriel, *Children Growing Up*, p. 202.

7. The child feels a continued need for exploration and experimentation.[16]
8. "Certainly by three children have turned the corner away from baby-hood and are 'on the straight' with the kindergarten and the Infant School ahead of them. Before the year is out they begin to talk about going to school and to look forward to it."[17]
9. "By three one sees more associative play in which activities are still individual but where there is interaction, the recognition of one child by another and simple exchanges between them."[18]
10. The three year old listens attentively to music and shows an interest in the instruments being played: bells, piano, flutes, and so on.
11. Jumping, running, rocking, walking, rolling, galloping, and clapping are favorite activities at this age.[19] (Skipping is sometimes substituted for galloping.)

Characteristics of Music for the Three Year Old

1. The attention span at this age is approximately ten or fifteen minutes for group music.[20]
2. It is advisable to acquaint children with the sounds of classroom instruments, possibly one at a time but never out of context.

Example:

In the song "Hickory, Dickory, Dock," the words directly coincide with the tick, tock of the tone block. The children can be guided to listen to the sounds of bells and the tone block and then decide which sound is more appropriate for "Hickory, Dickory, Dock."

3. The child at this age should not be coerced into participating in group musical activities. If the child becomes restless, he should feel free to leave the group.
4. Movement and dramatization of songs should be encouraged. The three year old should be made to feel as uninhibited as possible.
5. Playful, active, humorous songs which are accompanied by one or more percussion instruments are of great interest to this age group.
6. At this age the child can also be directed to listen attentively to environmental sounds.

Note:

The musical activities that follow are suggested as most appropriate for the three year old. The general characteristics of the growth pattern of this age child as will have been previously recorded by the teacher will serve as a basis for initiating these musical experiences. The songs here are arranged in a developmental sequence.

[16] McCall, loc. cit.
[17] Gabriel, op. cit., p. 202.
[18] Ibid., p. 218.
[19] McCall, op. cit., p. 9
[20] Ibid.

I Title of Song: " 'Round the Table"

'ROUND THE TABLE*

Traditional tune: " 'Round the Village"

1. Round and round the ta - ble,   Round and round the ta - ble,

Round and round the ta - ble,   As   we have done be - fore.

2. Let's sit down and sing now, etc.

3. Stand and wave good-bye now, etc.

*Public domain.

■ *Suggested Musical Class Activities for* " *'Round the Table"*

Singing: Repeated word patterns can be discovered through singing. Discovering melody patterns is done by following the rise and fall of the MELODY by reaching on high sounds (tones) and bending on low sounds (tones).

Playing: To identify the tonal sounds of the various classroom instruments have one child choose any instrument to play or tap throughout the singing of the song while the others describe its tonal characteristics.

Example:

The sound resulting from tapping a drum with the open hand might be described by the children as a banging or booming sound, whereas the shaking of bells might be described as producing a ringing or jingling sound.

Note:

Because vocabulary at this age is still limited, the children may choose to imitate vocally the sound of the instrument rather than describe its sound by giving it its word label.

Creating: Make up other ideas or motions that can be performed around or at the table. Through questioning techniques guide the children in remembering activities performed at the table throughout the day, such as coloring, handcraft, or art work of any kind; looking at picture books; enjoying refreshments, and the like. Then incorporate these ideas into the singable MELODY of this familiar song:

We will look at picture books.
We will look at picture books.
We will look at picture books.
As we have done before.

Dancing (free movement): Dramatize the directive movement expressed in each verse of the song:

1. All join hands and walk around the table.
2. Sit down while singing.
3. Stand and wave good-bye.

Listening: Listen to the words of the song and respond accordingly. After listening to one or more different classroom instruments, choose the instrument you want to play throughout the performance of the song.

Note:

It is recommended that these activities be rotated among the children to give everyone an opportunity to explore and discover for himself.

II Title of Song: "Hear the Drum"

HEAR THE DRUM*

M. Lament

1. Boom, boom, boom, boom, hear the drum
Boom, boom, boom, boom, rum, tum, tum.

2. Tick, tock, tick, tock, goes the clock, etc.
3. Oooo-oo-oooo, Ooooo-oo-ooooo hear the wind, etc.

*Original.

■ *Suggested Musical Class Activities for "Hear the Drum"*

Singing: Discover the repetition of word patterns and the similarity between the sound made by an object in the song and the word used to describe the sound: the boom of the drum, the tick, tock of the clock, and the oooo-oo-oooo of the wind.

Playing and Creating: Make up other verses related to the sounds in the environment. Explore the sounds of classroom instruments to discover which ones are closely associated to the sound of an object being sung about in a specific verse.

Example:

When sand blocks are rubbed together they produce a sound imitative of walking in autumn leaves (crunchy); or, for children who spend summer vacations at the sea shore, multiple sets of sand blocks when rubbed together produce a sound imitative of ocean waves rolling in to shore (swishy).

Dancing (free movement): Dramatize each verse of the song through free body movements. (Using large nylon or silk scarves can enhance the drama of movement, such as of the wind or the ocean's waves rolling into shore). The teacher's questioning techniques can serve as a guide in determining the action of object to be imitated: How does the wind blow? Can you make the sound of the wind with your voice? Does the wind blow straight ahead all of the time or does it blow up and down? By using your arms and your body can you show us how the wind blows on a cold winter day in a snow storm? How does the wind blow the flowers in a garden on a warm summer day?)

Listening: Listen quietly to the sounds of the room and to those outside and then sing together about these sounds of the environment.

III Title of Song: "Hear the Bells"

HEAR THE BELLS*

Austrian folk song

Hear the bells, hear their song. Ding ding dong,

Ding ding dong; Ding dong, ding dong ding dong.

*Public domain. Reprinted with permission from Ginn and Company.

■ *Suggested Musical Class Activities for "Hear the Bells"*

Singing: Note that the MELODY here moves up and down (in steps) but does not go as high as in "Looby-Loo" (p. 21); note, too, that many words are repeated.

Playing: Choose classroom instruments with bell-like sounds to play at will throughout the entire song; or only on such key words as "ding, dong," "bells," and "song."

Creating: Make up new words to sing to the same MELODY, but relate the words to environmental bell sounds heard daily, such as "Hear the door bell [chime], Hear it ring," or "Hear the church bell, Hear it ring," or, if necessary, alter the melodic RHYTHM to fit the RHYTHM of the words (syllables of words) that the children suggest they sing.

Example:

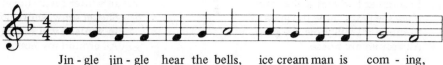

Jin - gle jin - gle hear the bells, ice cream man is com - ing,

Rin - gle jin - gle hear them ring, Rin - gle jin - gle jing jing.

Dancing (free movement): Dramatize the movement or sound of bells: church bells suggest big body movements for reaching and bending to high and low sounds; jingle bells suggest small body movements for bouncing or jigging up and down; and door chimes suggest slow body movements to dramatize the low to high sounds of the chimes as they are being played on resonator bells.

Listening: Listen to the different sounds of the classroom instruments and then choose the sounds that relate best to the words of the song. Use large cymbals tapped with rubber mallets for church bells; use bells on a stick or wristband to suggest the ice cream man or Santa Claus; and use several resonator bells of different pitches to correspond to the sound of door chimes. (The bells can be played individually with a rubber mallet.)

IV Title of Song: "My Hoop House"

MY HOOP HOUSE*†

M. Lament

1. Come and see my hoop house, my hoop house, my hoop house,

Come and see my hoop house, I live there all year 'round.

*Original.

†A hula hoop can be used as a hoop house or one can be constructed easily from vinyl or wood framing that measures 1 yard in diameter. This dimension will give the children enough room to perform activities inside the hoop. Lightweight construction materials are suggested so that the hoop can be manipulated easily and stored on hooks on the wall of the classroom.

2. In springtime I will plant the flowers,
   Plant the flowers, plant the flowers.
   In springtime I will plant the flowers
   All around my house.

3. In summer I will mow the grass,
   Mow the grass, mow the grass.
   In summer I will mow the grass
   All around my house.

4. In autumn I will rake the leaves,
   Rake the leaves, rake the leaves.
   In autumn I will rake the leaves
   All around my house.

5. In winter I will shovel snow,
   Shovel snow, shovel snow.
   In winter I will shovel snow
   All around my house.

■ *Suggested Musical Class Activities for "My Hoop House"*

Singing: Discover the word repetition in this song. Some of the same words are sung both low and high.

Encourage tonal memory by playing games. Intone "Come and see my hoop house" while the children continue to sing "My hoop house, my hoop house," etc. Observe the word patterns that are also repeated melody patterns: "Come and see my hoop house."

Playing: Choose a different classroom instrument to play during each verse. (As the children mature the teacher can guide them to the realization that different sounding instruments can imitate the sound of the activity performed in each verse.)

Example:

The "swish" sound produced by rubbing sand blocks together (and *not* the jingling sound of jingle bells) is similar to the sound of raking or sweeping.

Creating: Make up more verses to reflect the daily activities performed *inside* the house and dramatize the activities while singing new verses. (Encourage the children to think for themselves and to express their own ideas by posing such leading questions as "What could we do inside our hoop house to keep it clean?" Possible answers here are "We could mop the floor"; "We could sweep the floor"; "We could dust the room"; "We could paint the wall."

Children will respond to the question according to their experiences observing the performance of daily household chores.)

Dancing (free movement): Dramatize all the activities performed inside and outside the hoop house, as expressed in each verse of the song. (Some children will spontaneously perform the activity rhythmically.)

Listening: Listen for the words in each verse that are associated with a specific activity and then simultaneously dramatize the activity through free movement. (See Dancing.)

V Title of Song: "Looby-Loo"

LOOBY-LOO*

Traditional

1. Here we go Loo-by-loo, Here we go Loo-by-light,
Here we go Loo-by-loo, All on a Sat-ur-day night.___ I put my hand in,___ I put my hand out,___ I give my hand a shake, shake, shake, And turn my-self a-bout.___

2. I put my other hand in, etc.   3. I put my foot in, etc.
4. I put my other foot in, etc.   5. I put my head in, etc.
6. I put my whole self in, etc.

*Public domain.

Singing Game

All join hands and form a circle. Keep the circle while singing the chorus: "Here we go looby-loo." On the words "Saturday Night," stand still and face the center of the circle and sing the verse:

1. I put my hand in (reach one hand and arm in toward the center
    of the circle)
    I put my hand out (stretch an arm and hand outside and away
        from the center of the circle)
    I give my hand a shake, shake, shake
    And turn myself about.

Note:

To avoid confusion in teaching children the difference between right and left (which is a complex concept at this age), merely substitute words in the subsequent verses as follows:

2. I put my other hand in
3. I put my foot in
4. I put my other foot in

5. I put my head in
6. I put my whole self in

■ *Suggested Musical Class Activities for "Looby-Loo"*

Singing: Discover the repetition of word and melody patterns in this song. Observe that the syllable "loo" goes up; consequently, every time "loo" is sung, everyone in the class should reach their arms high and then lower them to their sides for the rest of the song.

Playing: Divide the class into two groups. Have group 1 tap large and small drums with the open hand to provide a rhythmic accompaniment to "Looby-Loo." Have group 2 sing "Looby-Loo" to the drum accompaniment provided by group 1.

Creating: Pretend to be squirrels, rabbits, cats, dogs, or any familiar animals and move in a circle singing "Looby-Loo" as the animal of your choice would move.

Example:

A rabbit hops; a dog walks; and a horse trots. Make up new verses related to the animal while increasing the song's vocabulary:

7. I put my paw in and shake it all about, or
8. I put my tail in and swish it all about

Dancing (free movement): Dramatize the meaning of the words of the various verses and react freely to the animal movements by using the whole body.

Listening: Respond spontaneously to the words of the song as they are sung, by listening for the key words.

THE FOUR YEAR OLD

General Characteristics of Early Growth

1. Children of this age have now acquired considerable physical and verbal dexterity as well as the ability to socialize with more ease.
2. Children of this age begin to have fun with speech since their vocabulary is gradually expanding. They enjoy playing games with words, especially discovering words that rhyme as well as words that are repeated in a song or poem.

The Four Year Old

3. The four year old finds pleasure in telling tall stories and oftentimes becomes more creative and imaginative as the spontaneous "yarn" proves to be of immediate interest to his listeners. This art of "story-telling" is also reflective of his growing capacity for becoming more creative and original in his manner of playing games and engaging in spontaneous conversation.

4. By four, the child desires to venture into cooperative play experiences and of special interest is dramatizing the social roles of familiar people to him, such as the postman, grocer, policeman, carpenter, plumber, window washer, doctor, and so forth. The four year old can easily become immersed in role playing the daily chores of mother and those of dad when he returns from work.[21]

Characteristics of Music for the Four Year Old

The following is a list of some musical activities appropriate to the four year old.

1. To encourage listening, at times the teacher should accompany the children's singing instrumentally, on the ukelele, guitar, autoharp, or bells, and so forth.

2. Also, to increase the attention span, the use of high quality recordings of songs and instrumental music is suggested. (Some inexpensive recordings of well-orchestrated and commendably performed nursery songs, folk songs, and current songs of interest are available in most novelty stores.)

3. Continue to permit children to explore and discover for themselves appropriate classroom instruments to accompany their singing and dancing.

4. A variety of songs to correspond with the children's interests should be included in the daily curriculum of the nursery school: action songs, echo songs, answer-back songs, game songs, and the like, all of which are appropriate for encouraging mental alertness.

5. Songs and poems appropriate for dramatization are of special interest to children of this age.[22]

6. Regarding movement, McCall suggests that the teacher "Continue as with three year olds, adding marching, skipping, stamping, hopping, sliding, crawling, swinging, whirling, shaking, nodding, walking on tiptoe, flopping, and bending."[23]

1 Title of Song: "Did You Ever See a Lassie?"

Singing Game:

All join hands and form a circle with one child in the center. Move in a circle while singing the song until words "go this way and that." At that point, the child in the center performs a motion and everyone in circle drops hands and imitates the motion (claps his hands or shakes his foot, etc.).

---

[21] Gabriel, op. cit., pp. 205–218.
[22] McCall, op. cit., p. 9.
[23] Ibid.

DID YOU EVER SEE A LASSIE?*

Traditional

Did you ev - er see a las - sie, a
lad - die, a

las - sie, a las - sie? Did you ev - er see a
lad - die, a lad - die?

las - sie go this way and that? Go this way and
lad - die

that way and this way and that way? Did you

ev - er see a las - sie go this way and that?
lad - die

*Public domain.

■ *Suggested Musical Class Activities for "Did You Ever See a Lassie?"*

Singing: Discover the word repetitions in this song and dramatize the rise and fall of the melody line through arm or large body movements—reaching and bending to the sound of the MELODY:

Example:

Playing: Divide the class into two groups. Have group 1 sing and tap percussion instruments (drums, sticks, and tone blocks) to the RHYTHM of the words or to the RHYTHM of the walking or skipping patterns of the children in group 2, who should form a circle. Allow the children to tap to the music and discover for themselves the way in which they want to keep time to the music.

Creating: Make up a variety of motions for the children to perform to hold their interest and gradually increase their attention span. Modify ways of performing this singing game:

Example:

Choose two or three children to stand in the center of the circle. Have each one do a different "trick." Give the children in the circle the freedom to choose the trick they want to imitate.

Dancing (free movement): Rotate the leader (the child in the center of the circle) to give everyone an opportunity to express himself or herself in performing a free movement—the primary purpose for this song.

Listening: Listen for each time certain key words or groups of words are repeated. Raise your hands whenever the repetition occurs.

Example:

While singing this song, have the group raise their hands or arms every time the words "Did you ever see a lassie?" are sung.

II Title of Song: "Three Little Kittens"

THREE LITTLE KITTENS*

Traditional

1. The three lit - tle kit - tens, they lost their mit - tens, And they be - gan to cry,__ "Oh, Mam-my dear, we sad - ly fear Our mit - tens we have lost!"__ "What! lost your mit -tens, you naugh - ty kit - tens? Then you shall have no pie!"__

Mi - ew, Mi - ew, We shall have no pie.____

*Public domain.

2. The three little kittens, they found their mittens,
   And they began to cry,
   "Oh, mommy dear, see here, see here,
   Our mittens we have found."
   "What! found your mittens, you good little kittens?
   Then you shall have some pie."
   "Mi-ew, mi-ew,
   We shall have some pie."

■ Suggested Musical Class Activities for "Three Little Kittens"

Singing: Point out to the class that the parts of the melody are alike, in that they move up and down in the same way, by humming the first two lines before singing the words.

Example:

Hum the first line on a neutral syllable ("la"). Have the children echo hum on "la," which is actually the second line of the song. The same procedure can be used when learning the last line: "Mi-ew, mi-ew, We shall have no pie," which is repeated.

Playing: Choose those classroom instruments that would be the most appropriate for reflecting the characteristics of the kittens, such as finger cymbals or triangles. Lead the class to reject the loud boom of a drum or the crash of cymbals here. Choose when to play the instruments while the song is being sung. Use this questioning technique: What kind of sounding instrument would you choose to play when mama cat is angry at the kittens for losing their mittens and tells them so? Listen to the sounds of the different instruments before deciding what to play.

Creating: Divide the class into three groups. Have group 1 sing the part of the three kittens; have group 2 sing the part of the mama cat; and have group 3 (comprised of four children) dramatize the entire song as it would be enacted by mama cat and the three little kittens, accompanied by groups 1 and 2.

Note:

Rotate the children portraying characters (group 3) so that all have an opportunity to dramatize. Introducing this and other nursery rhymes in a similar way is a memory-promoting activity that stimulates future recall or reinforcement of concepts.

Dancing (free movement): Have the three little kittens move around on their hind legs. Suggest that the children imagine sad or happy kittens reacting to losing or finding their mittens. Use these questioning techniques to stimulate individual thinking: How would the kittens act when they discovered they lost their mittens? Would they be happy? Would they be sad? Would they dance around the room? How would the kittens act when they found their mittens? Would they be sad? Would they be happy? Might they jump up and down and clap their paws together? How would mama cat act when scolding the kittens? How would she show her happiness when her kittens found their mittens?

Listening: Guide the children in listening for groups of words that, when sung consecutively, develop into a conversation between the characters that could be dramatized. The emphasis here is listening for key words in the song that call for a change in mood (happy/sad). The moods can be projected through various ways of singing the song (faster, slower, louder, softer) as well as through dramatization of the lyrics.

III Title of Song: "My Hands"

MY HANDS*

Louise B. Scott — Lucille F. Wood

My hands up - on my head I'll place, Up -
on my shoul - ders, on my face.
At my waist, and by my side, And
then be - hind me they will hide. Then
I will raise them way up high, And
let my fin - gers fly, fly, fly. Then

clap, clap, clap and one, two, three, Just

see how qui - et they can be.

*Reprinted from *Singing Fun* by Lucille F. Wood and Louise B. Scott © 1954 with permission of McGraw-Hill, Inc.

■ *Suggested Musical Class Activities for "My Hands"*

Singing: Emphasize the necessity of enunciation (clarity of speech) when singing words that are based on melody patterns that move quickly. Point out that many of the words move back and forth on the same tones.

Playing: Divide the class into two groups. Have group 1 choose percussion instruments (rhythm sticks, tone blocks) that produce a clicking sound with little, if any, resonance when the short, rhythmic patterns of the MELODY are tapped out:

— — — — — — ————
My hands up-on my head I'll place,

— — — — — — ————
Up-on my shoul-ders, on my face.

Have group 2 sing the song to the accompaniment of the percussion instruments.

Creating: Draw a life-size figure of a classmate: Place a five-foot length of brown or white wrapping paper on the floor. Have your classmate lie motionless on the paper while you trace the outline of his body with colored chalk. Fill in facial features and clothing by using colored chalk or crayons. Sing the song while facing your paper image. Respond to the words of the song by placing your hands on the head, face, waist, and so forth, of the paper image. (This activity requires individual thinking rather than imitation of a leader or fellow classmates. It reinforces knowledge of parts of the body, which is an example of developmental learning set in motion: simplicity of imitation, to the more complex activity of individual performance. Yet, we have here the total involvement of all the children within the nursery school classroom situation.)

Dancing (free movement): Dramatize the lyrics of the song by following the directions of the words, but in an informal position of choice: kneeling, sitting on the floor, or standing. Choose a partner and, in a face-to-face position, sing the song while responding to the words. (Encourage the children to maintain coordination throughout the song while facing their partners.)

Listening: Listen attentively to the words of the song so you can respond correctly to the required placement of your hands.

IV Title of Song: "Rig-a-Jig-Jig"

RIG–A–JIG–JIG*

English folk song

As I was walk - ing down the street,

Down the street, down the street, A lit - tle girl I

chanced to meet, Heigh - o, heigh - o, heigh - o.

Rig - a - jig - jig, and a - way we go, A -

way we go, a - way we go; Rig - a - jig - jig, and a -

way we go, Heigh - o, heigh - o, heigh - o.___

*Public domain. From Music Through the Day, Courtesy of General Learning Corporation.

■ *Suggested Musical Class Activities for "Rig-a-Jig-Jig"*

Singing: Observe the repetition of the word patterns here. However, also see that even though word patterns, such as "down the street" and "away we go" are repeated, they are sung on lower or higher tones. Thus, even though the word patterns are alike, the melody patterns are different.

Playing: Choose percussion instruments to be tapped that will best simulate the sound of walking (rhythm sticks, tone blocks, the rim of a drum) or, by granting the children freedom to explore the classroom sounds, have them tap on the floor, desk, tables, window sills, or on any object or surface in the room that will lead to individual decisions as to the most appropriate sound.

Creating: Have the children pretend to be riding ponies throughout the song to the accompaniment of coconut shells. In part A ("As I was walking..."), the pony walks down the street, but in part B ("Rig-a-jig-jig . . ."), the pony changes his movement to a gallop or a trot as illustrated here in the line duration of shorts (-) and longs (—). Have the RHYTHM tapped out with coconut shells.

Walk: – – – – – – – – – –

Gallop: – – – – – – – – – – – – – – –

Trot: – – – – – – – – – – – – – –

Dancing (free movement): Have the children execute locomotor movements (walking, galloping or skipping, trotting, and so on) to the rhythmic accompaniment of percussion instruments.

Listening: Have the children listen for the abrupt changes in the rhythm patterns of a walk, gallop (or skip), and trot that are produced by the tapping of a tone block or coconut shells. Encourage them to react spontaneously to these rhythmic differences. (See Dancing.)

V Title of Song: "Old MacDonald Had a Farm"

OLD MacDONALD HAD A FARM*

Traditional

*Public domain.

■ *Explanation of a Culminating Activity Based on "Old MacDonald Had a Farm"*

A culminating activity for a nursery school program, which would underline the increase in attention span gained by the age group, is to encourage the concepts through the medium of colored slides. A unit of a series of slides based on a specific concept proceeding from simple to complex can be made easily by the teacher:

1. Use colored felt-tipped markers or pens on manila tag board to initiate pictorially the gradual unfolding of a concept. (The project should contain 10–12 pictures.)

2. As an aid to the teacher questioning techniques or key words can be printed on each drawing to assure a smooth transition in sequence from one slide to the next. These words also serve as a teaching device for projecting pertinent facts related to the stated concept or objective for the specific slide series.

3. Use a 35mm camera (or facsimile) to photograph the drawings.

4. The mounted slides are used in a projector on a large screen. If a screen is not available, use a blank wall in the classroom.

The following slide series was produced by a group of students enrolled in an elementary music methods class at Central Michigan University, Mount Pleasant, Michigan, after they determined the concept to be explored for children in "Old MacDonald Had a Farm": Some melodies have long and short sounds that move up and down. Children can make these discoveries by becoming actively involved in musical activities that are initiated by slide shows.

Slide Series Initiating the Exploration of a Concept

Concept: Some melodies have long and short sounds that move up and down.

	Subject Matter On Each Slide	Questions and Procedures to be Initiated by Teacher for Pupil Response
 Here are some animal friends. Can you name them?	1. Picture of farm animals.	1. Here are some animal friends. Can you name them? (Encourage discussion of the animals.)

2. Picture of a barn, farmer, and animals.

2. What else do you see in the picture besides the animals? Do you know a song about this picture?

What else do you see in this picture? Do you know a song about this man and the animal?

Let's sing the song together.

3. Picture of the animals.

3. Lead a discussion of the song with the children and sing the song with them.

Let's sing the first part of the song on LA.

4. Picture of a stick man singing a melody using a neutral syllable, la, instead of the words of the song. (Musical notes encompass the man.)

4. All sing the first part of the song on "la."

Were some LA's longer than others?

Were some LA's shorter than others?

5. Question technique: Were some la's longer than others? Were some la's shorter than others?

5. Direct these questions to the children and then all sing the song again to test the answers.

Now Let's sing the song with words.

What words were longer? _____
_____
What words were shorter?
_____

6. Question technique: Which words were longer ? Which words were shorter ?

6. All sing the song. (Urge the children to answer the questions on the slide as asked by the teacher.)

Do all of the sounds move straight ahead?

Like this: _____ _____ _____ _____

or . . . Do some of the sounds move up and down?

Like this: _____ _____ _____ _____

7. Question technique: Do all of the sounds move straight ahead or do some of them move up and down?

7. Have the children respond to these questions after singing the song again and identifying those words of the song that move up and down.

Can you sing the 1st part of the song using your hand to show what words go up — — ⁻ what words go down — _ _ and what words go straight ahead _ _ _ _ ?

8. Question technique: Can you sing this song while using your hand to show which words go up, which words go down, and which words go straight ahead?

8. Demonstrate to the children what is being asked of them in this slide. Sing the song together.

Let's sing . . .

old Mac Don   had a   ei i
___ ___ ___   ___   ___
                                    ei i
                                    ___
        ald   farm
        ___   ___
                              o

9. Picture of the words in the first phrase of "Old Mac-Donald," with lines of duration over each word. Illustrate the words in an up-and-down arrangement as the contour of melody suggests.

9. Sing the song together and, using hands and arms, design the shape of the song in the air.

What do you see in this picture?

Do you know a song about a clock and a mouse?

"Let's sing the song."

10. Picture of a grandfather clock and a mouse close by.

10. Ask the children what song they think of when they look at this picture. Sing the song.

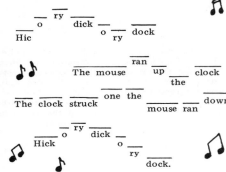

11. Picture of the words in the first phrase of "Hickory, Dickory, Dock," with lines of duration over each word. Illustrate the words in an up-and-down arrangement as the contour of the melody suggests.

11. Sing the song together and, using hands and arms, design the shape of the song in the air.

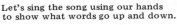

What song do we know about stars?

Let's sing the song using our hands to show what words go up and down.

12. Picture of stars in the sky.

12. Of what song does this picture remind you? All sing the song using your hands and arms to show which words go up and down.

Can you

make up your own

song?

13. Picture of children's faces. Question technique: Can you make up your own song?

13. Listen to short, individual melodies (sentence songs) of children and help them to make up their own words to fit their original tunes. Sing them often and post them on the bulletin board.

SUMMARY

The physical and mental characteristics of the early childhood years, also referred to as the preschool years, do not necessarily appear on schedule according to chronological age. As Gabriel asserts:

> there is little differentiation between the play of boys and girls during the preschool years. . . . children's play activities supply evidence of their physical development, for during the preschool years these activities progress gradually from bodily activity to the beginnings of finer movements. . . . while preschool children tend to progress from solitary to cooperative play, all kinds of play are in evidence during all ages.[24]

Therefore, the extent to which the musical activities of singing, playing, creating, dancing (free movement), and listening can be explored and experienced by children of preschool age depends largely on their physical development.

Consequently, it is imperative that the teacher be familiar with the general characteristics of early growth before delving into planning a developmental program of music for preschoolers.

The strategies and procedures suggested in this chapter for exploring musical learnings based on specific song materials are only indications of what can be achieved in a period of time. It must be emphasized here that the ways of initiating the aforementioned musical activities to increase child involvement and exploration are limitless in number and scope. The creative and imaginative teacher always strives to utilize a variety of procedures for achieving desired goals in learning. Hence, it might be well for the teacher to bear in mind this open and unending invitation to extend the horizons of musical learnings: Can you devise other strategies for incorporating the musical activities of singing, playing, creating, dancing (free movement), and listening as part of a learning event when experiencing this music?

Suggested Projects and Activities for the College or University Student

1. Visit a nursery school or day-care center for a period of time. Observe the daily behavioral patterns of the children at representative age levels. Record this data for future presentation in an open discussion in your methods class. Then, divide into groups, with each group being responsible for selecting an appropriate musical activity for a specified age level, planning the procedures for introducing the activity, and, finally, presenting the lesson before the class.
2. Volunteer as a teacher-aid at a day-care center or nursery school in your community for a prescribed period of time. Participate in guiding

[24]Gabriel, op. cit., pp. 218–219.

the children through musical experiences and observe the musical growth that occurs. Record your experiences in a daily or weekly log book that you have designed yourself. Make it a source book for your own future reference.

3. After investigating campus libraries for current information regarding early childhood (periodicals, textbooks, journals, source books) determine how other musical experiences would fit in to a readiness program in that area of child development. Record this data in a form—charts, pamphlets, series of visual aids—that you think will benefit you in later years as reference material.

Chapter 3

Early Experiences with Sound: Classroom Instruments

INTRODUCTION

An effective behavioral activity for guiding children through an exploratory process of discovering concepts, or musical ideas, uses classroom instruments.

> Many concepts of musical organization may be more easily acquired through the kind of concrete experiences that can be provided with musical instruments. Intervallic relationships and concepts of duration and of multiple sound may be much more clearly grasped when heard and played on an instrument than when experienced only through singing.[1]

This quotation emphasizes the importance and contribution of experiences with classroom instruments in acquiring and developing musical concepts.

Classroom instruments serve as a means through which the discovery, exploration, reinforcement, and growth of musical concepts occur. They also add another dimension by serving as a medium through which degree of muscular control and coordination can be expressed.

> Conceptualization of the constituent and expressive components of music is in itself behavioral.
> Such behaviors as listening, singing, playing, and moving are desirable in themselves and contribute to conceptual development.

[1] Bjornar Bergethon and Eunice Boardman, *Musical Growth in the Elementary School* (New York: Holt, 1963), p. 248.

> When a child has had sufficient firsthand experiences with music through listening, moving, singing, and playing tonal and rhythm instruments, he will be able to think musically. When a child thinks musically, he is conceptualizing musically and progressing toward lasting behavior in contrast to knowledge that will soon be forgotten.[2]

Because the use of classroom instruments in a developmental music program encourages musical growth, the purpose of this section will be to introduce particular instruments and illustrate and describe how each is played in the classroom. Suggestions for making classroom instruments also are given.

In subsequent chapters numerous musical examples will be given to illustrate how playing these instruments is a principal activity for exploring the elements of music in a conceptual approach to learning.

ENVIRONMENTAL AND UNCONVENTIONAL SOUNDS: (GETTING DOWN TO BASICS)

Environmental sounds, or the sounds that are a part of our environment from daylight to dusk, are infinite in number and variety. Elementary classroom teachers can devise strategies for encouraging children to be aware of the sounds around them.

For many children one of the basic activities experienced with members of a peer group in an organized classroom situation is the mastering of the quiet art of listening. Teachers are cognizant of the fact that numerous children enter the schoolroom totally unaware of the techniques of listening. At home they "hear" the blare of the television set; the hum of the washer and dryer; the startling ring of the telephone; and the anxious voice of mother calling out last-minute instructions for the day, such as, "Be careful to look both ways when you cross the street . . . ."

Undoubtedly, the children hear; but do they listen? One activity useful in motivating children to develop the skill of listening during the very first week of school is to take several quiet walking excursions up and down the street and around the school building. Urge the boys and girls to listen to the many sounds around them. Promise them that, upon your return to the classroom, they can take turns sharing everything they have heard: birds singing, trucks screeching, construction crews at work, and so on. Have the children make up their own rules for assuring the success of their walking adventure.

Examples of democratic rule making on the primary level:

1. We could walk with a partner.
2. We could walk quietly and not talk to anyone so we can listen for sounds.
3. We could follow a leader and walk on the sidewalk.

[2] Asahel D. Woodruff et al., "How Music Concepts Are Developed—And How They Are Applied," *Music Educators Journal,* LVI:58 (Feb. 1970).

This activity could prove to be of great value as a prerequisite to more formal disciplined attendance at concerts presented by the music department in a school system or in listening activities in general, such as in controlled listening to instructors and classmates within the confines of a classroom. Knowing how to listen will serve students well. They will be able to give undivided attention at a live performance in an auditorium or to recordings played in the classroom when listening for specific musical ideas or for concepts present within the structure of the composition being performed is required.

Listening plays a major role in the routine activities experienced by boys and girls during the course of a normal school day as well.

A more complex experience in exploring environmental and unconventional sounds that are suitable to and interesting for students on the *intermediate* level might proceed as follows:

Element: FORM
Component: Unity and Variety
Concept: Music is usually made up of sections (parts).

■ *Suggested Procedures and Strategies for Exploring the Concept*

1. On tape, record environmental and unconventional sounds. Some examples of sounds are the squeal of braked tires on pavement; rain on the roof, down gutters, on pavement, on windows, on an umbrella; the clink of ice cubes in glasses; the whir of an electric can opener or an egg beater; the jingling of keys and coins; the talking, laughing, or shuffling of students entering a classroom; the squeaking of a door; the scraping of chairs being repositioned on a wooden floor; the slap of books on tables; the click of typewriter keys; the rustling of newspaper; the sharpening of a pencil.

2. Listen to the tape. What kinds of sounds did you hear? Where might you hear some of these sounds? Which sounds were higher in pitch? Which sounds were louder? Which were softer?* Could these sounds be made into music? Could we structure an "environmental sound" composition?

3. Look at a chart of symbols that are representative of environmental sounds (Figure 1 and 2). What might these symbols represent? Can some of you go to these "instruments"? How would you play these instruments?

4. Divide the class into two groups. Let group 1 play the instruments using the first chart (Figure 1) as music. If we were to give this first part or section played a letter name what would it be? (A.) Have group 2 play the instruments using the second chart (Figure 2) as music. If we were to give this second part or section played a letter name what would it be? (B.)

5. Use these questioning techniques after groups 1 and 2 have played consecutively, as the charts of symbols indicate. How did the instruments sound? Were some heavy? If so, which ones? Therefore, which part consists of heavy sounds? (A.) Were some light? If so, which ones? Therefore, which

---

*The properties of sound are innumerable and variable and within this framework are modifications of the basic properties of high and low; loud and soft. However, they can be described effectively as a ringing sound, a rattling sound, a clattering sound, and the like.

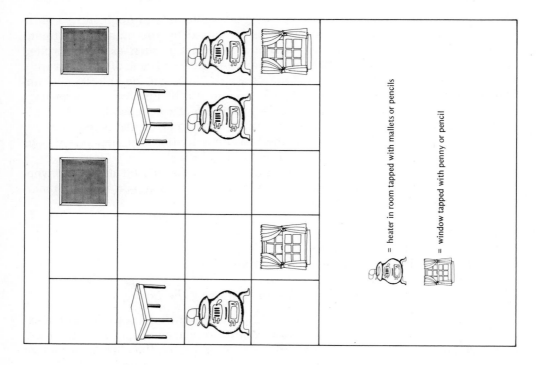

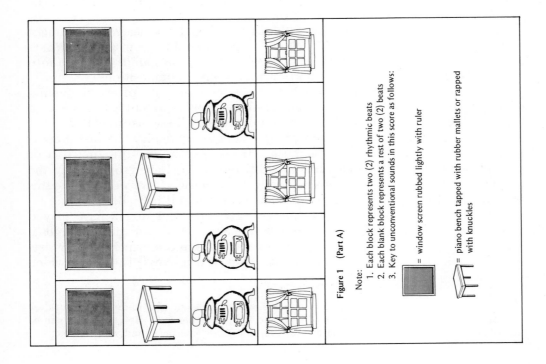

Figure 1 (Part A)

Note:

1. Each block represents two (2) rhythmic beats
2. Each blank block represents a rest of two (2) beats
3. Key to unconventional sounds in this score as follows:

= window screen rubbed lightly with ruler

= piano bench tapped with rubber mallets or rapped with knuckles

= heater in room tapped with mallets or pencils

= window tapped with penny or pencil

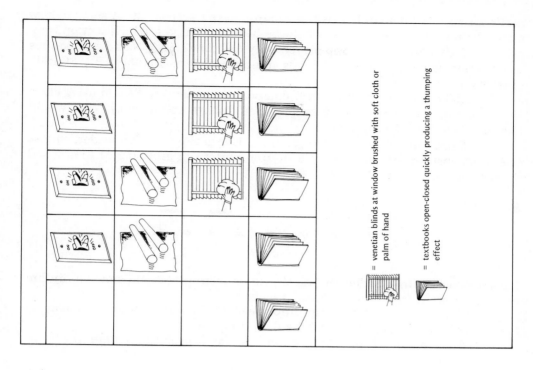

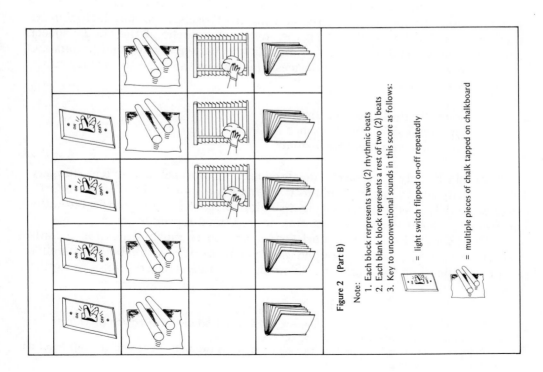

Figure 2 (Part B)

Note:

1. Each block rerpresents two (2) rhythmic beats
2. Each blank block represents a rest of two (2) beats
3. Key to unconventional sounds in this score as follows:

part consists of light sounds? (B.) If group 1 were to repeat the A section, how many distinct parts or sections would be heard? (Three.) Which section is repeated? (A.) Which section is played only one time? (B.) Name the sections using letter names. (ABA.) What is the musical term for the ABA FORM? (Ternary.)

6. Make up your own musical composition in ternary FORM using classroom instruments. How many groups should there be? (Two.) Who would like to be a leader of each group?

7. Divide the class into two groups. Have group 1, with a leader, choose classroom instruments and create a rhythm pattern (a grouping of longer and shorter tones).

Example:

Have group 2, with a leader, choose classroom instruments and create a rhythm pattern different from the one created by group 1.

8. Perform the entire composition in ABA FORM with group 1 playing the A section and group 2 playing the B section.

9. Make a tape of the composition and play it back to evaluate it.

The Body As a Musical Instrument

Carl Orff, an exponent of music education in Germany, has developed a purely sensorial approach to music education. It eschews an intellectual introduction to music by emphasizing the rhythmic element of the child's speech and movement pattern so that he may first experience, and then understand music. Orff uses several special devices which allow the child to explore music; for example:

a. specially designed instruments
b. children's jingles and rhymes
c. rhythmic and melodic ostinati

Zoltán Kodály's approach (music education approach adopted in Hungary) also uses rhythm to experience music. However, his method differs from Orff's in that Kodály uses a system of sight singing to teach children musical notation and employs hand signals for attaining desired tonal reproduction.[3]

The Zoltán Kodály and Carl Orff approach to music education includes *bodily movement* (the improvised movement of the entire body as well as clapping, stamping, patting[4] and snapping the fingers) as a response to rhythm;

---

[3] Lawrence Wheeler and Lois Raebeck, *Orff and Kodaly Adapted for the Elementary School* (Dubuque, Ia.: Brown, 1972), p. xix-xx.

[4] *Patschen* is the act of patting the right hand on the right knee and the left hand on the left knee simultaneously.

it accompanies speech, singing, and playing in conjunction with rhythmic notation and in response to musical FORM (rondo, canon, and so on).[5]

The approach is adapted here to the American public school system, by using regular classroom instruments instead of Orff instruments, together with a second **Orff-Kodály** technique, emphasizing the use of the normal childhood chant (falling minor third—5–3; refer to p. 71 or "sol-mi") to encourage an understanding of MELODY and a feeling for the contour of a MELODY.

Melody flutes or recorders can play the pentatonic MELODY (it begins with falling minor third) written as an accompaniment to the nursery rhyme "How Many Miles to Babylon?" (*This melody was composed by a group of Orff Workshop students at Ball State University, summer of 1971. The author was a member of the group.*)

HOW MANY MILES TO BABYLON?*

*Original.

[5] Ibid., p. xxvi.

Note:

The key to the symbols related to the body sounds used in the score is as follows:

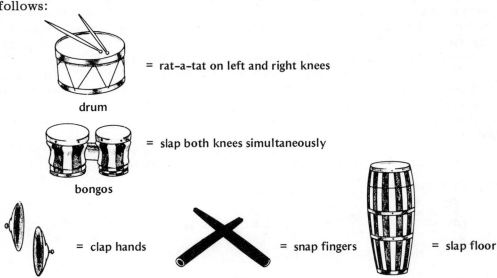

drum = rat–a–tat on left and right knees

bongos = slap both knees simultaneously

cymbals = clap hands   sticks = snap fingers   conga = slap floor

Pictorial Score of Body Sounds to be Performed with "How Many Miles to Babylon?"

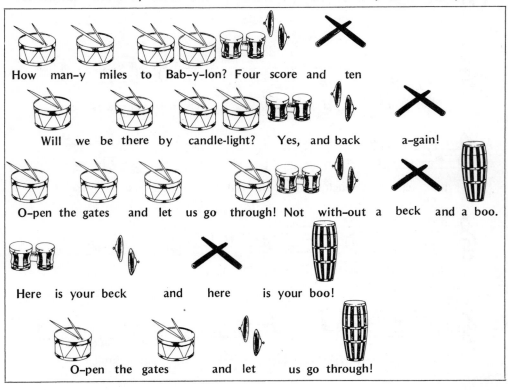

How man-y miles to Bab-y-lon? Four score and ten

Will we be there by candle-light? Yes, and back a-gain!

O-pen the gates and let us go through! Not with-out a beck and a boo.

Here is your beck and here is your boo!

O-pen the gates and let us go through!

Note:

Could you divide a class into two groups to perform this song as a question-answer sequence? Could you incorporate dance movements as an interpretation of the question-answer sequence? Could you also perform this activity using classroom instruments rather than body sounds?

Incorporating the use of body sounds (clapping, *patschen*, stamping and finger snapping) create your own rhythmic interpretation of the following:

"Counting-Out Rhyme"

Icker — backer
Silver cracker,
Icker-backer-boo.
En–gine
Number Nine
Out go you.
Out goes the cat,
Out goes the rat,
Out goes the lady
In the see-saw hat.
O – U – T spells OUT,
So go![6]

CLASSROOM INSTRUMENTS DESCRIBED AND ILLUSTRATED

After considering the categories of *melody*, *percussion*, and *chording* as appropriate for classifying the most common elementary classroom instruments, and after reading the following descriptions of individual instruments, can you identify an instrument's proper category? (Consult p. 56 for a classified listing of instruments by category.)

1. TOM-TOMS

    These drums are played preferably with hands, finger-tips, or with soft, padded mallets.

---

[6] Lena Barksdale, ed., "Counting-Out Rhyme," in *The Treasure Bag*, © Alfred A. Knopf, Inc., New York, 1947, p. 95.

2. TONE BLOCKS AND WOOD BLOCKS

These instruments produce a sharp tone when tapped with mallets. A guiro tone block has a fluted barrel that, when rubbed vigorously with a mallet handle, produces a sharp, rasping sound.

3. RHYTHM STICKS

A clicking sound is produced when rhythm sticks are tapped together; a scratching effect is produced when fluted sticks are rubbed together in a back and forth motion.

4. TAMBOURINES

These versatile instruments can be tapped or shaken to produce various tonal effects. Ribbons or crepe paper streamers can be tied to the rim for a colorful effect when used to accompany folk dances.

5. CYMBALS

Brass cymbals can be used in pairs to produce a loud crashing sound effect or they can be tapped with a mallet to simulate the sound of a gong.

6. FINGER CYMBALS

A delicate, resonant, bell-like sound is produced when cymbals are tapped lightly together. Young children can hold one in each hand from elastic finger straps (in this instance used as handles) and tap them lightly together. Older children may prefer to use them as professional dancers do: one pair on each hand with the elastic finger straps over the thumb and third finger.

7. TRIANGLES

A steel triangle of any size produces a resonant bell-like tone when struck with a steel tapper.

8. POINCIANA PODS

The source of these large pods is the poinciana tree, which grows in the south. The seeds within the dried pods produce a rattling sound when shaken.

9. COCONUT SHELLS

Hawaiians refer to these shells as *pu niu* (see p. 52). They produce a hollow clip, clop sound when tapped together.

10. JINGLE BELLS

Jingle bells are available in a wide variety of sizes and styles, as wrist bells, sleigh bells mounted on a wide nylon band that is attached to a wooden handle grip, and mounted on elongated wooden handle frames (available in various sizes).

11. MELODY FLUTES: TONETTE, SONG FLUTE, FLUTOPHONE

These instruments are usually introduced in grade 3 or 4 in elementary school systems. The range is limited to the C major scale (plus D above high C) and to the production of several accidentals. These melody flutes allow the individual child to become physically involved in numerous musical learnings, including (a) satisfactory tone production; (b) tonal direction, which is the discovery that the tones of a MELODY move up and down by step, skip, and sometimes stay the same; (c) experiencing the duration of pitch and other basic fundamentals associated with musical notation; and (d) the desire to increase sight-reading ability in this peer-group activity.

12. RECORDERS

This authentic melody instrument of the fifteenth century is available in different voicings (soprano, alto, tenor, and bass), which increases its flexibility and range as a fine instrument. The recorder cultivates a taste for serious music in the young student in the elementary school. Recorders are manufactured from wood as well as various synthetic materials.

13. STEP BELLS

Step bells are available in several ranges, which include chromatic tones. The step bells mounted on an elevated frame as illustrated serve as a visual aid in discovering that MELODY can move up or down by step and skip.

14. RESONATOR BELLS

Resonator bells are arranged in a luggage-style case in piano-keyboard position. Each bell is mounted on a wooden or plastic resonator block and can be removed to be played individually by class members.

Chord boxes are available and are convenient when selecting individual bells for building chords. The student can arrange the bells in the box in chord formation and play them using a double, triple, or quadruple mallet.

15. MELODY BELLS

Melody bells are arranged in the pattern of the piano keyboard and are mounted securely on a frame. These bells are available in various sizes and ranges.

16. AUTOHARPS: CHROMAHARPS

These string instruments are easily played by strumming or plucking. Various styles of picks, mallets, brushes, and so forth, can be utilized to produce different tonal effects when the proper chord bars are pushed down for immediate chord reproduction. Sizes of autoharps and chromaharps vary, the larger size offering a wider selection of chord bars for accompaniment.

17. GUITAR AND UKULELE

These popular string instruments are available in a wide variety of styles and sizes. They are manufactured of various kinds of wood or plastic materials.

The value of playing an autoharp, guitar, or ukulele to accompany singing in the classroom is in establishing eye contact with the children. Also, a free and casual rapport is possible and enjoyed by everyone involved, whether singing or playing. These instruments can be played by the young student as well as the teacher, especially if a peer group together learns the fingering of a simple chord progression (only two chords at first).

18. PIANO

The piano can be classified as a melody, percussion, and chording instrument and should be made available for use in every school.

Latin-American Instruments

CONGA DRUMS

These drums are available in various sizes and styles, in cone or barrel shapes.

BONGOS

Bongos can be held in the arm or between the knees to allow freedom for both hands to tap out exciting rhythms on both drumheads.

CLAVES

Claves differ from rhythm sticks in that they are tapped in pairs while being held in the following hand position: for the purpose of satisfactory resonance, one clave is balanced from the fingertips to heel of one hand while the partner clave is held in the opposite hand to tap the desired rhythm pattern.

CASTANETS

Castanets available in handle and finger styles and are designed for maximum clicking effect for dance or concert performance.

GUIRO

The guiro produces a high rasping sound when rubbed with an accompanying wooden scratcher; it is available in various sizes.

MARACAS

These "shakers" are instruments that produce a rattling sound when played individually or in pairs.

SPANISH CABASA

The cabasa is a pear-shaped gourd that is colorfully painted and covered with beads. It is an ideal instrument for children to explore to discover for themselves the tonal effects that can be achieved by tapping, twisting, and rubbing.

COPPER COWBELL WITH WOODEN TAPPER

The cowbell is available in various sizes; it gives an amusing tonal effect to the performance of some musical compositions.

Afro-American Instruments

KALIMBA OR MBIRA (AMBIRA)

This instrument produces a soft tinkling sound comparable to a music box. Thin, narrow rods extend over its bridge in varying lengths. It is held in both hands and touched lightly with the thumbs of either hand. Thirds and triads can be played by tapping more than one rod simultaneously; hence, it can be classified as a melody or chording instrument. (Refer also to the descriptions of drums, tom-toms, bells, and shakers that appear in this section.)

Oriental Instruments

CHINESE STYLE TOM–TOMS

These drums are available in several sizes; they produce resonant sounds of different pitches.

ORIENTAL BAN DRUM

This drum is available in several sizes; it produces a deep, resonant tone and is used for religious services, ceremonies, and dancing.

ORIENTAL TEMPLE BLOCKS

Different tonal effects for hollow, rippling sounds are achieved by tapping these blocks with hard rubber mallets or mallets whose heads have been wrapped in felt or lamb's wool. Each temple block has a distinct pitch and can be played individually.

ORIENTAL GONGS

These brass gongs of various sizes produce correspondingly high or low resonant pitches.

ARTFUL PLANKS

The sound emitted when these two pieces of cherry wood are struck together is comparable to the sharp resonant tone of the wood block.

FOUR-STRING LUTE

This instrument is played like a guitar or ukulele and plunked like a ukulele.

Instruments of the American Indian

TOM-TOMS

The heads of these drums are skins stretched over various sizes of tree trunks; each tom-tom is equipped with a rawhide handle and soft-headed mallet.

OCTO DRUMS

The heads of these eight-sided drums are decorated with brightly colored symbols. They are used on special occasions in the life of an Indian. (Also, refer to maracas, p. 50.)

DANCING BELLS

Rows of small jingle bells are attached to soft leather that is lined with felt and worn over the arm or ankle.

Hawaiian Instruments

ULI-ULI (pronounced oo'-lee)

These colorful feathered gourds are filled with beads and used with creative dance movement.

IPU (pronounced ee'-poo)

The ipu is a large, hollow calabash that is held in one hand while the heel and fingertips of other hand produce resonant tones when tapped.

PU NIU (pronounced poo-nee'-oo)

Better known as coconut shells, this instrument produces a clip, clop sound when the shells are struck together.

PUILI STICKS (pronounced poo–ee'–lee)

These bamboo sticks that have been slit produce a unique crackling sound when struck together against a foreign object or against the body. They are used by dancers for creative effects and are available in various lengths.

ILI–ILI (pronounced ee–lee)

These Hawaiian dancing stones are made of volcanic rock and produce sharp clicking tones when struck together.

UKULELE (pronounced yoo–ka–la'–lee)

This member of the guitar family is an Hawaiian instrument with four strings and a long fretted fingerboard. It is smaller than a guitar and is manufactured in various sizes for purpose of attaining differences in sound projection.

SUGGESTIONS FOR MAKING CLASSROOM INSTRUMENTS

MARACAS

Shakers that simulate the sound of maracas can be made from various sizes of tubular cartons with plastic lids that snap tightly. Also, cardboard mailing tubes or concentrated frozen fruit juice cans and various types of plastic containers with lids that snap (margarine, cottage cheese, and the like) can be made to produce different tonal effects with the addition of rice, sand, or popcorn kernels. Plastic contact material cut into colorful patterns instantly transforms the outside covering into a student's uniquely creative product.

Maracas can also be made from light bulbs.

1. Select two large light bulbs (150 watt).
2. Cover the light bulbs with papier mâché, which is made by immersing strips of newspaper in a mixture of wallpaper paste (wheat paste mix)* and molding many thicknesses around the light bulb.

*Wheat paste powdered mix is available in paint and decorating stores. Add water to the mix for a paste.

3. Allow the light bulbs to dry thoroughly (perhaps for several weeks).
4. When the papier mâché is completely dry, tap the maraca lightly to break the bulb within, which then provides a rattling tonal effect.
5. Paint original designs on the maracas.

SAND BLOCKS

Sand blocks can be made from wood blocks of odd sizes that have been discarded by lumber companies as scrap. Tack or staple a coarse grade of sandpaper to one side of the block. When two blocks are rubbed together in a rhythmic movement, they will produce a swishing sound imitative of ocean waves, trains, or walking in dry autumn leaves.

DRUMS

The sound of drums can be simulated by using various sizes of coffee cans or shortening cans with snap-on plastic lids. Each member of the class can be responsible for obtaining his own "drum." In this way each child will be motivated to become actively and physically involved in the rhythmic experience initiated in the classroom. A set of bongos can be improvised by joining one large- and one small-sized coffee can with wide bicycle tape.

TAMBOURINES

Tambourines can be constructed by lacing together two aluminum pie pans with colored yarn. Jingles made of small bottle caps or small metal can tops or actual jingle bells purchased in a novelty store or hobby shop can be tied around the rim of the pans. A rattling effect can be achieved with the addition of rice or sand to the inside of the instrument.

RHYTHM STICKS

Inexpensive wooden dowels, which can be obtained from a lumber company, are excellent substitute for professional rhythm sticks. The dowels can be cut to desired lengths and painted or decorated by the children.

TUNED WATER JARS

Water jars tuned to the C major scale and tapped with wooden mallets provide children with hours of pleasure. They also serve as an excellent visual aid for discovering that the tones of a simple MELODY move by step or skip and sometimes stay the same.

1. Select jars of the same shape and style: instant coffee jars are available in large and small sizes.
2. When tuning, be certain the jars are placed on the same wooden or formica counter top on which they will be played. (The pitches of tones are sometimes distorted when jars are moved to a different sounding board.)

3. When a desired pitch is achieved through the trial-and-error method of pouring an amount of water into the jar, add a few drops of red or green food coloring so that the water levels can be seen easily.
4. Jar tops prevent the evaporation of water (or pitch distortion) and offer the convenience of making the jars portable.

GONGS

Various sizes of gongs can be obtained by utilizing the large metal lids from detergent cartons that are shipped to school cafeterias and other large restaurants or institutions. Punch holes through the rim of a lid and insert colorful plastic cord as a handle to provide free and easy suspension. Make a soft-headed mallet by tying a woolen mitten stuffed with cotton to one end of a wooden dowel or drumstick.

CHORDING INSTRUMENTS

Plastic jugs and bottles as well as various sizes of soft drink bottles (12-, 8-, 6-ounce) can be tuned to different pitches by adding water to various levels. Using bottles of definite pitches, students can build specific chords and provide accompaniment to familiar songs. Blowing across the top of the bottle produces a different tone quality than tapping the bottle with a mallet.

The clip-clop of horses' hoofs can be simulated with inverted paper, plastic, or styrofoam drinking cups. Children can explore and discover for themselves which sounding boards in the classroom are the most satisfactory: window sills, the floor, desks, a chalk tray, the wall, chairs, a chalkboard, and so on. Also, coconuts that have been cut in half with an electric saw in the meat department of any grocery or supermarket and baked in a 325° oven for 15–18 minutes to dry up the white coconut meat, which can then be removed easily, can be used to simulate the hoofbeats as well. Tapping coconut shells together produces clip-clop sound.

Resonant bell-like sounds with distinct pitches can be achieved with various sizes of discarded metal bars or pipes suspended from a wooden frame and tapped with wooden or hard-rubber mallets. Also, discarded automobile parts (pistons, gears, etc.) when tapped with metal strikers can produce vibrant bell-like sounds. Obtaining these parts and assembling them for use in the school can be an appealing project for children on the intermediate level in an elementary school.

Suggested Project and Activity for the College or University Student

Divide the class into groups. Have the individual members of each group make up, design, or create a melody or percussion instrument. Then, as a group project, make up an accompaniment to a familiar song or melody and devise a strategy for preserving the accompaniment.

Example:

Using crayons or paints, illustrate the instrumental accompaniment on white shelf paper.

As a group, present your finished project before the class members in your methods course.

SUPPLEMENTARY NOTES

Classroom instruments common to many schools:

Melody*
    pianos
    resonator bells
    melody bells
    step bells
Percussion
    tone blocks
    rhythm sticks
    tambourines
    cymbals
    triangles
    temple blocks
    maracas
    large and small drums
    tom-toms
    claves
    bongo and conga drums (various sizes)
    coconut shells
    poinciana pods
Chording
    pianos
    autoharps
    resonator bells
    ukuleles (guitars generally are owned privately)

*List should also include melody flutes or recorders, if generally accepted in a school system.

Chapter 4

Skills for Guiding Musical Experiences in the Elementary School (Kindergarten-Grade 6)

THE CONCEPTUAL APPROACH: A BASIS FOR MUSICAL GROWTH

A concept, in the terms of this text, is an idea or a mental image established after experiencing and perceiving an element of music. This image may be quite general and vague in its initial stages, but it is refined and enhanced as experiences are added. A concept aids the teacher in organizing material and serves as a focal or unifying influence. Children learn that music is made of definite elements and that an understanding of these elements and their interactions will enable them better to understand the music.

Analyzing music for its elements and the components of those elements is the means of discovery. The following outline is an example of the structure of such analytical effort:

MELODY (musical element)
    direction of melody
    range of melody
    key or tonality of melody
    contour of melody
    interval relationship in building melody
    melodic phrases (like and unlike)

This same procedure of music analysis can be applied to the other elements present in music: namely, RHYTHM, HARMONY, FORM, DYNAMICS, TEMPO, and TONE COLOR.

In developing musical growth and understanding it is necessary and helpful to use many and varied activities to explore and develop a concept.

It is for this reason that the presentation of a simple primary song and strategies for its exploration are included in this section. It will illustrate and clarify the idea of musical growth, even though a specific concept is isolated and explored. Interaction with other musical elements and concepts is achieved simultaneously.

A suggested strategy for determining musical growth on the intermediate level is also contained in this section.

In this project, "The Indian Song" is explored for the purpose of discovering the accented beat and unaccented beats played on tone clusters at the piano keyboard (refer to p. 181). However, through the following exploratory sequence, the reader can be made aware of the possible existing interactions of other concepts related to the elements of music and their components. Also, reference to aesthetic sensitivity is not merely implied in this specific presentation, because various strategies and questioning techniques used for exploration also stimulate an imaginative and emotional response to the music.

THE INDIAN SONG*

M. Lament

I am a great big In - di - an Chief;

This is my ar - row and bow,

These are my moc - ca - sins and this is my drum,

And this is the way I sit just so!

*Original.

■ *Use of Classroom Instruments and Other Strategies for Exploring the Concepts Related to All of the Elements of Music: MELODY, RHYTHM, HARMONY, FORM, TEMPO, DYNAMICS, and TONE COLOR*

1. Listen to the song and tap along. Was your tapping even and steady or was it uneven? What is the song about? What is this Indian Chief singing about? Do you think he is tapping rhythm sticks or tone blocks while he is singing his song? What do you think he is using to keep time to the music? (Drums or tom-toms.)

2. Echo chant the words of the song in RHYTHM.

3. Divide the class in two groups. Have group 1 chant the words while tapping steady beat on drums and have group 2 chant the words while tapping rhythm sticks or tone blocks to the rhythm of the words. Were all of the steady beats loud or soft?

4. If you give the steady beats number names, what will you name the first beat? (One.) Now, chant the number names as you beat your drum. Is the first beat a strong or a weak beat? (Strong.) How many weak beats follow it? (Three.)

5. Design the strong and weak beats in the air or on the chalkboard:

/ / / /   / / / /   / / / /

6. Group the beats in sets of four:

/ / / / ¦ / / / / ¦ / / / / ¦ / / / / ¦

How many beats to a set? (Four.) Which beat is the strongest? (One.)

7. Notice that the piano keyboard is divided into black and white keys and that the black keys are clustered in two- and three-note groupings. Play these same beats on the piano keyboard on the black keys. On what group of black keys will you play the strong beats? (Three-note group.) On what group of black keys will you play the weak beats? (Two-note group.)

8. Sing and design the song using hand levels. How did the song move, up or down? On what words did it move up? On what words did it move down? Did it move up or down by step or skip? Did any of the tones of the song stay the same? On what words? Frame these words with your hands on the wall chart of the song or on the chalkboard.

9. Sing the song again as you play it on melody bells or resonator bells. If the MELODY moved up by skip, can you name the tones it skipped to as you play them this time? If you know that middle C in music looks like this,

can you draw the other tones of the MELODY on the staff since you played them on the bells and named them? How many did you draw? (Four.)

10. Place the resonator bells you played in a chord box and play them with a quadruple fan mallet: 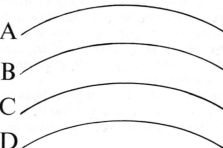 Do you know what we call these tones when they are played at the same time? (Chord.) Can you play this chord on the piano keyboard with your right hand? Place your thumb on C. Your third finger will fall on what key? (E) Your fifth finger will fall on what key? (G)

11. If the chord is built on C, the first note of the chord, what is the name of the chord? (C.)

12. Find and play the C chord on the autoharp, the bells, and the piano keyboard, and play along as you sing the song. Were you playing what you were singing? (No.) If not, did the tones you were playing and singing fit together even though they were different? (Yes.) What do we call this in music? (HARMONY.)

13. Sing the song again, but this time raise your hand whenever you come to the end of a musical idea or thought. (Raised hand = ↑ .)

I am a great big In-di-an Chief; ↑
This is my ar-row and bow, ↑
These are my moc-ca-sins and this is my drum, ↑
And this is the way I sit just so! ↑

How many musical thoughts did you discover in the song? (Four.) In music, what do we call these musical ideas? (Phrases.)

14. Design these phrases in the air using an arm movement in the shape of an arc: Were any phrases alike? Was each phrase different?

15. Design these phrases on the chalkboard giving letter names to the phrases.

A ⌒
B ⌒
C ⌒
D ⌒

Did each phrase have a different letter name? (Yes.) Why? What would you call the design or form of this song? (A B C D.)

16. Make up an Indian dance to perform while you sing the song. If you base the design of your dance on the phrase structure of the song, will you move in the same direction for each phrase or will you move in a different direction for each phrase? Why?

17. Draw the design for your Indian dance on the chalkboard:

On phrase A move clockwise:

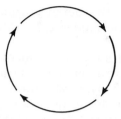

On phrase B move counterclockwise:

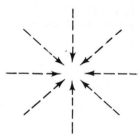

On phrase C move in to the center:

On phrase D move out from the center:

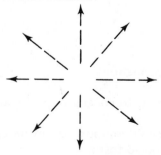

For the climax go from a high jump to a sitting position as the MELODY and words of the song dictate.

18. Sing this song and perform the dance accompanied by autoharps, resonator bells, melody bells, piano, and percussion instruments of your choice including maracas, tom-toms, drums, and Indian dancing bells (which can be worn by the dancers).

19. Listen as you perform this activity again. Is the TEMPO, or the speed, of the song fast, slow, or moderate? (Moderate.) Is the TEMPO steady? (Yes.)

20. Listen to the sounds of all the instruments used in this performance. Close your eyes and name the instruments as you hear each one played alone. Did you like these sounds? Why? Did the sounds of all these different instruments playing together add tonal color to the music?

21. After you perform this song again, can you pretend the Indian begins to steal away into the deep forest as the drum beats gradually become softer? The Indian is a brave hunter and although we cannot see him, we know he must have heard or seen some wild animal because we hear his jubilant cry from far, far away; now even the Indian drums are silent.

Additional Strategy for Exploring the Concepts Related to All the Elements of Music: MELODY, RHYTHM, HARMONY, FORM, TEMPO, DYNAMICS, and TONE COLOR on the Intermediate Level

1. While listening to a musical composition list the elements of music (except FORM) represented in the work.

2. Listen again to the same composition and expand the list into a brief outline that designates which aspect (component) of a specific element is represented.

Example:

MELODY
　repeated phrases
RHYTHM
　4/4 meter (accented beat falls on 1s)
HARMONY
　major tonality
TEMPO
　moderate throughout
DYNAMICS
　mf (moderately loud throughout)
TONE COLOR
　orchestral accompaniment to vocal group of male soloist and chorus

3. Listen once more to the composition in its entirety to determine its FORM, such as, A B, A B A, and so forth.

4. Within an allotted period of time elaborate on or expand the outline to explain the techniques used or how the composer achieved the interaction of these elements of music in his composition.

CONSIDERATION OF THE DEVELOPMENTAL GROWTH PATTERN OF CHILDREN IN THE ELEMENTARY SCHOOL[1]
(five to eleven years of age)

An awareness of this growth pattern can serve as an effective aid in planning activities for exploring musical concepts on the elementary level. At this time, children begin to participate in group activities and to acquire independent attitudes. They begin to desire individual recognition and achievement and display a growing independence. Five year olds desire to improve the skills of running, jumping, and skipping and are preoccupied with observing the activity going on around them rather than being an eager participant in the activity itself. This age child is generally docile and contented. Six year olds tend to fluctuate in mood and behavior, however; one minute they may be excited and happy and then suddenly they may become depressed or disappointed. Similarly, they are momentarily docile and cooperative and then quite unexpectedly stubborn and uncooperative. Seven year olds appear to be more poised and settled. They more readily accept a task to be performed, become engrossed in performing it, and resent being interrupted or disturbed. Therefore, the school and teachers of this age level must strive to organize activities that demand a child's attention but that are flexible enough so that they can be changed often and quickly. They must provide a varied curriculum that "gives opportunity for group cooperation, creative and constructive work, for reading and reading-readiness programs, and for general bodily activity" (p. 240).

Eight and nine year olds are increasingly interested in initiating informal play groups and also tend to flit from one activity to another. Thus, "eight year olds do not usually persevere at any one task . . . . Yet, despite this, children certainly make great progress socially, emotionally, and in creative and academic skills during the eight to nine period" (p. 282). Nine year olds can also be described as "always on the move," but their actions are more controlled than those of the eight year olds. Ten year olds are more consistently persevering and have developed the ability to act independently.

Eleven year olds generally can be described as possessing an enthusiastic drive for learning, for adventure, and for social experiences. Therefore, the school and teachers of this age level must strive to: provide a planned environment that is not solely academic but includes art, crafts, hobby sessions, and activities of an expressive nature, such as drama, mime, poetry, story writing, and music. Classroom group activities must be initiated in which children can share social experiences that are planned as a means toward their academic growth and development. Children naturally seek to exercise their developing physical and mental capacities, to further their new interests and to fulfill their new purposes. This they can do most readily in groups, because groups provide them with an opportunity to engage in activities that are more complex and varied than is possible when playing alone or with a single companion.

[1] Data obtained from John Gabriel, *Children Growing Up* (London: University of London Press Ltd., 1969), p. 222-291.

CHARACTERISTICS OF MUSICAL GROWTH IN THE ELEMENTARY SCHOOL[2] (THROUGH LISTENING)

Equipment

It is vitally important that record players, tape recorders, and all types of sound equipment for the reproduction of musical compositions be of good, if not the best, quality. Equipment should be checked periodically for such inadequacies as defective needles, which produce a scratchy reproduction of the music and unbalanced turntables, which can produce undesirable surface sounds.

There are many different types of record players and tape recorders on the market, so before attempting to use any equipment, be certain you understand the directions for use. Actual live demonstrations of how to operate the equipment are usually more beneficial than reading or following a diagram of steps and procedures.

Use of Background Music in the Classroom in the Lower Grades

The use of background music in the classroom to establish mood (at resting time or play time) is frowned on by some educators as serving no specific purpose, encouraging distraction, and possibly causing the child to become restless and fidgety. However, other educators maintain that the expressive quality of the music creates an awareness of differences in musical texture and may encourage desirable emotional response.

Thus, the value of using music in this manner should be determined by the individual teacher in his or her unique situation.

Example of a Listening Lesson

The March from *Soirees Musicales*, by Rossini-Britten, is comprised of various rhythm patterns (even and uneven) that are the principal focus of the following listening lesson. The suggested procedure for conducting the listening lesson is developmental and suggests numerous activities for exploring the

---

[2] Bjornar Bergethon and Eunice Boardman, *Musical Growth in the Elementary School*, 2nd ed., Musical Growth Charts (New York: Holt, 1970). In this text these characteristics of musical growth are recorded developmentally (simple to complex).

Activities—listening, singing, free movement, creating, playing, reading—for exploring concepts related to musical growth are included in all suggested lesson plans and procedures as follows: Kindergarten, p. 36-37; Grade 1, p. 56-57; Grade 2, p. 82-83; Grade 3, p. 112-113; Grade 4, p. 142-143; Grade 5, p. 182-183; Grade 6, p. 224-225.

concept, which must be extended over a period of several lessons. In this way, reinforcement of the concept will be assured.

Primary Level

Element: RHYTHM
Component: Even and Uneven Rhythm Patterns
Concept: Some music is made up of both smooth and bouncy rhythm patterns (even and uneven).

> Rossini-Britten: March from *Soirees Musicales*,
> from *Adventures in Music*, Grade 1, Volume I

Suggestions for Presentation:

1.   Listen to this music as you tap along. What kind of a beat are you tap-ing? Is it steady? Does it move along smoothly? What do we call this beat that keeps a steady time with the music? (Steady beat.)

2.   Listen to this music again. Do you hear any other rhythmic beats that are different from the steady beat? Even though the steady beat keeps going throughout the music, do you hear any rhythms that move faster?

3.   Tap this RHYTHM alone for your classmates to hear. Do you hear it played again? Do you know what we call this RHYTHM that is played over again and again and is different from the steady beat? (Rhythm pattern.)

4.   Play an echo game with your classmates by tapping out the rhythm pattern you heard on a drum and asking your classmates to echo this pattern on rhythm sticks.

5.   Design the pattern you played on the chalkboard in line duration.

Example: ____   ____   __   __   ____

Chant the pattern as you play it on rhythm sticks and drums:

<u>long</u> <u>long</u> <u>short</u> <u>short</u> <u>long</u>

6.   (Divide class into two groups. Have group 1 play a steady beat on tom-toms, and have group 2 play a rhythm pattern on rhythm sticks. Can both groups play together at the same time?)

7.   Discover other rhythm patterns that might be present in the musical composition you heard. On the wall chart point out the different rhythm patterns that you heard and played on classroom instruments. Are there many different kinds of rhythm patterns?

8.   Tap a steady and smooth rhythm pattern on a tambourine. Design it on the chalkboard:

Example: __   __   __   __   __   __   __   __   __

In music what do we call a steady rhythm pattern? (Even rhythm pattern.)

9. Tap a bouncy rhythm pattern on rhythm sticks. Design it on the chalkboard:

Example: ⸻ — ⸻ — ⸻ —

In music what do we call a bouncy, or not so steady, rhythm pattern? (Uneven rhythm pattern.)

10. Listen to other musical compositions and discover the different kinds of rhythm patterns you hear in the music.

The characteristics present in this sampling of a procedure for conducting a listening lesson can be summarized: (1) The listeners are given specific directions as to what to listen for and then are further requested to demonstrate recognition by some overt action, such as raising a hand, tapping along, and so on. (2) Related questioning techniques are used to support the concept and encourage individual thinking as well as the involvement of the entire class. (3) Various activities for exploring the concept are included throughout the presentation and serve as an aid for reinforcement. (4) Suggestions for exploring the concept involve the entire class in a variety of activities.

Suggested Listening Materials for the Elementary School

I Program Music

Program music is reflective of extramusical ideas that may be indicated in the title itself or in an explanation or brief description in the introductory remarks about the composition.

It might be well to state here that even though the various types of program music provide interesting listening activities, because of the descriptive character of the music, its weakness may be its constant association of stories or pictorial representations, which negates the artistic value of the music.

Therefore, combining the patterns of musical growth related to the understanding of the elements of music (as recorded developmentally early in this chapter) with the descriptive character of the music will strengthen the value of such listening presentations.

Program music can be divided into various categories:

1. Stories in music

Examples:

Mother Goose Suite by Maurice Ravel. This composition is a series of fairy tales represented musically in a set of little story tunes.

Peter and the Wolf by Sergei Prokofiev. The structure of this musical composition affords an excellent opportunity for an introductory experience with the instruments of the orchestra.

Peer Gynt Suite by Edvard Grieg. Peer Gynt is a mischievous boy who is also a dreamer and roams the countryside in search of adventure. Grieg succeeds in musically describing Peer's adventures.

2. Picture music, or a composition that musically describes an image, conveys an idea, or creates a mood

Examples:

Carnival of the Animals by Camille Saint-Saëns. The traits and physical characteristics of various animals are portrayed musically in this work.

Nutcracker Suite by Peter I. Tchaikovsky. This expressive music usually is interpreted in dance, specifically, ballet. It is the story of a little girl, Marie, and her adventures in dreamland with her beloved Christmas gift, a nutcracker in the figure of a handsome prince.

Scenes from Childhood by Robert Schumann. This is a group of short musical compositions that reflects the spirit of a child at play, a child preparing for an important event, a child listening to an interesting story, and so forth.

II Music Representative of FORM and Design

1. Rondo (refer to p. 199)
2. Two- and three-part FORM (refer to pp. 196–199)
3. Theme and variation (refer to p. 202)
4. Suite: *Mother Goose Suite, Nutcracker Suite, Peer Gynt Suite*

III Operas

Examples:

Hansel and Gretel by Engelbert Humperdinck
Amahl and the Night Visitors by Gian Carlo Menotti

IV Marches

Examples:

Pomp and Circumstance, by Sir Edward Elgar. This dignified march is associated with such ceremonial festivities as school graduations.
Stars and Stripes Forever, and other marches by John Philip Sousa

V National dances—folk dances

Examples:

Hungarian Dances nos. 5 and 6 by Johannes Brahms
Slavonic Dances nos. 1 and 3 by Anton Dvorak
English Morris dances by Percy Grainger
Irish reel, "Molly On The Shore," by Percy Grainger

VI Additional music representative of all ethnic groups

VII Consideration of historical and world events (and inventions) along with the music and composers of the same era

Examples:

> Historical event: signing of the Declaration of Independence, 1776
> Classical period of music composition
> Representative composer of this period: Wolfgang Amadeus Mozart (refer to pp. 293-296)
> Representative composition: Minuet from *Don Giovanni*

After repeated experiences in guiding listening activities in the classroom, it is further suggested that additional categories of current interest be developed by the teacher and children planning together.

Example:

Compare and contrast the structure, design, and texture of current music heard on radio and television to music composed during the historical periods of the development of music composition

Composers and Music	*Approximate Dates*
Baroque period	1600-1750
Classical period	1750-1820
Romantic period	early, 1820
	late, 1920

For an excellent quick reference guide to composers and music of these historical periods see the Musical Calendar, Boston Music Co., 116 Boylston Street, Boston, Massachusetts 02116.

Note:

Actual demonstrations of orchestral and band instruments by class members and attendance at school concerts are valuable experiences. They encourage enthusiasm for a listening program, which is an integral part of the school music curriculum.

Suggested references:

See this series of books for listeners by Lillian Baldwin, published by Silver Burdett Company, 1951: *Music for Young Listeners* (The Green Book); *Music for Young Listeners* (The Crimson Book); *Music for Young Listeners* (The Blue Book); and *Music to Remember.* Write to General Learning Corporation (Silver Burdett), 250 James Street, Morristown, New Jersey 07960.

Adventures in Music edited by Gladys Tipton, is available from RCA Educational Sales, 1133 Avenue of the Americas, New York, New York 10036.

This record series of twelve albums (two each for grades 1 through 6, with individual albums available) is organized to give elementary school children experience in listening to, responding to, and understanding music by master composers of many periods and styles. A comprehensive Teacher's Guide accompanies each album, providing analysis of the music, suggestions for responding to it, its correlation with art and poetry, and so on.

Bowmar Orchestral Library

This record series of twelve albums (two each for grades 1 through 6, with and offers music of master composers representative of many periods.*

Young Keyboard Jr.

This is a monthly publication of Keyboard Jr. Publications, Inc., 1346 Chapel Street, New Haven, Connecticut 06511, publishers of music and art appreciation magazines for children. Allied teaching aids and recordings, charts of orchestral instruments and pictures of composers are included.*

GUIDING MUSICAL EXPERIENCES
THROUGH SINGING

Early Singing Activities

Early singing activities, proceeding from the most simple to those that are complex, will have to differ widely as a result of each child's home environment, peer-group associations, and experiences in imitating environmental sounds of varying pitches (the door bell; the sirens on fire trucks, ambulances, and police cruisers; and animal sounds—of cats, cows, chickens, horses; and the like).

Educators also must consider the impact of current children's television programs on youngsters of preschool age. These programs offer numerous opportunities for boys and girls to become involved in musical activities, especially singing, which inadvertently can effect their aural perception of how MELODY moves.

Preliminary singing experiences also emphasize the natural flexibility of the voice as it intones such childhood chants as:

*An annotated description of materials appears in *The Music Educator's Business Handbook*, Washington, D.C.: Music Industry Council, 1970, 1201 Sixteenth Street, N. W. 20036.

time signature*

One, two, buck-le your shoe; Three, four, shut the door, (etc.)

or

One po - ta - to, two po - ta - to, three po - ta - to, four (etc.)

or such nursery rhymes as:

Hump - ty Dump - ty sat on a wall,

Hump - ty Dump - ty had a big fall (etc.)

Lit - tle Jack Horn - er sat in a cor - ner

eat - ing his Christ - mas pie_____ (etc.)

*Note: Refer to "Conducting a Song," pp. 93–100 for an interpretation of meter (time) signature.

    This natural chant is built on two pitches only and the distance (interval) between the two is termed the *minor third.* The minor third refers to a specific interval present in any musical scale. *Scale* is defined as the arrangement of eight tones ordered in particular steps. A *whole step* is the distance between two keys with a single key between them. A *half step* is the distance between two keys with no key between them.

    The following representation of the C major scale as intoned on a piano keyboard illustrates whole steps and half steps presented in an ordered arrangement of tones:

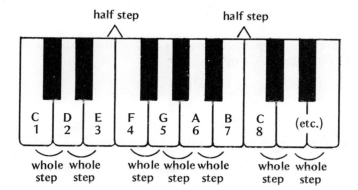

Notice that the half steps appear between numbers 3-4 and 7-8 of this C major scale. This same arrangement of half steps occurring between 3-4 and 7-8 is present in all major scales. (Refer to the chart on pp. 103-104.)

This is an illustration of the C major scale as notated on a musical staff:

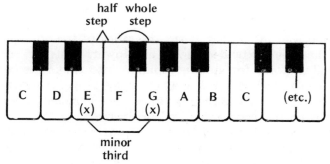

This is an illustration of a minor third present in the preceding scale as intoned on a piano keyboard. It is isolated for scrutiny of the step arrangement (1½ steps):

This is an illustration of the same minor third as notated on a musical staff:

It is the intonation (from high to low) of this or any minor third within the most common vocal range of a child's voice that constitutes a natural childhood chant.

Extending the Range of the Voice

Most children enjoy participating in action songs that incorporate body movement to dramatize the words.

TEDDY BEAR*

Traditional

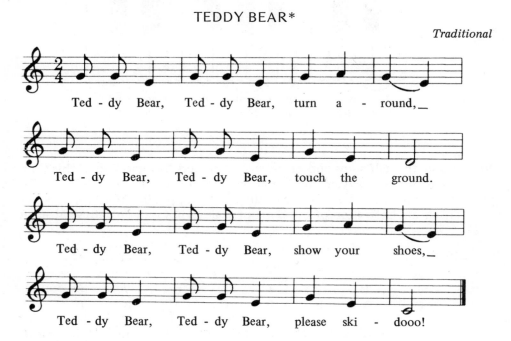

Ted - dy Bear, Ted - dy Bear, turn a - round, __

Ted - dy Bear, Ted - dy Bear, touch the ground.

Ted - dy Bear, Ted - dy Bear, show your shoes, __

Ted - dy Bear, Ted - dy Bear, please ski - dooo!

*Source unknown.

It should be noted that in "Teddy Bear" the range of the voice intonation of the minor third has been extended higher and lower. This can serve as an example of a starting point for guiding children into singing experiences that demand flexibility to produce tones in an extended range. Singing games, such as "Here We Go 'Round the Mulberry Bush," are excellent activities for encouraging all children to become involved in singing.

Also, many play activities, such as skipping rope (referred to in some localities as playing jump rope), rely on the singing of such songs as "Teddy Bear" and other childhood jingles as an accompaniment to the rhythmical movement of the activity.

A teacher can be very effective in encouraging children to make up their own brief songs, also referred to as sentence songs. By using everyday activities (such as painting, first experiences in reading about their pet animals, and so forth), and correlating these interest areas with singing experiences (possibly to the accompaniment of melody bells or resonator bells, which can be removed from their cases), the child can begin to perceive aurally and visually how a song can be made up of more than two tones. Furthermore, when ready, they can play their own songs on the bells.

This song is notated in a directional pattern of tones:

John-ny, Sus-ie, will you come out-side to play?

Answer:

We can play out-side to-day, First we'll put our books a-way.

Here is the same song notated on a musical staff:

M. Lament*

John - ny, Sus - ie, will you come out - side to play?

*Original. We can play out-side to-day, First we'll put our books a - way.

The range of a child's voice (boy or girl) varies, but it is most commonly accepted as being:

In some instances, the range is not so extensive and may center on a few tones above and below the middle tones of the C major scale:

However, as previously suggested, with increased singing experiences over a period of time, the range of singing higher and lower tones can be experienced and realized by both the teacher and children. Thus, continued singing experiences in the intermediate grades include songs of a more extensive range than suggested for early or primary grades.

Note:

The teacher should try to sing within his or her most comfortable range, which usually corresponds to the range of the child's voice. There are exceptions, of course. Remember that a man's singing voice will sound one octave (eight tones) lower than a child's singing voice.

Using Recordings to Teach Singing

Most elementary music textbooks include recordings of all or many of the songs in the books. These recordings are beneficial for the music teacher as well as the children when used as an aid for learning a song. However, teachers should be aware of the negative aspects associated with learning from recordings.

1. If one sings with the recording, one may not be listening for the concepts of musical organization that will benefit understanding: contour of MELODY, melody patterns, phrasing, various rhythmic patterns or groupings, the harmonic blend of the accompaniment with the solo voice or ensemble group, and any additional interaction of other elements of music that may be present in the song.

2. The teacher may ineffectively use the recording for learning a song if he or she is preoccupied with other tasks, thereby demonstrating a lack of interest in the song while the record is being played.

3. The use of a defective needle can cause a scratching, abrasive reproduction of the composition or song to be learned.

Therefore, keep these points in mind when using recordings as a teaching aid:

1. Be familiar with the recording *before* introducing it to the class, having previously ascertained the musical concepts present in the song.

2. Invite the children to listen for, and then to identify, a specific "happening" on the recording. This happening may refer to the text or some musical aspect of the song.

3. Be enthusiastic and totally involved with the boys and girls in learning the song.

4. Avoid being distracted by environmental sounds. Maintain eye contact with the children and register facial expressions or some reactionary response to what's going on to let them know you, too, are interested.

5. Often permit the element of surprise which is present in some music to pave the way for an enjoyable learning experience.

Using Elementary Music Textbooks or Other Books to Teach Singing

Effective methods for learning to read music by means of books can be tried and tested in numerous ways:

1. Keep books closed while learning a song aurally and then use the books to check the rise and fall of the melody line through visual perception of the notation of the song on the musical staff.

2. Encourage aural perception of repeated melody patterns, followed by visual perception of the same melody patterns on the musical staff. Play the patterns on melody instruments.

3. Promote additional experiences in the aural perception of all musical concepts present in the song and related to the elements of music followed by noting the visual representation of the same concepts in the book.

4. At times, encourage aural and visual perception to occur simultaneously. Direct boys and girls to listen quietly and follow the notated score in the books while the same song is being played or sung.

As you become an experienced music teacher (classroom teachers, too, are music teachers when they teach music), you will undoubtedly discover many varied ways to use recordings and elementary music textbooks effectively for introducing learning experiences and for reinforcing previously learned concepts related to musical ideas.

Voice Production and Repertoire

Two factors related to singing—voice production and repertoire—will be considered simultaneously because satisfactory voice production in the classroom, to a large extent, depends on the interest engendered through carefully chosen song materials.

Guiding children through proper breath support for favorable intonation, satisfactory posture (sitting position or standing position), pronunciation (words spoken correctly), and enunciation (clarity of pronunciation) is more often achieved through actual experiences in singing and through the music itself rather than through more formal, isolated drills in vocalizing. However, formal vocalizing (vocal exercises) also has a place in the elementary school situation in specialized singing groups: the intermediate chorus, the choir ensemble, and so forth.

In the early grades, special attention to voice production can be accomplished by singing songs that demand a lightness of quality, in contrast to songs of a more vigorous nature.

Example:

"Snowflake Song" (p. 139) or "Raindrop Song" (p. 82 in contrast to "This Old Man" (p. 132) or "Walking, Walking" (p. 287).

Note:

The words (lyrics) of the song "Walking, Walking" (as well as of many songs) can be altered to show children how the words of a song can change the over-all texture or quality of performance.

Example:

"Marching, marching down the street," or "Tiptoe lightly down the street." Use these questioning strategies: As you tiptoe down the street, will you sing loudly or softly? Why? When you march down the street in a parade, will you sing as softly as when you tiptoed? Why not?

Relating to familiar objects in early childhood and considering environmental characteristics of urban or suburban living can serve as an aid in achieving proper posture for satisfactory tone production.

Examples:

"Stand tall and pretend you are touching the white, fluffy clouds with your fingertips. Now, with arms down at your sides, are you ready to sing?"

"Stand as tall as the tallest tree in your front yard (or, in the park)."

"Pretend you are Humpty Dumpty and sit up in your seats as Humpty Dumpty sat straight up on the wall before he had a big fall."

"Pretend you are a puppet dangling from a string at the top of your head. Pull up on the string to make yourself sit up. Raise your hands, puppets, when you think you are ready to sing!"

"If you sit crooked and twisted in your seats, the way this pretzel is

how do you think your singing will sound? But, look at this pretzel stick!

If you sit up straight and tall in your seats, as this pretzel stick is, how do you think your singing voices will sound?"

With reference to the intermediate level, proper tone production through the performance of the music can be accomplished in numerous ways. To experience (rather than verbalize) diaphragm breathing, sing a sea chantey.* It will invite a vigorous production of tones that are the result of successful diaphragm control:

Ya ho! ye lub-bers, Ya ho! ye lub-bers, Ya

ho! Ya ho! Ya ho!

*Source unknown.

After the experience of singing this part of the song, refine the initial experience to each student "feeling" the action of his own diaphragm at work supporting the production of the tones.

For example, the instructor (who is also participating) can suggest that (1) everyone stand and stretch his arms, legs, and whole body; that (2) all stand erect with hands on hips; and that (3) all sing out "Ya ho! ye lub-bers" and, from a position of hands on hips, feel the tones being supported from the diaphragm, rather than experience shallow breathing from the chest.

Such singing activities are usually appealing and encourage proper tone production in an informal atmosphere. They are in contrast to a lengthy oration on the values of diaphragm breathing with accompanying charts and instructions for achieving proper breath support. This latter presentation generally antagonizes young boys and girls in a regular classroom situation and discourages them from further participation in singing alone or in groups.

However, favorable singing in the classroom usually can be achieved with the entire group (including the teacher) observing the following basic rules:

1. Listen for the beginning pitch (refer to p. 101 for a suggested procedure for finding "do" and tuning up to sing a song).

2. Listen to the song (several times if necessary) *before* singing it to discern the shape or contour of the MELODY, and thereby discover the up-and-down movement of the MELODY.

3. Listen to each other while actively singing in a group and then, while learning and rehearsing the song, make every effort to refine and improve the performance through a better understanding of (a) the text, or lyrics, of the song, which leads to expressive interpretation; (b) melodic phrasing, which can be determined through the use of dynamic effects (loud and soft) as they are incorporated in the over-all interpretation; and (c) the interaction of all the elements of music that may be present in a specific song (the elements of music will be explored in detail in subsequent chapters).

Additional Aids for Encouraging Favorable Tone Production

1. Avoid singing behind clenched teeth; allow the jaws to open freely—about the width of two fingers is suggested by authorities in vocal instruction.
2. For satisfactory enunciation (clarity of word pronunciation), refrain from permitting the tongue to roll back into the mouth; rather, place the tip of the tongue behind lower front teeth when producing vowel sounds.
3. When striving to sing higher tones, avoid tilting the head high with the jaw thrust forward. This head movement results in tightening of the throat muscles, and voice production becomes distorted and strident. Open the jaws freely and think the high tone before producing it.

Often, in a classroom situation, vocal techniques for insuring favorable results emerge from an immediate need for eliminating such problems as harshness of tone quality; shallow breath control, which results in a chest tone instead of resonant head tones; and poor enunciation, which results from a combination of deficiencies (poor reading skills; speech defects; incorrect posture).

Therefore, additional aids for developing satisfactory tone production should be devised, tried, and tested spontaneously as the need arises.

Note:

Playing a guitar or any folk instrument as an accompaniment for informal singing activities in the classroom is strongly recommended. It is a valuable motivating force for encouraging positive attitudes toward singing; it creates an atmosphere conducive to singing and thereby evokes an enthusiastic response from everyone involved.

Enthusiasm for learning is contagious. If the teacher transmits an enthusiastic attitude by participating in all musical activities in the classroom, the children will respond with a similar eagerness to learn.

Further Consideration of Repertoire

The choice of appropriate song materials for children of specific age levels is most important. In fact, the success of the general music program will depend to a great extent on the song repertory. It must have significant value for the conceptual development of musical ideas as well.

Therefore, it is advisable for the teacher to be very familiar with a song before introducing it in the classroom. An evaluation of its musical worth and general appropriateness should be based on the following considerations:

1. The range of the song (refer to pp. 102–106 for a procedure for transposing a song to a more comfortable singing range).
2. The children's interest areas. The following list is suggestive of interest areas of boys and girls from kindergarten through grade 6. It is organized developmentally (from the most simple levels of interest in the early grades to more complex levels of interest in the intermediate grades):

Action songs and games
Songs related to animals and nature
Songs for dramatization
Songs for rhythmic activities
Songs related to home and community
Song stories
Songs for special days:
> birthdays
> patriotic days: Veterans Day, birthdays of presidents, Columbus Day,
>> and Election Day
> holidays: Halloween, Thanksgiving, Christmas, Hanukkah, Valentine's
>> Day, Easter, Passover, Memorial Day, and so forth

Fun and nonsense songs
Songs of the seasons:
> autumn, winter, spring, summer
Songs of praise and thanksgiving
Current popular songs:
> television, motion pictures
Folk and foreign language songs correlated with nations being studied in a
related arts program:
>> foreign language songs can be studied from phonetic pronunciation

For an example of phonetic pronunciation, refer to p. 258, "Aloha Oe," with phonetic pronunciation of the Hawaiian language derived from:

Roes, Carol. *Eight Children's Songs from Hawaii.* 988 Kealaolu Avenue, Honolulu 15, Hawaii: Carol Roes (publisher), 1958.

Most publishers of current elementary music textbooks that include foreign language songs supply or make available to teachers a guide to phonetic pronunciation of the specific language or languages involved.

> Art songs or composed songs reflective of various historical periods in music. (When possible, correlate them with related arts programs.)

Review songs

3. The text. Consider whether a text is appropriate for the age level and if the words fit the flow of the melody line.

4. The cohesive characteristics. Consider the results of the interaction of the elements of music: MELODY, RHYTHM, HARMONY, FORM, TEMPO, DYNAMICS, and TONE COLOR. These elements are studied individually and in detail in Chapters 5 through 9.

5. Are the songs suitable for assembly or group singing? Base your selection on the following criteria:

a. appropriate text for age level
b. comfortable vocal range for age level

    c. "singable" melody line
    d. melody line that lends itself to an easy chording accompaniment
    e. songs that are known well *before* the assembly for the performance to be labeled successful
    f. songs of general appeal
    g. variety that is evident by the easy recognition of differences in TEMPO, mood, RHYTHM, and so on
    h. a time limit for the program to avoid boredom and the waning interest of the group
    i. song selection based on the season, holidays, patriotism, and all current or timely centers of interest in the locality

From your own experiences can you expand this list of criteria to include additional points you would deem valuable for structuring a program of this type?

Aids for the Uncertain Singer

Follow these melody-pattern techniques to strengthen aural perception and accuracy in singing on pitch.

    1. Echo singing

New songs and familiar songs made up of patterns, melodic phrases, or motives (very short tonal patterns) that are suitable for echo responses are usually enjoyable to sing. They also function as an aid in encouraging singing on pitch because the singer or singers must listen attentively to the correct intonation of the melody pattern in order to echo (repeat) it satisfactorily on pitch.

Example:

ECHO SONG*

(Echo notated in parenthesis)　　　　　　　　　　　　　　　M. Lament

GOOD MORN-ING (Good morn-ing) GOOD MORN-ING (Good

morn-ing)　　I'D　　LIKE TO SAY GOOD MORN-ING　　(I'd

like to say good morn - ing) GOOD MORN-ING (Good

morn - ing) GOOD MORN-ING (Good morn - ing) ON
ON

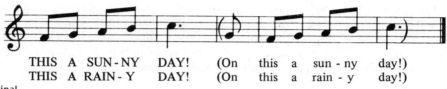

THIS A SUN-NY DAY! (On this a sun - ny day!)
THIS A RAIN-Y DAY! (On this a rain - y day!)

*Original.

The creative teacher can make up ways and arrange for children to sing parts of familiar songs as an echo response. Many songs are composed of an echo concept: "The Happy Wanderer" (chorus: "fol de ri, fol de ra," etc.); "Little Sir Echo" ("HELLO! hello! HELLO! hello!"); and "The Cuckoo Bird" (an Austrian folk song in which the sound of the cuckoo bird is echoed).

When the melody pattern (which is intoned vocally or on melody bells) is echoed it can be performed as a solo or by a small group of children, depending on the immediate classroom situation. In any event, the teacher should strive to avoid embarrassment for the uncertain singer or singers involved in the activity. The suggestion to "listen well *before* repeating a melody pattern" is an effective aid in encouraging the uncertain singer to sing in tune and on pitch.

2. Singing repeated patterns

Another aid for the uncertain singer is to sing songs made up of repeated patterns, as "The Angel Band" (p. 312).

Suggestion for performance:

Because there are ten little angels in the band, designate individual children to sing the part of each of the ten angels:

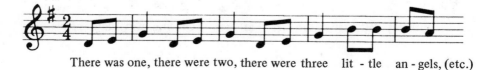

There was one, there were two, there were three lit - tle an - gels, (etc.)

Note:

This repeated melody pattern can also be played on melody bells as an accompaniment for the individual singer. It also serves as an aid for strengthening aural awareness of accurate pitch.

In the seating arrangement of the ten singers, integrate the uncertain singers with children who sing on pitch.

Suggested placement of singers:

Angel 1	*Angel 2*	*Angel 3*	*Angel 4* (etc.)
(singer)	(uncertain singer who hears pattern intoned correctly by Angel 1)	(singer)	(uncertain singer)

Perhaps, at first, the song can be performed with *two* children singing the repeated melody patterns rather than with individual (solo) singing of the patterns. Again, there is no one way for guiding these experiences to insure a successful result. Thus, by means of trial-and-error procedures, the teacher can explore and discover ways and means for helping the uncertain singer.

3. Use of an ostinato (pronounced os–ti–nä′–tō)

A simple ostinato (the same melodic pattern or sound pattern persistently repeated throughout a song or segment of a song) related to the environment can be made up by the teacher or children and serve as an effective aid in promoting in-tune singing. The ostinato in the following song ("pitter, patter") encourages a keen sense of singing on pitch.

Example:

LISTEN TO THE RAIN*

M. Lament

Hear the rain-drops gen - tly fall - ing, Lis - ten to the rain;

Pit - ter Pat - ter   Pit - ter Pat - ter   On my win - dow - pane.

*Original.

Suggested lesson procedures:

a. Have the class listen as you sing this raindrop song. Ask these questions: From where do the raindrops fall? Do they fall from the sky?
b. Have the children stand on their tiptoes and reach toward the sky. Ask them if they can make the raindrops fall ever so gently.
c. Have the children sing the song as they make the raindrops fall from the sky. Because this MELODY moves mostly by step, ask them if it would be easy to play the song on the resonator bells or melody bells.
d. Play the song and sing it with the class.
e. Have the class listen as you chant "pitter, patter" on the "do"-"la" pattern (minor third).

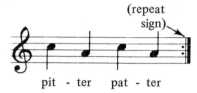

(Refer to pp. 70–72 for the definition of a minor third interval)
f. Have the children find the sound of the pitter, patter on the bells and play them steadily throughout the song.
g. Divide the class in two groups. Have group 1 sing "pitter, patter" and group 2 sing "Listen to the rain." Have groups 1 and 2 sing together.
h. Divide the class into four groups. Have group 1 sing "pitter, patter"; group 2 sing "Listen to the rain"; group 3 whisper "pitter, patter" steadily throughout song; and group 4 tap large and small drumheads lightly with their fingertips steadily throughout the song. Also, have group 4 tap finger cymbals now and then to imitate the sound of raindrops.
i. Play this raindrop song on a piano keyboard and add this accompaniment to the entire musical activity.
j. Listen as you take part in this musical performance. Are there many sounds going on at the same time? Do all of the sounds blend?
k. Rotate the performing groups so that all of the children have an equal opportunity to be involved in performing each of the accompaniments.
l. Perform the "ding dong" ostinato in "Are You Sleeping?" (p. 181), or imitate the sound of the wind in the song, "Wind, Sing Through the Trees" (p. 129).

4. Singing song stories

Singing familiar melody patterns either as a solo or in small groups is a satisfactory remedial aid for the uncertain singer. This activity can be performed in many different ways. For example, the teacher or a group of children can intone a melody pattern or phrase while one child (or several) continues the familiar "song story" by singing the next melody pattern or phrase.

Example:

SEE THE LITTLE DUCKLINGS*

German folk song

(teacher)   (child or children)

See the lit - tle   duck - lings, swim-ming here and   there

(teacher)   (child or children)

Heads down in the wa - ter, tails up in the   air.

*Public domain. Courtesy of Ginn and Company.

Suggested lesson procedures:

   a. The group sings "See the little ducklings."
   b. One child completes the tone thought by singing "Swimming here and there."
   c. The group continues to sing "Heads down in the wa–ter."
   d. One child completes the tone thought by singing "Tails up in the air."

Rotating children in this type of activity and permitting them to choose their favorite well-known songs to perform in this manner may lead to an enthusiastic effort to sing on pitch.

    5. Selecting melody patterns that are within the context of the song being studied

Various strategies for encouraging the singing of melody patterns in tune or on pitch frequently materialize from an immediate need to sing a new song or even a familiar song in tune. Whatever the case, avoid any isolated tonal drills of melody patterns that are unrelated to the specific song being learned. Select a melody pattern that is within the context of the song being studied.

Example:

   "Down in the Valley" (refer to p. 182)

Suggested teaching procedures:

   a. Sing the entire song for the class.
   b. Intone the melody pattern (that is not being intoned accurately on pitch by the children) on melody bells or a piano keyboard while the

children are listening. (In this way the children are directed to listen intently to the melody pattern *before* singing it, thus emphasizing aural awareness to direction or shape of the pattern.)

c. Have the children (individuals or in small groups) sing the melody pattern on a neutral syllable ("la") and then sing the words of the pattern. The following bars are a melody pattern from "Down in the Valley" that can be isolated for this type of practice:

the   val - ley   so   low,

d. Finally, sing the entire song again and, hopefully, the specific melody pattern isolated for practice in singing accurately and on pitch now will be intoned satisfactorily.

Additional aids for the uncertain singer can be devised, tried, and tested by the individual teacher. If a specific technique proves beneficial for encouraging in-tune singing, record it for future reference and use.

This technique will aid the uncertain singer in intoning wide interval skips in tune.

FOR HEALTH AND STRENGTH*

Old English round

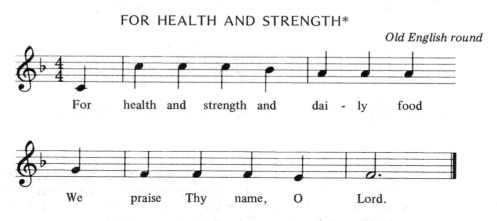

For   health   and   strength and   dai - ly   food

We   praise   Thy   name,   O   Lord.

*Also known as "Round of Thanks." Reprinted with permission of Cooperative Recreation Service, Inc., Delaware, Ohio, from *Joyful Singing*, p. 80.

Such songs as "For Health and Strength" are made up of wide skips, or leaps, and provide an opportunity for the teacher to stress the value of thinking the tone before singing it. This technique is used repeatedly by instrumentalists who play such brass instruments as trumpets, trombones, and bugles. They also are required to think the placement of the tone in question (high or low) before they reproduce it. (However, it is necessary to note that, in addition to thinking the placement of a tone, the instrumentalist usually observes several techniques simultaneously to insure satisfactory sound intonation.)

Case Study:

A graduate student in music education was to resolve the following problem within a limited time: devise techniques for helping Mary, an uncertain singer, to sing in tune.

The student was given her freedom to try any strategies that might prove successful in solving the problem and to record the strategies and results for subsequent evaluation.

In the course of the six-week time period allotted for this project, the student used various methods and techniques for encouraging Mary to sing in tune. The strategy that proved most successful was followed for singing a song such as "For Health and Strength":

   a. Mary was directed to listen to the wide interval leap as intoned on a piano keyboard:

   b. To sing the high tone in tune, Mary was directed to visualize herself throwing a basketball into a basket mounted high on the wall of the gymnasium whenever she was to intone the interval:

   c. Thus, Mary was directed to think the high tone before producing it.

The student recorded Mary's results:

> I was amazed! This simple technique proved successful when every other strategy I tried failed. Also, because Mary was overjoyed by her accomplishment, she was willing to try her skill at singing many different songs using various other techniques devised by me for helping her to sing in tune.
>
> Because of that successful experience and sense of accomplishment, Mary was henceforth enthusiastic about striving to sing in tune and exerted every effort to do so.

Part Singing

   A. These aids will encourage the singer to think independently.

   1. Rounds, ostinato, simple descants, whispered sound patterns or chants, and partner songs

In former years, music educators generally believed that the simplest technique for initiating part singing was through the singing of rounds; that is, to have the same melody sung several times by two or more groups starting in time at different points. Thus, the purpose for introducing the singing of rounds in a classroom was to initiate the concept of a harmonic blend of voices. At times this activity proved frustrating to the teachers as well as to the children because the group members had to cover their ears to carry their own part in order to exclude the sound of the others. Group singing was in direct opposition to the purpose for singing rounds.

However, of late it has been determined that an effective way to initiate successful independent part singing is through the use of the ostinato; simple descants (a MELODY intoned above the song); whispered sound patterns or chants (refer to "Ocean Waves," p. 298 or by singing two well-known songs simultaneously, which is commonly referred to as singing partner songs.

Example:

"Three Blind Mice" and "Are You Sleeping?" (pp. 181-182)

In the upper elementary grades the system of rotating parts when singing two- or three-part songs is considered by many instructors to be an asset in strengthening aural and reading skills. Because the general characteristics of range and quality of boys' voices in the elementary grades is basically the same as for the girls, there is little difficulty there in rotating parts for simple two- and three-part singing. (In grade 6, a few boys may experience a beginning change in voice. However, the changing voice is associated particularly with the junior high school years.)[3]

2. Part singing in easy intervals of thirds and sixths

Easy and satisfying basic experiences in singing in parts can be realized by singing part of a song in unison (singing together on the same part, which, in this instance, refers to the MELODY), and then periodically dividing into easy part singing in intervals of thirds or sixths. (The distance in pitch between two tones, or notes on the musical staff, is termed an *interval.*)

Example:

An interval of a third

Example:

An interval of a sixth

[3]Duncan McKenzie, *Training the Boy's Changing Voice* (New Brunswick, N.J.: Rutgers University Press, 1956), p. 20.

Example:

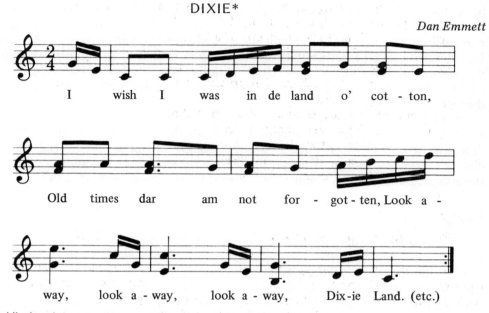

DIXIE*

Dan Emmett

I wish I was in de land o' cot - ton,

Old times dar am not for - got - ten, Look a -

way, look a - way, look a - way, Dix -ie Land. (etc.)

*Public domain.

Easy arrangements of songs for introducing part singing are usually available in current elementary textbook series.

3.   Aural recognition of chord changes through the use of an autoharp

Another procedure for introducing harmonic experiences encourages aural perception of the basic chord changes that provide harmonic accompaniment to a melody line.

Aural recognition of chord changes through the use of the autoharp (chording instrument) is, perhaps, the easiest procedure for the classroom teacher, because pushing down on the designated bar or button with the index finger and strumming the strings of the instrument produce the desired chord. (See p. 48 for an illustration of autoharp in playing position.) For additional aids for playing chording instruments and building chords on melody instruments, refer to HARMONY, pp. 183-189.

4.   Vocal production of simple chord progressions as an accompaniment to a MELODY

Simple chord progressions that serve as an accompaniment to a MELODY can be produced vocally:

a.   Sing a familiar MELODY that requires only two chord changes (I–V–I) in the accompaniment, such as for "Down in the Valley," p. 182, which is written in the key of G major. (Refer to pp. 103–104 for the names of the scales and key signatures most commonly used in the elementary grades.)

b. Everyone sing the MELODY in unison to an autoharp accompaniment. Identify the MELODY aurally when the chord changes (I-V^7) by raising a hand.

c. Divide the class members into groups to provide a harmonic accompaniment vocally to this MELODY as follows:

Group 1: sing the MELODY

Group 2: sing the high part   so → so → so

Group 3: sing the medium part mi ↗ fa ↘ mi

Group 4: sing the low part   do ↘ ti ↗ do
                               I   V^7 I

Syllables notated on staff:

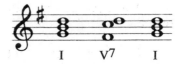

I   V7   I

Note:

The teacher or student can strum the I (G) chord on an autoharp or sound the individual pitches on bells or a piano keyboard before intoning vocally.

The following analysis is of the chord structure used in harmonic accompaniment to "Down in the Valley." The song is built on a G major scale. In Figure A, the G major scale is notated on the musical staff; the number names, and letter names of the tones of the scale appear:

Figure A.: G major scale

	1	2	3	4	5	6	7	8
	Do	Re	Mi	Fa	So	La	Ti	Do
	G	A	B	C	D	E	F	G

In Figure B the chords required in the harmonic accompaniment to "Down in the Valley" are illustrated:

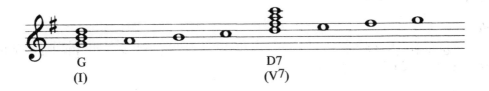

G   D7
(I)   (V^7)

Notice the awkward distance between the two chords as they appear on this staff in root position; that is, the chord is built on the fundamental, or lowest, note of the chord. Therefore, the I–V^7 chords will be intoned vocally as illustrated in Figure C:

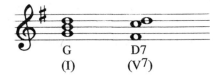

G   D7
(I)   (V^7)

Note:

The I (G) chord is said to be in root position because it is built on G, or the first tone of the chord.

However, notice that the V^7 (D^7) chord is not in root position, as illustrated in Figure B, but is in an inverted position for ease in chording vocally using syllables as notated previously on the staff. (Refer to p. 89.)

If it were so desired, the same groups could sing the number names (rather than the syllable names) of the tones present in the chords as follows:

Group 1: sing the MELODY

Group 2: sing the high part   5 → 5 → 5

Group 3: sing the medium part 3 ↗ ^{4} ↘ 3

Group 4: sing the low part   1 ↘ 7 ↗ 1
                                         I V^7 I

Number names of tones notated on staff:

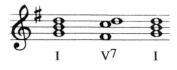

I   V7   I

Note:

Refer to Figure A and notice that number names of tones directly correspond to the syllable names.

Whichever names you use (number or syllable names of tones in chords), immediately relate them to the notated chords on the musical staff as illustrated. In this way, a reading of notation or a visual perception of chord movement on the musical staff is immediately provided.

Note:

Refer to p. 187 for a listing of familiar songs using a simple harmonic background of I–V^7 chords.

This same procedure can be observed in the singing of familiar songs that use the simple harmonic background of I–IV–V^7 chords. (Observe the IV (C) chord as it appears in root position on the musical staff in relation to I–V^7 chords in the key of G major:

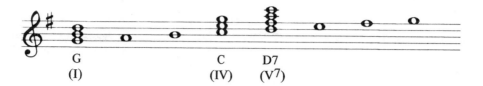

G   C   D7
(I)   (IV)   (V⁷)

Divide the class members into groups as follows:

Group 1: sing the MELODY

Syllables notated on staff:

Group 2: sing the high part   so ↗ la ↘ so → so

Group 3: sing the medium part mi ↗ fa → fa ↘ mi

Group 4: sing the low part   do → do ↘ ti ↗ do

I   IV   V⁷   I

      Singing the number names of the tones present in the chords might be preferred and would appear as follows:

5 ↗ 6 ↘ 5 → 5

Notated on staff:

3 ↗ 4 → 4 ↘ 3

1 → 1 ↘ 7 ↗ 1

I   IV   V⁷   I

Note:

      Refer to p. 189 for listing of familiar songs using simple harmonic background of I–IV–V⁷ chords.

      Invite the children to think the syllable or number names of the tones as they sing or hum them softly on a neutral syllable (such as "la"). This will encourage further aural perception of the blending of tones while providing a harmonic accompaniment to a simple MELODY.

      Building these same chords on resonator bells and playing them on the autoharp or other string instruments will also strengthen aural perception of tones and add enrichment to the final presentation.

     B. Seating Arrangements

      Seating arrangements for part singing can be determined by both teachers and children after considering those physical features of the individual classroom that would either enhance or detract from the performance. In any case, a desirable seating arrangement is conducive to encouraging aural awareness of small-group intonation as well as to strengthening aural perception of the total harmonic blend of all the groups singing together. Thus, it may prove necessary to move seats from a conventional seating plan (vertical rows) to a semicircle. Inviting groups to sit on the floor in a semicircle (for a short time) may relax the atmosphere enough to increase attentiveness.

Again it must be emphasized that the teacher should be totally involved and should strive to be flexible in his or her approach to any musical activities.

C. Materials for early experiences in part singing

Consult any current elementary textbooks for their arrangements of songs appropriate for early experiences in part singing. Also refer to the Appendix in this text for a listing of music publishers from whom a graded classification of materials—easy, medium, and difficult—for part singing can be obtained. Most materials are made available for a limited time "on approval." This service policy provides ample time for a thorough examination of materials before purchasing the same. For example, the following choral collections are available from Neil A. Kjos Music Co., Publisher, 525 Busse Street, Park Ridge, Illinois, 60068. This listing offers a sampling of choral materials of general appeal for today's boys and girls.

Songbooks by Beatrice and Max Krone

For Language and Music Classes

> *Cantemos ninos!*—Introductory
> *Cantos de Mexico*—Supplementary, Beginning Classes
> *Chantons en français*—Book 1, Introductory
> *Singen wir auf Deutsch*—Book 1, Introductory

Records: 12-inch LP records for all books aid learning songs and pronunciation.

Student's Books: Texts in original languages. MELODY and some easy two-part arrangements with autoharp or guitar chords.

Teacher's Books: All the material of the Student's Books plus piano accompaniments, literal English translations, and information and suggestions about the songs.

For the Elementary School Choir and Classroom

> Folk Songs with Descants (Arranged by the Rineharts)
> Christmas Carols with Descants (Arranged by the Rineharts)
> Mexican Folksongs
> Inter-Americana
> Folksongs of Brazil
> Songs of Sweden and Finland
> Songs of Norway and Denmark
> Songs and Stories of the American Indians
> Christmas: Its Origins, Music, and Traditions
> Songs of Travel and Transport
> Very Easy Descants (with records)

Conducting a Song

■ Use Hand Levels[4] in the Early Grades

Directing or conducting singing in the very early grades (kindergarten through grade 2) is often confined to the use of hand levels because both the duration of tones and the direction or contour of the melody line are illustrated simultaneously through this bodily movement. Also, the value of using hand levels for leading a song may manifest itself in the children's natural inclination to use hand levels along with the teacher, especially when learning a new song. Through this activity they can become aware of the rise and fall of the melody line and recognize that some tones are shorter or longer than others. Using both arms and hands is advisable for children's early experiences in following the movement of hand levels.

■ Conducting Pattern for Songs Moving in 2s

In later years beginning possibly with the last half of grade 2, children are able to follow a rhythmical conductor's beat and are even quite capable of conducting easy rhythmic patterns themselves.

A short, easy song such as "Are You Sleeping?" is appropriate for a first conducting experience if the children are quite familiar with the song and if, through body movement (swaying in their seats while singing the song) they can feel the RHYTHM of the song moving in 2s. Using a percussion instrument or pencils and simply tapping the pulse (steady beat) of the song while singing it also provides an opportunity to foster the natural inclination to accent or stress the first beat in every group of two beats.

The following example is a pictorial representation of steady beat (pulse) illustrating the stronger beat on 1s as experienced when singing and moving to "Are You Sleeping?":

Are you sleep-ing, Are you sleep-ing, Broth-er John? Broth-er John? (etc.)

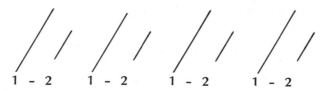

1 - 2   1 - 2   1 - 2   1 - 2

[4]Kodály refers to "hand signals." (See Laurence Wheeler and Lois Raebeck, *Orff and Kodály Adapted for the Elementary School* (Dubuque, Ia.: Brown, 1972), pp. xxiv–xxv.)

Following these preliminary experiences of singing while feeling the rhythmic motion of the song, the children in the room can lead or conduct the song in unison while sitting in their seats, using both arms, and observing the conducting pattern of

(down) (up)

The accented, or strong, beat they experienced when swaying or tapping a percussion instrument is now manifested through the motion of a strong downbeat on the count of 1 and the weaker upbeat on the count of 2:

1 ((2

Note:

The conducting patterns illustrated in this section are basic. It should be remembered that every conductor, through years of experience, develops his own style of conducting using these patterns but adding personal variations.

For an additional and more complex experience (tried and tested successfully by this writer), divide the class into two groups to perform the same song, such as a round, and assign a conductor or leader to each group. The conductor is then responsible for the vocal entrance of his or her group, which makes the experience more challenging and quite gratifying for the conductors as well as the group members when, through a period of trial and error, the final performance is satisfactory and vocally intact.

■ *Interpretation of the Time Signature (Meter)*

Songs moving in 2s, 3s, 4s, 6s, and so forth are identified by a sign placed on the musical staff preceding the musical notation of the song. This sign is referred to as the time signature and is interpreted as follows:

Example:

   2 → music moves in sets of 2s (set is designated as a measure).
   4 → symbol for a quarter note (♩) designates that there are two quarter notes, or their equivalent, to a set or measure.

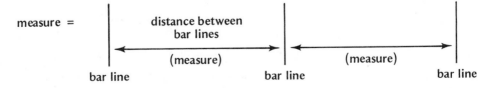

Now, we already know that music is made up of short and long tones (notes), so the RHYTHM of a MELODY may be composed of quarter notes or their equivalent, as illustrated in the following chart:

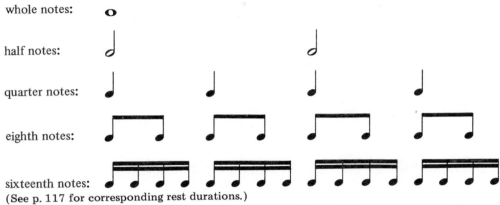

whole notes:

half notes:

quarter notes:

eighth notes:

sixteenth notes:

(See p. 117 for corresponding rest durations.)

Here is an example of a direct correlation of this chart to a MELODY composed in $\frac{2}{4}$ meter:

You may notice in musical notation that eighth notes (♪) and sixteenth notes (♬) can be notated as illustrated here, referring to ♪ or ♬ as flags. However, when several of these notes appear in consecutive order as

they are usually beamed together as

for ease in comprehending or in determining each grouping of notes as a unit.

Thus, in the following notated example (as in the preceding melody) of the song "Are You Sleeping?" in $\frac{2}{4}$ meter, beamed notation in the melody line can be observed. The steady beat in the lower line is represented by quarter notes, which also serve to illustrate how two quarter notes or their equivalent (refer to melody line) equal two pulses, or beats, to a measure.

To reinforce this concept of interpreting the time signature (meter), the same tune, "Are You Sleeping?," is notated in $\frac{4}{4}$ meter in its entirety, remembering that

4 → music moves in sets of 4s (feeling of 4 beats to a measure).

4 → symbol for a quarter note (♩) designates that there are four quarter notes, or their equivalent, to a set of measure.

■ A Conducting Pattern for Songs Moving in 4s, Including a Preparatory Beat

The conducting pattern for $\frac{4}{4}$ meter when the song begins on the first beat is illustrated here:

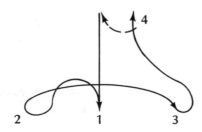

Notice the dotted line preceding the first beat. It designates a slight movement, or preparatory beat, before the strong downbeat. Taking a short breath while giving a preparatory beat is oftentimes an aid to the conductor in executing a smooth movement into a firm downbeat.

Note:

The conductor's arm should be flexible; it should move freely from the shoulder with the elbow slightly away from the body, and even feel a bounce when designing a rhythmical pattern. Patterns are designed for a right-handed conductor; thus, if one is left-handed, the opposite left-to-right directions should be used.

■ *A Conducting Pattern for Songs Moving in 3s*

The conducting pattern for a $\frac{3}{4}$ meter when the song begins on the first beat is

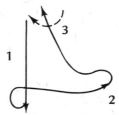

OCEAN WAVES

(refer to p. 298)

O - cean waves so foam - y white,

Toss me high with all your might!

Note:

A dot after a note increases its value by one half, as,

$$\text{𝅗𝅥. } = \text{𝅗𝅥} + \text{♩} \qquad \text{♩. } = \text{♩} + \text{♪} \qquad \text{♪. } = \text{♪} + \text{♬}$$

Therefore, in songs notated in $\frac{3}{4}$ meter,

$$\text{𝅗𝅥. } = \underset{2 + 1}{\text{𝅗𝅥} + \text{♩}} = \text{three pulses or beats per measure.}$$

DOWN IN THE VALLEY

(refer to p. 182)

Down in the val - ley, the val - ley so low,*____

■ *A Conducting Pattern for Songs Moving in Slow 6s and in Fast 6s*

The conducting pattern for a slow TEMPO in $\frac{6}{8}$ meter is

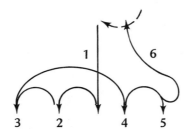

Note:

> 6 → in slow TEMPO the music moves in 6s
> 8 → symbol for an eighth note (♪) that designates that there are six eighth notes or their equivalent to a measure

Example:

*A tie is a curved line joining two notes on the same pitch, as in the preceding notated example:

The second note is not sounded, but is merely sustained and added to the value of the first note.

The following notated example is of a song moving in slow $\frac{6}{8}$ meter:

SILENT NIGHT*

Joseph Mohr   *Franz Gruber*

Si - lent night,   Ho - ly night,   All   is calm,   All   is bright, (etc.)

*Public domain.

However, the conducting pattern for a fast TEMPO in $\frac{6}{8}$ meter is the same as if the song were moving in 2s because the feeling of the rhythmic movement is in 2s. Therefore, the pattern is also

1   2

(1-2-3)   (4-5-6)

The following bars are notated examples of songs moving in a fast $\frac{6}{8}$ meter:

6 → in fast TEMPO the music moves in 2s rather than 6s
8 → (same as for slow TEMPO)

SAILING, SAILING*

Godfrey Marks

Conducting pattern:
(down)   (up)

Sail - ing,   sail - ing,   o - ver the bound-ing   main;＿ (etc.)[†]

*Public domain.

[†]For review, refer to the explanation of dotted and tied notes on pp. 97, 98.

ROW, ROW, ROW YOUR BOAT*

Traditional

Row, row, row your boat, Gen - tly down the stream,_(etc.)

*Public domain.

■ *Conducting the Upbeat*

Every song does not always begin on a strong downbeat. Many songs begin on the upbeat, or, in musical terminology, the *anacrusis*.

The upbeat is a note or a group of notes that occurs on the weak beat preceding the bar line and the beat in the following measure. The following example is of a song beginning on the upbeat:

SHE'LL BE COMIN' 'ROUND THE MOUNTAIN*

Southern mountain song

She'll be com - in' 'round the moun - tain when she comes (etc.)

A partial conducting pattern for "She'll Be Comin' 'Round the Mountain" in $\frac{4}{4}$ meter, illustrating the preparatory beat *before* the song begins on the upbeat, is represented here:

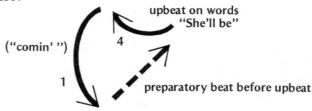

*Because the upbeat at the beginning of a song constitutes an incomplete measure, the last measure of the song is also incomplete. (*The last measure in this example is identical to the last measure in the song.*) The combined value of the beginning incomplete measure and the last incomplete measure equals one full measure.

SUPPLEMENTARY NOTES

Tuning Up to Sing a Song

A song does not always begin on "do," or on the first tone of the scale on which the song is built. That is evident here in the notated example of "Three Blind Mice," which begins on the third tone of the C major scale, or "mi."

However, merely intoning the pitch of the first tone of a song does not provide aural awareness of the over-all tonality of the song. This can only result from hearing and singing the scale on which the song is built. In this way, boys and girls are alerted to the sound of "do" and its relationship (higher or lower) to the beginning tone of the song.

Suggested learning procedure for finding "do":

1. Listen to the beginning pitch of song intoned in melody bells and sing it on a neutral syllable ("la").
2. Listen to the sound of "do" (the beginning pitch of the scale on which the song is built) intoned on melody bells.
3. Sing the scale slowly on "la," listening to each tone while singing it. Raise your hands when you aurally recognize that you are intoning the beginning pitch of the song.
4. Sing the principal tones (ascending and descending) of the scale as an additional tuning-up technique:

Note:

Singing various tones of the scale *slowly* when tuning up encourages aural perception of the over-all tonality of the song. This procedure (tuning-up activity) reinforces the tonality of the song before it is sung.

5. Encourage increased skill in the ability to aurally perceive the tonality of a song by thinking various tones of the scale and then singing them *without* the tonal aid of melody bells or a piano keyboard. Observing the teacher using hand levels to build the scale in the air is a valuable visual aid while one is intoning the scale. While the teacher moves

hand levels to the approximate interval skips, attempting to sing them can become a game that is fun to pursue. It simultaneously builds tonal alertness.

Note:

Refer to pp. 103–104 for the key signatures of the scales most commonly used in the elementary school.

Transposing a Song to a More Comfortable Singing Range

There are times when a teacher may discover that a song to be presented in the class lesson is notated in an uncomfortable singing range for the children. When this problem is evident it means that the song must be transposed to a different key; then, the melody notes of the song will be intoned satisfactorily. The following information is essential to anyone proceeding to transpose a song:

1. Refer to p. 70 for an explanation of the arrangement of tones in a major scale.

2. Be familiar with the following symbols and their meanings:

   a. Sharp sign (♯)

      ♯ is the music symbol that indicates a pitch should be raised a half step.

   b. Flat sign (♭)

      ♭ is the music symbol that indicates a pitch should be lowered a half step.

   c. Natural sign (♮) is the music symbol that cancels the previous alteration.

   d. Key signature

      A key signature may be composed of one or more flats or sharps, which are placed immediately on the staff after the clef sign and indicate the key in which the music is to be performed. The key signature denotes which notes are to be flatted or sharped throughout the performance of the musical composition, unless otherwise indicated. (Refer to the chart on pp. 103–104 for examples of various key signatures.)

3. Be familiar with the most common key signatures and scales used in notating children's songs. (Refer to the chart on pp. 103–104.)

Key Signatures and Scales Most Commonly Used in the Elementary School*

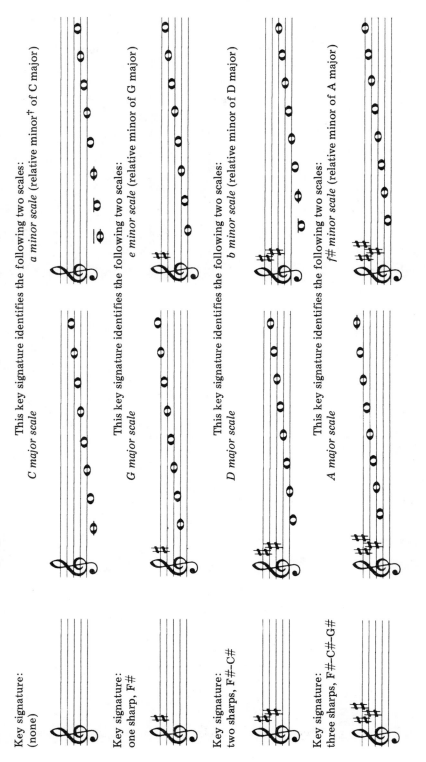

*Children's songs are seldom written in key signatures of more than three sharps or three flats.)

†The relative minor scale is built on the sixth tone, or degree, of the corresponding major scale; therefore, because the home tone and the placement of half steps in the relative minor scale are different, the sound of the scale will also be different (home tone = beginning tone).

Key Signatures and Scales Most Commonly Used in the Elementary School (continued)

Key signature:
four sharps, F#–C#–G#–D#

This key signature identifies the following two scales:

E major

c# minor (relative minor of E major)

Key signature:
one flat, B

This key signature identifies the following two scales:

F major

d minor (relative minor of F major)

Key signature:
two flats, B –E

This key signature identifies the following two scales:

B major

g minor (relative minor of B major)

Key signature:
three flats, B –E –A

This key signature identifies the following two scales:

E major

c minor (relative minor of E major)

Key signature:
four flats, B –E –A –D

This key signature identifies the following two scales:

A major

f minor (relative minor of A major)

Example:

"See the Little Ducklings" is identified as being notated in the key of A major:

SEE THE LITTLE DUCKLINGS

German folk song

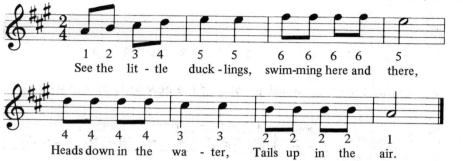

Because the range of this song as notated here is rather high, you may want to transpose it to a different key. A suggested step-by-step procedure for transposing a song follows:

1. Identify the key signature of the song. (The key signature of this song is A major.)

2. After notating the A major scale on the musical staff and identifying the number names of the notes of the scale as illustrated,

ascribe the corresponding number names to the notes of the song as illustrated above.

3. From your knowledge of key signatures and corresponding scales from the preceding chart, choose a different and more appropriate key for notating the song to assure a more comfortable singing range.

Example:

Choose the key of C major.

4. Notate the C major scale on the musical staff and identify the number names of the notes of the scale as you did in step 2:

5. Write the number names of the song under a blank staff:

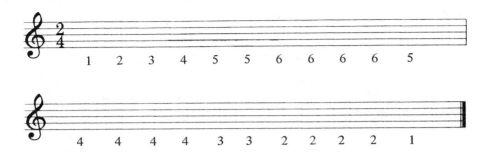

6. Supply the corresponding notes of the new scale on the staff as:

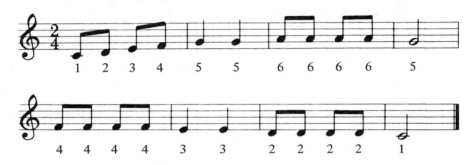

Thus, by transposing "See the Little Ducklings" from A major to C major, a more comfortable singing range has been achieved for everyone.

Suggested Activities for the College or University Student

1. As a group project, design and search out materials for several categories of listening activities that you think would be of interest to children of one or more grade levels in the elementary school. Record your data as a permanent file for future reference. If time permits, individual members of the group should present a brief listening lesson before the group for the purpose of practice in oral delivery (especially in questioning techniques) and evaluation of performance by the peer group.
2. In a campus laboratory school or in a nearby elementary school, volunteer your services as a teacher's aide during the music period once or twice a week. After observing the music period for a time, make known your desire to teach the children a song. If you are granted the opportunity, following your presentation, request an evaluation of your performance from the regular teacher. The more experience you have in guiding children through musical activities, the more adept you will become in your presentations.

Chapter 5

Continued Analysis of Skills Needed for Guiding Musical Experiences in the Elementary School

GUIDING MUSICAL EXPERIENCES THROUGH FREE MOVEMENT

Free Movement Defined and Illustrated

The term *free movement* may have different connotations for different people, but basically it implies freedom to express oneself through some body movement or gesture.

For example, freedom to respond to the pulse, or rhythmical swing, of Sousa's "Stars and Stripes Forever" might be manifested by some children in beating a drum, clapping hands, tapping feet on the floor at their seats, or otherwise engaging in some overt action. However, others might not be satisfied by remaining at their seats and merely keeping time with the music. To them, free movement might mean keeping time by vigorously marching around the room, perhaps with everyone moving in the same direction, thus forming a parade.

In any case, freedom to express oneself through some body movement as an initial reaction to the music, to a poem, to a painting, or to a combination of all three is in direct contrast to following specific directions in performing a square dance or a national folk dance. This is *not* to oppose folk dancing in the classroom during the music period. In fact, in what better way can children experience a feeling for the movement of music in phrases than through the actual performance of the various directional patterns present in folk dances? Too, by participating in folk dancing, children can grow in understanding the structure or form of the music.

Example:

The melodic contour (rise and fall of the melody line) usually serves as the basis for planning the dance pattern. Thus, the artistic value of the music itself becomes an integral part of the lesson.

Also, correlating the traditional dances of ethnic groups with the social studies of corresponding nations is commendable and, if the physical characteristics of the room allow dancing (movable seats, adequate space for movement, and so on), it should, by all means, be initiated. In this regard, consultation should be made with the instructor of physical education for the purpose of avoiding conflict in scheduling the use of the gymnasium. Presenting the instruction of folk dancing in conjunction with the physical education department is also a popular activity. It will warrant the use of the gymnasium or all-purpose room.

The reference to folk dancing here is merely for the purpose of comparing and contrasting free movement to the specific directions necessary to the performance of a definite dance pattern.

The following presentations were initiated in a classroom situation and are included here as examples of free movement.

Primary Level

Element: RHYTHM
Focus: Free Creative Movement
Concept: Acting out (dramatizing) poems, songs, and movements of familiar animals and related experiences in a child's life can be transferred to direct rhythmic experiences in music.

The following lesson was planned and successfully taught by student teachers enrolled at Central Michigan University, Department of Music Education, Mt. Pleasant, Michigan.

■ Suggested Use of Strategies for Early Grades

1. Sing and move around the room to a familiar marching song, such as "Marching to Pretoria" or "When the Saints Go Marching In." Refer to "Walking," p. 287, and sing the words "Marching, Marching" instead of "Walking, Walking." What did singing this song make you want to do? Why did you feel like marching or walking briskly around the room?

2. Sit anywhere on the floor and see if you can answer these questions: Who was Columbus? What did he do? Do we explore today as the famous explorers did many years ago? Where and what do we explore now? Are we exploring outer space? How big is it? Where does it go? What do we find there? How do we get there? Can you walk in outer space? What do you have to wear when you are in outer space? How do you think that it feels to be in outer space?

3. Listen to a recording of "Atmospheres," by Ligeti, from *2001: A Space Odyssey*, or *Thus Sprach Zarathustra*, by Richard Strauss (fanfare section, approximately the first 1½ minutes, the opening music for the film *2001: A Space Odyssey*), and the poem "Walking in Space," by Grace Nash.

Excerpt from Walking in Space

... Walking in space a new thing to me
As one foot I lift the other hangs free
Like riding a bicycle?—no pedals to race
No wheels and no bars, just treading in space
No traffic, no hurry, no possible race
Its lonely to walk in Big Outer Space.
I feel like a feather slowly in flight
And stepping in clouds with one foot or two
I can draw circles wherever I choose. . . .[1]

4. Locate your own spaceship (the children are free to move to any part of the room).

5. Listen and move to the poem *and* the music, which are being played simultaneously. When you were moving what things did you think of? Did the music make you feel this way? Do you think that you could sing this music? Do you think that you could march to this music? Why not? How is this music different from the song we sang and marched to before? (We cannot and do not feel we want to march to this music.) How are the space heroes honored when they return from outer space? (Homecoming parades and festivities.)

6. Dramatize the return of a space hero by forming your own parade and marching around the room while singing a favorite marching song. (This activity would reinforce the concept of free movement in contrast to movement to music that has a specific rhythmic beat.)

7. Make up your own poem related to outer space and create your own musical effects by strumming on the open strings of an autoharp (not pressing down on the bars). Experiment with different techniques for performing on self-constructed instruments as well as on various percussion and melodic instruments.

---

[1] Grace C. Nash, "Walking in Space," *Verses and Movement.* © Nash Publications, Scottsdale, Arizona, 1967.

Intermediate Level

Element: RHYTHM
Focus: Free Creative Movement
Concept: Creative arts projects and various moods and/or occasions can be the source of motivation for free expressive movement.

Note:

The following happening is an actual example of group participation in which the group first listened to the music and then shared orally their individual emotional reactions, which culminated in this descriptive poem:

> Cold   Black   World
> silence surrounds . . .
>
> Still full night
> dark . . . sullen . . . mysterious

Hope lies hidden in unseen light and color!

There! . . . (pointing to the lighting effect produced by colored
water in cut glass bowls or dishes and projected on
the wall with an overhead projector)

There! . . . (pointing to a revolving prism of light splashing color
on another wall)

Here! . . . (pointing to blinking lights on a string)

There! . . . (pointing to the lighting effect produced by a black
light bulb)

Color brings smiles, warmth, life, movement, and ideas.
Rise now in the orange and coral rays of the sun. It's dawn! Reach
out and spread with the colors of the new day.
Float with the early morning dew as it settles slowly to the ground
and covers the still, quiet world.

Awake creations of the world and scatter your colors around!

Fly with the wings of the seagull, bob on the white caps of the sea;
Bloom with the blossoms of flowers and shade the world with your
branches.

The sun is reaching to the height of the sky—stretch till the tips of your fingers tickle the clouds.

(Pause . . .)

Suddenly, dark clouds pass overhead making the day gray.

The still branches become alive and sway in the world.

The rain begins to trickle and splatter as it hits the ground.

Lightning flashes as thunder rolls; sheets of rain drench the once bright day and encloses the world in drabness;

When . . . Presto!—we're rescued by the bright colors of a new rainbow as they blend together in the promise of another great day.

As we set with the sun, life becomes still and darkness sets in.

As the beautiful colors of the day slowly begin to disappear, we once again return to our still, dark world.

This poem, synchronized with the music *Rite of Spring* (*Le Sacre du printemps*) by Igor Stravinsky, motivated experiments in creating illusions of psychedelic lighting effects and expressive body movement.

■ *Suggested Strategy for Further Experiments*

Listen and then compile a list of recordings that would serve as motivations for freedom of expression, such as *Grand Canyon Suite* by Ferde Grofé. Also, include recordings of Afro-American rhythms and chants; music of various ethnic groups; and contemporary compositions, such as "Banshee," by Henry Cowell (Folkways FX 6160, *Sounds of New Music*), and "Gargoyles," by Otto Luening (Columbia MS 6566, Columbia-Princeton Electronic Music Center).

Additional Suggestions for Incorporating Free Movement into the Music Lesson on the Primary Level

1. Use the body to pantomine animal movements when singing animal songs: "The Elephant Song," p. 135. "Mister Rabbit," p. 305 and songs related to prancing ponies, sauntering bears, and so forth. Pantomine a trip to the zoo (either a pretend trip for which portraits of animals are a visual aid or an actual

field trip) during which the observation of various animals might provide the ideal motivation for making up brief sentence songs or poems that can be accompanied by appropriate animal movements; the strut of the proud peacock, the waddle of the ducks, the patter of the penguins, and so forth.

Suggested references:

Crowninshield, Ethel. *Songs and Stories About Animals* and *Stories That Sing.* Boston, Mass.: The Boston Music Company, 1947.

2. Pantomine numerous activities that can be accompanied rhythmically on percussion instruments: coconut shells, all sizes of drums or drumheads, rhythm sticks, tambourines, and the like.

Examples:

Playground Activities:

baseball game
"bounce and catch"
seesaw
jump rope
swinging

Occupational Activities:

sailors: swabbing the deck
hoisting the sails
painting the masts
pulling the anchor
circus performers: tight rope walkers
acrobats
circus clowns
jugglers
carpenters: pounding or hammering nails
painting the walls
sawing wood
farmers: planting crops
pitching hay
picking apples in the orchard

3. Dramatize storytelling songs.
This type of song may be very brief (a nursery rhyme) or may consist of many verses (a ballad). The song may be descriptive of the daily activities of a historical figure such as Abraham Lincoln who, when a boy, chopped down trees in the forest and sawed them into logs for the fireplace in his log cabin.
The song may possess the element of adventure. Whatever the principal focus of the song is, a few children can dramatize the movements or activities of the characters in the story while the others form the chorus and sing the song.

4. Through the use of body movement, interpret the text of a song that has a reference to snowflakes falling, ocean waves rolling into shore, or wind blowing through the trees (*you* are a tree). Refer to the song "Wind Sing Through the Trees" on p. 129. Interpret the instrumental texture of a composition:

Examples:

Use arm movements to interpret

> Elgar: "Fountain Dance" from *Wand of Youth Suite* no. 2 from *Adventures in Music*, Grade 2, Volume I

Use body movements to interpret the short pecking movement of unhatched chickens while listening to

> Moussorgsky: "Ballet of the Unhatched Chicks" from *Pictures at an Exhibition* from *Adventures in Music*, Grade 1, Volume I

Intermediate Level

5. Through improvised dance movements interpret the text of an entire folk song, such as "He's Got the Whole World in His Hands" or "Shenandoah."
6. Dramatize the structure or form of a composition. (Refer to "Sing for the Wide, Wide Fields," p. 200.)
7. Working in groups as a laboratory activity, improvise drum beats on all shapes and sizes of drums available, including bongos, conga drums, kaluba drums (refer to p. 245), tambourines, wood blocks, and so forth. Other members of class can improvise appropriate rhythmic movements to the drum beats—perhaps some students can plan synchronized movements. Later, the performers (drummers and dancers) should devise some method (possibly symbolic) of notating the rhythmic patterns of the drum beats and dance movements.
8. Dramatic interpretations of the music of ethnic groups, characterized by such songs as "Zuni Sunrise Song" (Zuni Indian song), can be experienced successfully if children are permitted to work in groups and are granted freedom to experiment through group performance.

GUIDING MUSICAL EXPERIENCES THROUGH CREATING

The ability to encourage children to think and respond creatively while exploring a musical concept is a valued skill that reflects the creative talent of the teacher. For creative musical growth is really not an activity that can be thought of apart from all others. Rather, if the music program is complete and varied, it will spark creative thinking as a part of its function.

Children are inquisitive by nature; they are imaginative and enthusiastic about life and living things. The screaming siren of a fire truck, the cheerful song of a red bird, the chirping of crickets, the sight of feathery, light snowflakes falling from the sky, the aroma of freshly baked ginger cookies, the taste of a smooth, frosty ice cream cone are all among the joys of childhood. To keep alive this spirit of enthusiasm for living and learning more about life should be the desire of every educator.

And so it is with music. Discovering and exploring music—where it comes from, how it grows, the stories it can tell so beautifully—can be exciting experiences for children, especially if they are encouraged to make up their own songs and their own dances, to initiate their own way to play a classroom instrument, to initiate their own ideas about how to listen to music, and to respond freely to music. This is creative thinking being nurtured! The process calls to mind this happening:

> One day in early spring the music teacher introduced a song entitled "April." The first words of the song (chanted rhythmically) were something like "A-pril, gen-tle breez-es blow-ing." At this point, whispered softly by a sixth-grade student were the words "cha, cha, cha." The alert teacher was so excited and overjoyed at this spontaneous rhythmic response that immediately she distributed the Latin-American instruments—maracas, bongos, guiro—and an entirely new and different rhythmic rendition of the same song was created. It was not contrived; it was a natural involuntary reaction to the introduction of a new song.

This experience is just another example of creative growth occurring spontaneously in a classroom situation and of a teacher who recognized the possibility for creativity in an involuntary response to the music. It is the purpose of this text to encourage creative thinking and growth as it can occur throughout musical development.

GUIDING MUSICAL EXPERIENCES THROUGH PLAYING AND READING

Because the activities of playing melody and chording instruments naturally indicate to many teachers the ability to read musical notation, the two activities have been combined here for consideration and discussion. Many educators also have discovered that isolating the reading of notation to merely assimilating facts, rather than considering it an integrated activity with singing or playing instruments, is virtually unproductive. Therefore, in this section musical growth occurring through a combined association of activities will be illustrated.

It must be remembered that early experiences in playing instruments (as well as with all other musical activities) are basically aural. Only after aural activities have been reinforced over a period of time is visual perception (reading notation) gradually introduced.

Melody and Percussion Instruments*

Early experiences in playing melody bells, resonator bells, any xylophone-type instrument, or percussion instrument are in a short two- or three-tone motive representative of environmental sounds—the pitter, patter of raindrops (p. 83), the ding, dong of a bell (p. 182), and so forth. These motives can be used as an ostinato accompaniment to a MELODY, and in this way they function as an introduction to harmony or two-part singing. Playing brief passages on melody instruments also serves to embellish and enrich the performance of a song. Children should be encouraged to rely on aural perception to attain any desired sound available through the experimental playing of melody instruments or the tapping, beating, rubbing, or shaking produced by various percussion instruments.

Transferring Aural Perception to Visual Perception (Reading Notation)

Admittedly there are numerous methods for transferring the ability to play by ear to reading musical notation. The following procedure embraces the educational philosophy of synthesis → analysis → synthesis:

general perception of the whole	→	study of individual parts related to the whole	→	final over-all perception of the whole

If this procedure is followed, a complete learning experience should be the end result.

Example:

1. Sing and play by ear several short familiar songs, including a song that moves mostly in steps, such as "See the Little Ducklings" (p. 105).
2. Show the notated score of "See the Little Ducklings" on a screen from an overhead projector, but *omit the title and words of the song* from the score:

*For illustrations and descriptions of the instruments discussed in this section refer to Chapter 3.

3. Observe that the notes on the score seem to move by step. Design it in the air using hand levels.
4. Repeat the activity of singing the same two or three songs (including "See the Little Ducklings") and, while singing each song, design its shape in the air using hand levels.
5. Identify the design of the visual score on the screen as "fitting" the design of the hand levels used while singing "See the Little Ducklings."

6. Label and identify the individual symbols of notation that comprise the entire musical score as follows:

five lines and four spaces (▭) = musical staff

𝄞 = treble clef

= middle C (identify middle C on the notated score of the song and chant the names of the following notes as they appear on the staff in step-wise arrangement)

$\frac{2}{4}$ = time signature (a sign at the beginning of a composition to indicate the meter (time) (Refer to pp. 94–96.)

♩ = half note

♩ = quarter note

♫ = eighth notes

Analysis

7. While viewing the notated score, sing the entire song using the letter names of the notes rather than words.
8. Sing the same song again, using the letter names of the notes, while playing it on melody bells, resonator bells, a piano keyboard, or tuned water jars.
9. Finally, *sing the words* of the song ("See the Little Ducklings") while playing it on all the melody instruments available.

Synthesis

In the music lesson subsequent to this one, include reinforcement of these learned concepts by introducing *another* song that is comprised of notes that move by step *and skip.* In this way, learning experiences will gradually move from the simple to the complex. The experiences will be new and yet familiar. They will tend to stimulate interest while they provide a challenge to the students.

Transferring Aural Rhythmic Activities to Visual Perception

The transfer of aural activities involving the tapping of percussion instruments also can be achieved through classroom techniques.

Examples:

1. Transfer a pictorial representation to a music notation of accented and unaccented beats (pp. 158-160) and the reading of a symbolic musical score for a rhythm instrument as illustrated on p. 299.
2. Transfer a line duration (blank notation) to music notation as illustrated on RHYTHM, p. 152.

Assembling and Using the Flannel Board As a Visual Aid to Reading Music

One method for conducting the reinforcement of learned concepts is through the use of the flannel board—a teaching aid that usually can be purchased through the school system or from an educational agency such as T. S. Denison & Company, Inc., 5100 West 82nd Street, Minneapolis, Minnesota 55437.

However, satisfactory flannel boards can be assembled easily:

1. Cut a section of a corrugated box to measure approximately 25" X 36".
2. Cut a piece of cotton flannel fabric to the same measurement. Secure it with glue to one side of the box. (This will become the front of the flannel board.)
3. Cut five black felt strips of ½" X 36". Spaced and secured to the board, these will represent the musical staff.
4. Trace and cut out symbols of notation in black felt in sizes that correspond to the size of the staff.

Examples:

treble clef sign (𝄞)

musical notes of varying durations:

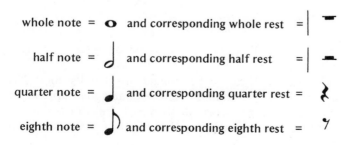

meter signatures: 4 2 3 and so forth
                     4' 4' 4'

sharp signs (♯)

flat signs (♭)

natural sign (♮)

bar lines

repeat sign

Cut out all other signs and symbols in black felt as they appear in new songs. The felt symbols will adhere to the flannel so that even when the board is displayed in a tilted or upright position the symbols will remain in position.

To increase the effectiveness of the flannel board as an aid for fostering musical growth, have every child in the room make his own smaller flannel board. Total involvement in the activity will be assured, as each child can identify the symbols and build the same notated phrase that the teacher is designing on the master flannel board at the front of the room. There are many additional uses for the flannel board in the music class.

Examples:

1. Reinforce previous reading experience by reconstructing the melody patterns present in "See the Little Ducklings" (or any song) on the musical staff on the flannel board:

Then sing and play the pattern as it is being *read* from the flannel board.
   2. Make up scale songs (pp. 137–139) and build them on the flannel board.
   3. Transfer an ostinato played by ear to the flannel board (pp. 82–83).

Melody Flutes and Recorders

Fingering charts for the melody flute and recorder are usually included with the instrument at the time it is purchased. These charts also appear in most current elementary music textbook series, so they will be omitted from this text. However, a procedure for introducing this melody instrument to children needs to be outlined here:

1. Practice the mechanics of holding the instrument in "play position" (up to the lips) and "rest position" (down on the desk).

2. Play the echo game: intone a short phrase or melody pattern and have the pupils observe your finger placement. Have them listen to the tones and repeat each melody pattern; the resulting sound will provide an echo effect:

After completing this response activity, all play the entire song. It will be identified as "Hot Cross Buns."

3. Include many aural activities of this type in the music period but steadily move from simple to more complex songs in an extended range. This will increase skill in finger dexterity and in the coordinatioh of ear with performance.

A procedure for transferring these aural activities to the actual reading of notation is suggested here:

1. Project a notated score of a familiar song on a screen from an overhead projector. Omit the title and words of the song.

2. All together, chant rhythmically "shorts-longs" or ("ta, ti, ti")[2] while tapping them to identify the varying notes of duration:

♪ = short ("ti") or a series of ♪ represented as ♪ ♪ or ♫

♩ = long ("ta")

An illustrated example of these notes, combined in a notated phrase with rhythmic chants, follows:

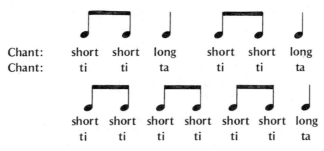

Chant:	short	short	long	short	short	long
Chant:	ti	ti	ta	ti	ti	ta

short	short	short	short	short	short	long
ti	ti	ti	ti	ti	ti	ta

[2] Rhythmic duration is based on the educational philosophy of Zoltán Kodály. See Mary Helen Richards, *Threshold To Music* (New York: Harper, 1964).

3. Chant "longs-shorts" while tapping the rhythm of the notes.

4. Divide the class in two groups. Have group 1 chant and tap the steady underlying beat and group 2 chant and tap the RHYTHM of the notes.

5. Chant the letter names of the notes while rhythmically tapping them:

C   E   G   C   E   G   A   A   G   F   E   D   C

6. Finally, play the entire song on a flute or recorder.

Suggestions for Reinforcement:

Divide the class into two groups. Have group 1 chant rhythmically the letter names of the notes and tap them as group 2 plays them. (Immediately rotate this group activity.) Then have group 1 sing the song and group 2 play the accompaniment. (Immediately rotate this group activity.)

Additional Reinforcement Aids for Recalling Signs, Symbols and Terms of Musical Notation

■ *Musical Bingo*

See the "Bingo" card on p. 121, labeled "Music." (Answer key to this card appears below the card. Have each child in the class make his own card of musical terms, symbols, and signs that have been introduced in a previous music lesson. A large hat box that has been covered with white shelf paper and colorfully decorated as a drum can serve as a receptacle for holding the call cards.

After terms are identified and covered on an individual's bingo card, in specified arrangement (horizontal, vertical, diagonal), the winners can be awarded the privilege of choosing a favorite song to sing and play together.

■ *Music Spelling Games*

Directions for Playing the Game. If you know the names of these musical notes, you can fill in the blanks and discover that you have spelled a word."

M U S I C

♩	*mp*	♪	𝄐	𝄾
<	*ff*	4/4	*f*	𝄇
𝄞	| - |	free	≡	♯
o	≡	D. C.	𝄽	>
≡	♩ ♩	D. C. al fine	*p*	♭

Answer Key to the Bingo (Music) Game

Under **M**	Under **U**	Under **S**	Under **I**	Under **C**
1. half note	medium-soft	eighth note	hold	eighth rest
2. crescendo	very loud	time signature	loud	repeat sign
3. treble clef	whole rest	FREE	staff	sharp sign
4. whole note	bar line	da capo (return to beginning)	quarter rest	decrescendo
5. staff	quarter notes	da capo al fine (return to beginning and play to the fine)	soft	flat sign

Directions for the following game: "Spell the following words on the musical staff using whole notes."

E G G   D A D   F E E

Directions for the following game: "Make up two words and notate them on the staff using whole notes."

Example:

(Ans. = BEEF)

Now, notate your words on the staff:

Chording Instruments

Chording instruments and reading for chording instruments can be found on p. 88 (autoharp). An additional source is *The Many Ways To Play The Autoharp*, Vols. I and II. (Jersey City, N. J.: Oscar Schmidt-International, Inc., 1966) See pp. 184–189 for a discussion of resonator bells, piano keyboard, and ukulele.

Suggested Activities for the College or University Student

1. While engaged in practice-teaching activities or as a student-teacher's aid in an elementary school, devise ways and means for motivating children to participate in free movement. This can be achieved by following the suggestions outlined in this chapter. If gaining experience in teaching in an elementary school is not possible at this time, divide your methods class into groups and verbally share strategies for incorporating free movement as a valued segment of the music program. Then, transfer the strategies that have been discussed into actual class participation in a planned lesson so that free movement can be realized as a natural response to and an integral part of, the music lesson.
2. Choose various songs in a current elementary music textbook series and use them to devise strategies for incorporating creative ideas and techniques to help children understand and enjoy music. The elements

of music—MELODY, RHYTHM, HARMONY, and so forth—can serve as a basis for exploring and discovering the constituents of music through various creative facets. Record these creative ideas and evaluate their worth after incorporating them in an actual classroom situation in your methods class or in an elementary school.

3. Place yourself in a teaching situation in which you introduce first experiences in playing an instrument—melody flute, piano, autoharp, bells, or the like. After referring to the ideas in this text for initiating a transfer from aural perception to visual perception, plan your own method for motivating students to learn and interpret correctly musical terms, signs, and symbols of notation.

Introduce these ideas in your methods class and observe and note the reactions to your procedures. An evaluation of your lesson by you and your peers should prove beneficial to your future plans for introducing reading experiences through a developmental approach.

Chapter 6

Melody—
An Element of Music

The following preliminary remarks should clarify the method used in Chapters 6 through 10.

1. Because more than one concept often is present in a particular song, the same songs will be suggested for exploring various concepts. However, it must be remembered that these songs have been selected with care for the purpose of analysis. The procedures offered in this text are intended to encourage ideas for becoming actively involved in music. The creative and enthusiastic teacher will expand them to include a variety of additional activities to reinforce and stimulate musical growth.

2. Manipulative devices (strategies) and questioning techniques are based on the assumption that the children are already familiar with the songs.

3. Even though these procedures are written primarily for the teacher, manipulative devices are most often addressed to the pupils and concepts are verbalized for children on the primary level. The concepts are developed from simple to complex.

4. Childhood experiences often can relate well to the exploration of musical concepts based on the elements of music, and, for this reason, are included here as a device for clarifying ideas.

5. Even though several concepts are explored simultaneously in the same lesson, each concept is isolated for the exploration of an element of music. In making direct reference to the development of concepts, *The Study of Music in the Elementary School—A Conceptual Approach*, states:

As every musician knows, music consists of the interactions which exist among its constituent elements. If these interactions are to be understood, however, it is necessary first to investigate and understand the nature and structure of each of the individual elements which are interacting.[1]

MELODY

Percival Symonds's declaration "one learns what, and only what, one does"[2] is pertinent to all areas of the curriculum. In considering education for today's child, many teachers, philosophers, and students agree and attest to the validity of Symonds's statement.

Music, then (of which MELODY is a part), must be experienced to be understood. If the interaction of the elements of music can be experienced by everyone exploring and discovering for himself, under skilled leadership, the learning process will have been set in motion; concepts, no longer abstract ideas, will become realities. The numerous strategies and manipulative devices available to teachers and students provide a challenge to creative ingenuity.

To illustrate this explore-and-discover technique, and to support another educational philosophy that suggests that "we teach and learn best from the music," refer to "The Angel Band," p. 312. The song will serve as a basis for exploring the components, or parts, of MELODY—an element of music—through the procedure presented.

ANALYSIS OF THE COMPONENTS OF MELODY
THROUGH THE MEDIUM OF A MELODY

Suggested Procedure for Exploring "The Angel Band"

1. Sing the song "The Angel Band" as a group.
2. Analyze the components of the MELODY of "The Angel Band."

Components

DIRECTION AND DISTANCE OF THE MELODY

This component, direction and distance, refers to MELODY and sound moving up, down, and sometimes straight ahead. Thus, when discerning the direction and distance of this MELODY consider the following: Does the MELODY of "The Angel Band" move up, down, and sometimes straight ahead? Where? On what words?

---

[1] Charles Gary, ed., *The Study of Music in the Elementary School—A Conceptual Approach* (Washington, D.C.: Music Educators National Conference, 1967), p. 3.

[2] Percival M. Symonds, *What Education Has to Learn From Psychology*, 3rd ed. (New York: Teachers College Press, 1968), p. 37.

RANGE OF THE MELODY

The highest and lowest tones in a MELODY constitute the range of the MELODY. Therefore consider on what words the highest and lowest tones occur in "The Angel Band."

MELODY PATTERN

A series of tones in a MELODY may group themselves into a unit or pattern. By singing the song again and observing "The Angel Band" notated on the staff, can you discover for yourself a series of tones in the MELODY that group themselves into a unit or pattern?

Example:

Oh, was - n't that a band, Sun - day morn - ing,

REPEATED PATTERN

A melody pattern that recurs is termed a repeated pattern. Can you find a repeated melody pattern in "The Angel Band"?

Example:

There was one, there were two, there were three

SEQUENCE

When a melody pattern is repeated higher or lower it is called a sequence. Is there a sequence in "The Angel Band"? (No.)

INTERVALS

The distance in pitch between two tones (or notes on the musical staff) is termed an interval. However, children generally refer to intervals as "tones in the MELODY that move by skip or step."

Examples:

an - gels   Was - n't that a band

HOME TONE (TONAL CENTER)

Tones in a MELODY often move around a home tone. The home tone may be experienced as a final tone of rest. The feeling of reaching the home tone in "The Angel Band" occurs in the second line when singing the word "band" and on the final word, "soon."

Example:

Ten lit - tle an - gels in the band._____

Sun - day morn - ing soon?_____

KEY OR SCALE

When eight tones are arranged in a particular steplike order or arrangement, a scale is formed. The scale is named for the tone on which it begins and ends.

Example:

When a MELODY is composed of the tones in a specific scale, such as the G major scale, the MELODY is said to be written in the key of G. Therefore, from the previous discussion of home tone, what is the home tone of a MELODY written in the key of G? (G.) "The Angel Band," as notated on the musical staff on p. 312, is written in the key of ___? (key of G.) (Refer to pp. 103–104 for an additional reference to the scales and scale chart.)

PENTATONIC SCALE

A MELODY may use only five tones or be made up of only five tones in a particular arrangement, which forms a pentatonic scale. This component is not present in "The Angel Band."

3. Sing the song as a group once more for the purpose of being totally involved in producing the whole MELODY after having analyzed the individual components that make up the whole.

Hopefully, by being involved in this exploratory procedure you will have discovered for youself how a MELODY is put together.

Primary Level

The following songs and listening activities illustrate the musical concepts to be explored. Each concept is related to a component of MELODY and is structured from simple to complex. The suggested musical activities for exploring the concepts also are presented developmentally for children of primary age.

Concepts are based on the following components of MELODY:

Direction and Distance
Range
Pattern and Repeated Pattern
Sequence
Intervals
Home Tone (Tonal Center)
Key or Scale
Pentatonic Scale

SAMPLING OF PROCEDURES AND LESSON PLANS FOR EXPLORING MUSICAL CONCEPTS RELATED TO MELODY

Element: MELODY
Component: Direction and Distance
Concept: Melody and sound move up and down and sometimes straight ahead.

WIND, SING THROUGH THE TREES*

M. Lament

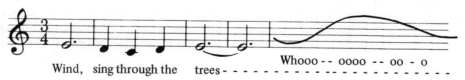

Wind, sing through the trees - - - - - - - - - - - - - - - -
Whooo - - oooo - - oo - o

Wind, whis-per to me - - - - - - - - Whooo - - oooo - - ooo - oo - o

*Original.

Sway-ing and bend-ing and reach-ing so high _____

Sing to me wind through the trees. _____

■ *Suggested Musical Class Activities for "Wind, Sing Through the Trees"*

Listening: Listen to the wind. When it blows very strong does it sound the same or does it seem to move very high and then very low?

Free Movement: Pretend you are the wind. When you blow, move your arm the way the wind is blowing (high, low, and sometimes straight ahead).

Singing: Sing the wind's song as you have designed its motion.

Listening: Holding a piece of soft flannel or terry cloth (or wearing a mitten), sweep your hand over the piano keyboard. Listen as you play. Did you play from low to high? Did you play from high to low? Can you play high and low back and forth quickly? Can you play straight ahead?

Playing and Listening: Play the piano again while another classmate designs the direction of the sound you are playing on the chalkboard. Let the rest of the class design the direction using arms, hands, or full body movement.

With the toe of your shoe, press lightly on the sustaining pedal, or soft pedal, of the piano. Repeat this activity as you sing the song. What sound do you hear? Do you hear the sound of the strong wind blowing you around the corner? Can you make this sound on other classroom instruments? On melody bells? On resonator bells? On step bells? On tuned water jars? Can you make this sound by strumming the open strings of the autoharp? What other classroom instruments would add excitement to this activity? (Large brass cymbals, tiny finger cymbals, triangle, and sand blocks.) Can you decide when in the song you might choose to play these instruments and why?

Tell familiar fairy tales in your own words and explore the sounds of classroom instruments that would enrich the meaning of the words of the story. Move freely about the room exploring the table of classroom instruments and play them or tap them whenever needed to accompany the words of the story.

Example:

Goldilocks and the Three Bears

A little girl named Goldilocks (finger cymbals) went tripping up the hill (intervals in triplet rhythm played on keyboards, bells, and temple blocks in an UP direction). Then, Goldilocks (finger cymbals) came tripping down the hill (same as above only in a DOWN direction) looking for violets that grow wild in the forest. She saw over yonder three brown bears: She saw *Papa Bear:* low, loud tone clusters (any group of tones lying close together) played on keyboards as well as on conga drums in simultaneous RHYTHM. She saw *Mama Bear:* intermediate tone clusters in the middle register played on keyboards and resonator bells, as well as on smaller drums in simultaneous RHYTHM. She saw *Wee Baby Bear:* as for Mama Bear, only high tone clusters played lightly with mallets on resonator bells or sounded on piano keyboards while small bongo drums are tapped lightly. (The same procedures are used throughout the improvised storytelling activity.)

Creating: Make up sentence songs to add interest and enrichment to the storytelling activity.

Singing and Playing: Sing and play the sentence songs by ear whenever they are needed to help tell the story musically.

Example:

Here is a notated sentence song that could be played by ear.

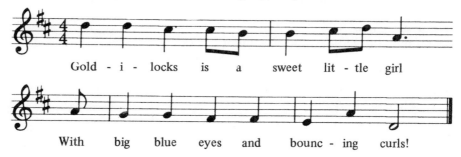

Gold - i - locks is a sweet lit - tle girl

With big blue eyes and bounc - ing curls!

Playing: Accompany the sentence songs with the proper-sounding classroom instruments (triangle, melody bells). Recite familiar poems and accompany the words with the proper-sounding classroom instruments.

Element: MELODY
Component: Range
Concept: Some tones in a MELODY are high and some tones are low.

FOR HEALTH AND STRENGTH*

Old English

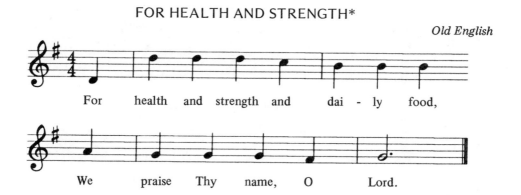

For health and strength and dai - ly food,

We praise Thy name, O Lord.

*Public domain.

■ *Suggested Musical Class Activities For "For Health and Strength"*

Listening: Listen to the song as it is played by the teacher on melody bells or resonator bells. Listen again and raise your hand when you hear the highest tone. On what word do you sing the highest tone? Play it on the bells. Repeat the activity listening for the lowest tone.

Listening, Singing, and Moving: Listen as you sing the song and design its shape in the air using arm movement or hand levels.[†]

Playing: Repeat this activity while another classmate plays it on the bells.

Reading: On musical staff (on flannel board or chalkboard) place the highest note you sing about where you think it should be. (Your teacher will help you.) Do the same with the lowest note. As class sings the highest and lowest tones, find and play them on the bells.

Creating: Recalling and naming things or objects that are high and low (example: airplanes can fly high, up to the sky; airplanes can fly low, down to the ground), make up songs with high tones and low tones.

Element: MELODY
Components: Pattern and Repeated Pattern
Concept: Several tones of a MELODY may group themselves into units or patterns.
Concept: A pattern may be repeated on the same tones. It is then called a repeated pattern.

THIS OLD MAN*

English singing game

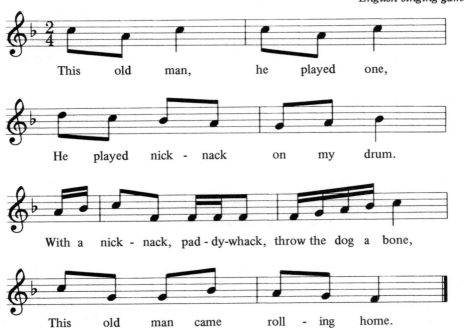

*Public domain.

†Kodaly refers to "hand signals." (See Wheeler and Raebeck, *Orff and Kodaly Adapted for the Elementary School*, p. xxiv-xxv.)

■ *Suggested Musical Class Activities for "This Old Man"*

Listening and Singing: Listen as you sing "This Old Man." Identify the places in the song in which the tones group themselves into a unit or a pattern.

Examples:

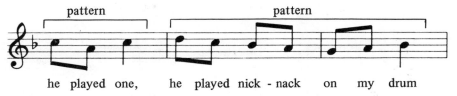

he played one, he played nick - nack on my drum

Free Movement: Sing and design these patterns using arm movements or hand levels.

Reading: Read the song "This Old Man" on a wall chart or chalkboard and identify a melody pattern that is repeated:

This old man, he played one

Playing: Design this pattern in the air while singing it. Now, play it on the melody bells.

Creating: Make up your own song containing a repeated pattern; or, using the classroom percussion instruments, make up a repeated sound pattern and use it as an accompaniment to a familiar song.

Example:

Tap a long-short sound pattern on a drum:

long	short	short	long
		or	
ta	ti	ti	ta

and, while singing "This Old Man," tap the pattern as an accompaniment. This recurring sound pattern then becomes a repeated pattern.

Note:

A repeated pattern can be compared to a cookie cutter or a dress pattern because all are used repeatedly.

Element: MELODY
Component: Sequence
Concept: When a pattern is repeated higher or lower, it is called a sequence.

SKIP TO MY LOU*

U.S. folk song

Flies in the butter - milk, shoo, fly, shoo!

Flies in the butter - milk, shoo, fly, shoo!

Flies in the butter - milk, shoo, fly, shoo!

Skip to my Lou, my dar - ling.

*From *Music Through the Day*, courtesy of General Learning Corporation.

■ *Suggested Musical Class Activities for "Skip to My Lou"*

Listening and Singing: Listen to, sing, and then identify a melody pattern in the song "Skip to My Lou" that moves in the same direction—up, down, or straight across—but sounds higher or lower. (Observe and compare the first three lines of the song.)

Free Movement: Design this pattern in the air using arm movements or hand levels. Observe that the pattern is repeated, but it is repeated higher or lower.

turn a - round right, clap, clap, clap

turn a - round left, clap, clap, clap

turn a - round right, clap, clap, clap

Playing: Play this pattern on a resonator or melody bells and then repeat it higher or lower, forming a sequence.

Singing: Sing this song again, and every time you hear a pattern and its sequence, raise your hand. On what words did the sequence happen? ("Flies in the buttermilk, shoo fly shoo.")

Creating: Make up your own pattern and sequence and play them on the melody bells or resonator bells. Do they move higher each time you play them? Do they move lower? Do they move higher and lower?

Reading: Listen as you sing a familiar song and find the patterns and their sequences. Play the sequences on various classroom instruments. How many times in the song did you play a sequence? Can you draw your sequence on the chalkboard or design it on the flannel board? Can you design it with your hands?

Element: MELODY
Component: Intervals
Concept: Some tones in a melody move by a wide skip, or leap.

THE ELEPHANT SONG

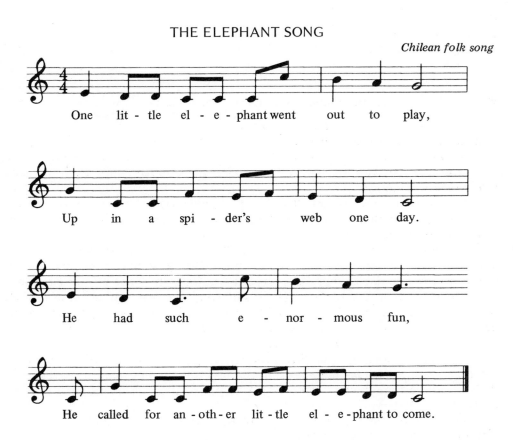

Chilean folk song

From *Making Music Your Own*, Book 2, Courtesy of General Learning Corporation.

■ *Suggested Musical Class Activities For "The Elephant Song"*

Listening: Listen while your teacher sings and, using hand levels, designs "The Elephant Song." Raise your hands when you hear tones in the song that have a wide skip (interval) or leap.

Listening, Singing, and Free Movement: Listen as you sing the song and design it in the air with your arms, your hands, or your whole body.

Singing and Playing: Sing the entire song again and when you come to the tones that leap, play them on the melody bells or resonator bells. How far apart were the two tones? Count the number of bells from the first (lowest tone) to the last (highest tone) and see that they are eight tones apart. This wide skip is called an octave.

Creating: Make up a song of your own using the leap of an octave and play it on melody bells, resonator bells, or a piano keyboard.

The following presentations are samplings of lesson procedures (including questioning techniques) as they might evolve in a classroom situation.

Each presentation directly relates to a component of MELODY as it might be explored conceptually in a developmental program.

Element: MELODY
Component: Home Tone (Tonal Center)
Concept: Tones in a MELODY often move around a home tone, or a tonal center.

■ *Use of Classroom Instruments and Other Strategies to Explore the Concept*

1. Listen as you sing a familiar song such as "Yankee Doodle." Stop singing whenever your teacher signals you to do so. When you stopped singing, did the music sound unfinished? That is, did you want to keep singing or did you stop on a tone that seemed to be a resting place in the song? On what word did you stop singing?

2. Close your eyes and just listen as your teacher plays the song again and stops at the same place. When the music stopped, did you feel as if the song had come to the end?

3. Play a short song, such as "Hot Cross Buns," on the melody bells or on the piano for your classmates, but stop playing on any tone you choose. When you stopped playing, did everyone feel that they had reached home or were they on their way home? That is, did everyone feel that the music should have continued until it finally reached home? Whenever music stops playing or we stop singing on a tone that feels "ended" or "final," we know we have reached the home tone, or tonal center.

4. Stand and sing a familiar song in its entirety except for the last tone. At that point ask a classmate to sing the last tone as you play it on resonator bells or a piano keyboard. If it sounds to you as if the last tone sung were the home tone, sit down.

5. Play this ear game (aural activity) using a piano, bells, tuned water jars, or any other melody instrument.

Element: MELODY

Component: Key or Scale

Concept: When eight tones in a MELODY move by step from low to high or high to low, a scale is formed.

MY ROCKET SHIP*

M. Lament

My rock - et ship and I will take a trip up to the moon

Zoom-ing high - er, high - er, oh I know we'll get there soon!

Oh, Mis - ter Moon, hel - lo! good-bye! We have - n't long to stay,

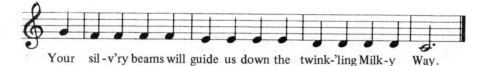

Your sil - v'ry beams will guide us down the twink-'ling Milk-y Way.

*Original.

■ Use of Classroom Instruments and Other Strategies to Explore the Concept

1. Listen to the song "My Rocket Ship" as your teacher plays or sings it.

2. Sing the song as you design its shape using arm or hand movements. Does the song move from low to high? Does it begin high and move downward? Do the tones in the song move by step or skip?

3. Listen as you sing the song again and design its shape on the chalkboard or flannel board. Does its shape look like anything you have ever seen before? Does your design look like the steps up to the slide on the playground? Does it look like a stepladder or like the stair steps in your home? Listen to the sound of the beginning tone and then play the song on the melody bells.

4. Play the song as you sing it and have one of your classmates point to each step of the design as the song is heard to move up and down in a stepwise direction. How many steps up in the song? (Eight steps.) How many steps

down in the song? (Eight steps.) Play a note on the bells and its octave above. Then play all the notes in between and you will discover that this is the scale. Can you transfer your design of the song onto the musical staff using musical notes to shape the design? What is the name of the first note of your design? (C.)

■ *Use of Additional Material and Teaching Guides to Explore the Concept*

FLYING KITES*

M. Lament

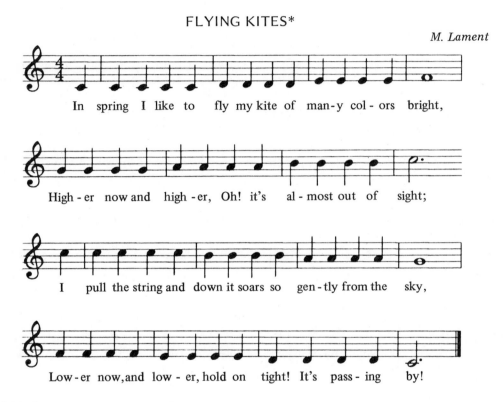

In spring I like to fly my kite of man-y col-ors bright,

High-er now and high-er, Oh! it's al-most out of sight;

I pull the string and down it soars so gen-tly from the sky,

Low-er now, and low-er, hold on tight! It's pass-ing by!

*Original.

HALLOWEEN NIGHT

Source Unknown

Hal-low-'een is com-ing, the moon is shin-ing bright;

There's gob-lins and witch-es, and black cats out to-night,

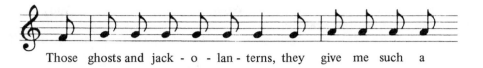

Those ghosts and jack - o - lan - terns, they give me such a

fright! Oh, but it's scar - ry on Hal - low - 'een Night BOO!

Listen and notice that the preceding songs move along the scale from low to high. (⟶) Compare them to "My Rocket Ship" (p. 137) which moves in the same direction.

SNOWFLAKES

M. Lament

See the snow - flakes gen - tly fall - ing

See them fall - ing, See the snow - flakes

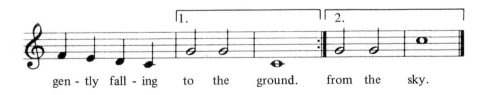

gen - tly fall - ing to the ground. from the sky.

*Original.

Listen and notice that this song moves along the scale from high to low (⟶).

Element: MELODY
Component: Pentatonic Scale
Concept: A MELODY may use only five tones or be made up of only five
tones, which forms a pentatonic scale.

■ *Use of Classroom Instruments and Other Strategies to Explore the Concept*

 1. Close your eyes and listen as one of your classmates plays on the black
keys of the piano or on the black resonator bells or melody bells. What kind
of sound does this music have? (Oriental; Chinese.)

 2. Play the first tone of a group of three black keys on a piano or bells
and then continue playing up and down on each black key in this black-key
pattern:

How many tones are in this scale? (Five.) Therefore, this scale has a name
meaning five tones, which is pentatonic. What does the word *pentagon* mean?
(A five-sided geometric figure.)

How many sides does the government building in Washington, D.C., called the
Pentagon have? (Five.) Therefore, what does the prefix *penta* mean? (Five.)

 3. Make up a song on the black keys on the pentatonic scale in a pattern
as illustrated here using a combination of short and long tones.

Example:

— — — — — — — — — — — — — — —
 1   1   2   3   3   4   5   5   4   3   3   2   1   1   1

Write this notated pattern on the chalkboard showing the contour, or shape,
of the song:

```
                          5  5
                        4        4
                   3  3            3  3
                 2                       2
              1  1                          1  1  1
```

4. Transfer the line notation to musical notation and play this same pattern again with this note ♪ as the short tone and this note ♩. as the long tone.

Where does the longest tone occur? Point to it on the chalkboard. Can you make up words to this music?

5. Play and sing one of the songs you learned that was built on the scale made up of eight tones ("My Rocket Ship," "Snowflakes," "Flying Kites") and compare the sound of the two scales. Are they built alike or differently? Close your eyes as you listen to each scale played on the bells. Raise your hands when you hear the pentatonic scale.

Additional Music Literature for Listening Experiences on the Primary Level

Element: MELODY
Component: Direction and Distance
Concepts: Some tones in a musical composition are high and some are low. Some tones in a MELODY stay the same or move up and down by step and skip.

    1. McDonald: *Children's Symphony*, Third Movement from *Adventures in Music*, Grade 2, Vol. I

Suggestions for Presentation:

1. Listen as your teacher plays a MELODY you might hear in the *Children's Symphony.*
2. Listen to the music. Did you hear just one MELODY or was there more than one?
3. Sing or hum the MELODY or melodies you heard.
4. Point to the MELODY on the chalkboard or wall chart and also point to the notes that go up, down, and sometimes stay the same. Do they go up by step or skip? Do they go down by step or skip?
5. Design the MELODY with your hands and on the chalkboard while you sing.
6. Use arm movements and make designs whenever you hear the MELODY soar from low to high or swoop from high to low.

7. Have you ever seen an airplane take off? Pretend you are an airplane and, using arm movements, take off into the wild blue yonder. What does the plane look like when it's gliding? Does the melody you hear ever glide or seem to move straight ahead?

8. Using arm movements, pretend that you are coming in for a landing. Are you going from high to low or from low to high?

9. "Swoosh" high and low or up and down the piano keyboard holding a piece of soft flannel or terry cloth in your hand so that you can move faster and not stick to the keys.

10. Play an autoharp, "swooshing" back and forth on its open strings in the direction of the music. Can you also do this on resonator bells? Melody bells? A xylophone? Tuned water jars?

11. Sing the MELODY when it goes from high to low or low to high.

Additional Material for Use on the Intermediate Level

Element: MELODY
Component: Direction and Distance
Concept: Songs and melodies move in steps, chords, and sometimes straight ahead.

■ *Use of Classroom Instruments and Other Strategies to Explore the Concept*

1. Sing a familiar song, such as "Dixie."

2. See the charted melodic patterns of three familiar songs, "Dixie," "Yankee Doddle," and "Battle Hymn," on p. 143.*

3. Sing the first few measures of "Dixie" again, designing the contour of the MELODY on the chalkboard or in the air with hand levels. Which visual-aid pattern matches "Dixie"? (Chart 1.)

4. After choosing which visual aid most closely fits the melodic contour of the song, sing the song and simultaneously play it by ear on the melody bells. Have a student, using a pointer, follow the contour of the melody pattern on a chart as a visual aid.

5. Sing another familiar song.

6. By means of an overhead projector, view the melodic notation of one of the songs just sung omitting the words and title of song.

7. Match the melodic notation to the pictorial representation of the same melodic pattern on the visual-aid chart.

Example:

"Yankee Doodle"

*Use any object, such as baseball, in place of actual notation to design the contour of a song for use as a visual aid.

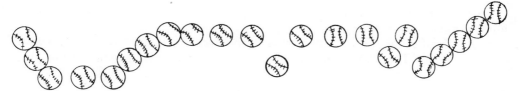

Chart 1. "Dixie." Omit the title and words of the song from the chart when projecting it for students.

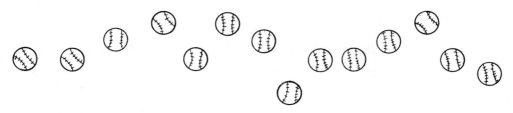

Chart 2. "Yankee Doodle." Omit the title and words of the song from the chart when projecting it for students.

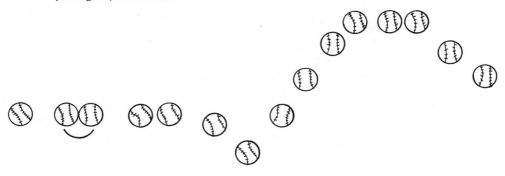

Chart 3. "Battle Hymn." Omit the title and words of the song from the chart when projecting it for students.

Which pattern looks like this music? Which song that we just sang corresponds to this musical notation as well as to the pictorial pattern on the charts?

8. After matching the music notation of "Yankee Doodle" to chart 2, sing the song and play it on melody bells, resonator bells, melody flutes* or

Song flute, a type of melody flute. Cover the thumb hole on the back of the song flute with your left thumb. Blow gently into the instrument. You are playing C on the major scale. Using one finger at a time, starting with the left hand, begin covering the holes on the song flute. You will now be playing *down* the C major scale. Reverse this procedure removing one finger at a time. You will now be playing *up* the C major scale. (See current elementary music textbook series for more detailed instruction and information.)

recorders* while reading the notation as projected on the screen to verify the choice of song as correct.

9. Divide the class into groups with leaders and invent other ways of playing "Name This Tune" that might encourage greater facility in sight singing.

Element: MELODY
Component: Key or Scale
Concept: When eight tones are arranged in particular steps, or in an arrangement, a scale is formed.

■ *Use of Classroom Instruments and Other Strategies to Explore the Concept*

1. Listen and play the C major scale on melody bells or resonator bells. Why is the name of this scale C instead of E or D, for example? (Because the scale is named for the tone on which it begins and ends.)

2. Review the scale songs that are built on the C major scale (pp. 137-139).

3. Listen to a different scale played on resonator bells beginning on G and moving in steps on all of the *white* bells. Did it sound different from when we began our scale on C and played all the *white* tones?

4. Listen to the G scale again played on bells and when you hear a tone that sounds "different" raise your hand.

5. Watch the teacher play the G scale again and raise your hand when you hear the sound that is different or that doesn't sound exactly right. Can you sing the scale the way you think it should sound beginning on G? Therefore, which tone should be changed when you play the G scale using all the white bells? (F.) Does your ear tell you to play F higher or lower? (Higher.) A whole step or a half step higher? (Half step.) What is the musical term for raising a tone a half step? (Sharp.) Therefore, the G major scale has one sharp. What is its name? (F#.)

6. Play the C major scale on bells chanting the number names of the tones. Between what numbers of the scale do the half steps occur? (3-4, and 7-8.) Therefore, in building major scales, where do the half steps occur? (Between 3-4, and 7-8.)

7. Now, play the G major scale on the bells while chanting the number names of the tones.

8. Build a major scale beginning on any tone of your choice, being certain to raise or lower the tones one half step as demanded by your ears and your eyes. Between what numbers of the scale do the half steps occur? (3-4, and 7-8.) What is the musical term for lowering a tone one half step? (Flat.)

*Recorder (soprano). For fingering technique in playing the recorder, consult current elementary music textbook series or see Hugh Orr, *Basic Recorder Technique*, vol. I (Scarborough, Ontario: Berandol Music Limited, 1969).

9. Make up your own scale songs.

10. Sing and play your songs on different scales to discover for yourself the number of sharps and flats in each scale.

11. Write the scales on the chalkboard, notating in their proper position on the musical staff the sharps or flats present in each scale—the key signature of the scale.

Examples:

F Major   G Major   A Major

Key Signature: B♭ Key Signature: F♯ Key Signature: F♯, C♯, G♯

Concept: When a MELODY is composed of the tones in a specific scale, such as the C major scale, the MELODY is said to be written in the key of C.

Concept: Different melodies can be made up of the same tones of a scale. These MELODIES can move in steps or chords.

■ *Use of Classroom Instruments and Other Strategies to Explore the Concept*

1. Listen to RCA's original soundtrack album of Rodgers' and Hammerstein's "Do-Re-Me" from *The Sound of Music*. What did you notice about the MELODY? Did you hear just one MELODY or more than one?

2. Sing the first MELODY you heard and recognized as "Do-Re-Mi."

3. Listen again to the recording and raise your hands when you hear a different melody introduced by Maria. Hum or sing this MELODY, designing its shape in the air using hand levels. Does this MELODY move mostly by step, as does the scale MELODY "Do-Re-Mi," or by skip? (Skip.)

4. Sing and play this MELODY by ear on the melody bells and resonator bells.

5. Notate the MELODY on the chalkboard.

6. Divide the class in two groups. Have group 1 play and sing "Do-Re-Mi," and have group 2 play and sing the countermelody.

7. Groups 1 and 2 playing and singing the two melodies simultaneously, as heard on the recording, is termed counterpoint. (Counterpoint is often used interchangeably with the term *polyphony*. Refer to HARMONY, pp. 181 and 190.)

8. Compose your own countermelody to a major scale of your choice.

9. Divide the class into groups and play and sing your contrapuntal (counterpoint or polyphonic) composition. (Refer to HARMONY, p. 181.)

10. Sing other partner songs and songs with descants.

Suggested Sources

Krone, Beatrice, and Max Krone. *Songs for Fun with Descants.* Growing Up With Music Series. Park Ridge, Ill.: Neil A. Kjos Music Co., 1956. Most of the songs in this book are recorded in the Bowmar record album entitled *Songs for Fun with Descants.* The album is available from your educational record dealer or Bowmar Records, 622 Rodier Drive, Glendale, California 91201.

Krone, Beatrice, and Max Krone. *Intermediate Descants.* Growing Up with Music Series. Park Ridge, Ill.: Neil A. Kjos Music Co., 1954. Most of the songs in this book are recorded in the Bowmar record album entitled *Intermediate Descants.* The album is available from your educational record dealer or Bowmar Records.

Krone, Beatrice, and Max Krone. *Descants and Easy Basses.* Vol. 1. Book X. *A World in Tune.* Park Ridge, Ill.: Neil A. Kjos Music Co., 1950.

Beckman, Frederick, Arr. *Partner Songs.* Boston: Ginn, 1958.

Beckman, Frederick, Arr. *More Partner Songs.* Boston: Ginn, 1962.

Concept: Melodies built on scales other than major scales in which the whole steps and half steps are rearranged have a different sound.

■ *Use of Classroom Instruments and Other Strategies to Explore the Concept*

1. Sing "Row, Row, Row Your Boat" to the accompaniment of an autoharp while pushing down on the C major button. What tones are played and heard when you push the C major button and strum the autoharp? (Chord tones in C major scale.)

2. Now, sing the same song, "Row, Row, Row Your Boat," to the accompaniment of an autoharp while pushing down on c minor button. Is the sound of the song different than when you sang it to the accompaniment of chord tones in the C major scale? Can you describe the sound? Is it mysterious? Does it sound as if you are rowing your boat down the stream on a foggy or rainy day? What tones do you think you heard and played when you pushed down the c minor button? (Chord tones in the c minor scale.) Therefore, would you say that the same MELODY or song can sound different when built on a different scale?

Concept: Bitonality results when a MELODY is played simultaneously in two different keys.

■ *Use of Classroom Instruments and Other Strategies to Explore the Concept*

1. Play a simple tune such as "Are You Sleeping?" in a key of your choice, perhaps G major, on the melody bells.

2. Write the song in musical notation on the chalkboard. (Key of G major.)

3. Play the same tune in a different key, perhaps F major. (The musical term for playing the same tune in a different key is *transposing*.)

4. Write the song in musical notation on the chalkboard. (Key of F major.)

5. Divide class in two groups. Have group 1 play "Are You Sleeping?" in G major, and have group 2 play "Are You Sleeping?" in F major simultaneously. How would you describe the resulting sound? Does the music seem to fit, or go well together? Would you say that the resultant sound is different, pleasant, or clashing? Do you hear sounds similar to this in contemporary music?

6. Rotate the groups for playing the same tune in two different keys on song flutes or recorders in combination with the piano keyboard.

7. Learn the definition of *dissonance* and *consonance*. (Refer to HARMONY, p. 179 for definitions and exploratory experiences.)

8. Choose other familiar tunes and experiment with the various combinations of melody instruments.

Concept: A tone row is made up of all twelve tones of the chromatic scale, which are not arranged in consecutive order.

■ *Use of Classroom Instruments and Other Strategies to Explore the Concept*

1. "Accidentally" spill (ever so gently) on to a table every black and white bar from C to C in a set of resonator bells.

2. Direct twelve volunteers to choose any bell from the table and to form a line in the front of the room.

3. Play each bell individually and, with help from members of the audience (classmates), rearrange yourselves by sound to build the chromatic scale from C to C. How many tones are there in a chromatic scale? (Twelve.)

4. Scramble the bells again by giving your bell to a member of the audience. Hurriedly reassemble the bells in the front of the room but, once again, keep them tonally disorganized as to consecutive order of tones in the chromatic scale.

5. Play each bell individually, creating a tone row. (No tone or bell is repeated.)

6. Notate each tone as it is played on the musical staff using whole notes.

7. Experiment with rhythmic ideas, notating them on the staff with proper note values that reflect the ideas to create a MELODY. Does this MELODY have a tonal center? (No.) Can you play it on the piano keyboard or on melody bells?

8. Create other tone rows and compose various atonal melodies, void of a home tone or tonal center, and play them on melody instruments.

9. To preserve your creative projects, notate these melodies on music staff chart paper.

10. Listen to

> Thomson: "The Alligator and the Coon" from
> *Acadian Songs and Dances* from *Adventures in Music*, Grade 3, Volume II

Raise your hands when you hear the "climbing tune" or theme that tonally describes the boy in the story pulling up a rope hand over hand that was dangling over the boat down into the water. Would you call this climbing tune a tone row? Why?

Suggested Activity for the College or University Student

1. Choose a song suitable for children of elementary school age. (Consult elementary music textbooks, if you wish.)
2. From your knowledge of the components of MELODY, decide which component present in the song would be most suitable for exploration through the musical activities of listening, singing, free movement, creating, and playing. (If it is advisable, considering the children's previous experiences with other activities, add reading to this list.)
3. Record your ideas for experiencing musical growth developmentally as a procedure or lesson plan.

Chapter 7

Rhythm–
An Element of Music

A principal character of most music is RHYTHM. That is to say, music has RHYTHM. It is true that some music, because of its sound movement ("free" movement encouraged by changes of TEMPO), seems to lack the quality of RHYTHM, but this can be attributed to the absence of *meter*, which is the organization of beats (time values) into groupings or sets, each set constituting a measure.

Because RHYTHM is made up of various components (including meter), the following procedure is suggested for exploring and discovering them through the song "Jamaican Farewell" (p. 233).

ANALYSIS OF COMPONENTS OF RHYTHM THROUGH
THE MEDIUM OF A FAMILIAR MELODY

Suggested Procedure for Exploring the
Rhythmic Components in "Jamaican Farewell"

1. Sing, as a group, the song "Jamaican Farewell."
2. Analyze the rhythmic components of the song.

Components

STEADY BEAT

Most music has a steady beat (underlying pulse). Tap along as you listen to and sing "Jamaican Farewell." Was it easy to tap a steady beat while listening to this music? Would you say that there is a steady beat or an underlying pulse in "Jamaican Farewell"? Why?

ACCENTED BEATS-UNACCENTED BEATS

Some tones in music have a stronger beat than others. The stronger beat is the accented beat and the weaker one is the unaccented beat. Tap the steady beat while singing the song again; tap the first beat stronger (accent the first beat) and also sing with the number names:

$$1 - 2 - 3 - 4, \qquad 1 - 2 - 3 - 4, \text{ etc.}$$

Does this song begin on the stronger beat (first beat) or accented beat? Clap the accented beats (which occur on the 1s) and tap the unaccented beats, or weak beats, as

1– 2 – 3 – 4,   **1**– 2 – 3 – 4,   **1**– 2 – 3 – 4, etc.

How many unaccented beats follow the accented beat? (Three.)

METER

Music moves in sets of 2, 3, 4, 6, and so forth. While classmates tap the steady beat of "Jamaican Farewell," accenting the 1s, design the steady beat on the chalkboard in some way to show that the 1s are stronger.

Example:

Now, show how you would group in sets (perhaps using a dotted line):

In what sets would you say this music moves? (Four.) On the musical staff sets designated by bar lines instead of a dotted line appear as follows:

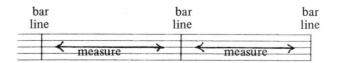

and the distance between the bar lines is termed a *measure*.

The time signature (meter sign) placed on the staff at the beginning of the music tells the performer that the music moves in sets of 2, 3, 4, 6, and so forth.

Example:

The time signature for "Jamaican Farewell" follows:

4 → music moves in sets of 4 (a set is designated as a measure)

4 → symbol for a quarter note ($\quarternote$) and designates that there are four quarter notes, or their equivalent, to a set, or measure. (Refer to the chart on p. 95 illustrating the relative duration of quarter notes.) View every measure in "Jamaican Farewell" and determine whether there is the equivalent of four quarter notes per measure.

POLYMETER

Polymeter simply means that music can move in different sets at the same time. In viewing the notated score of "Jamaican Farewell" do you notice the presence of different meter signs? (No.)

RHYTHM PATTERNS

Rhythm patterns are groupings of shorter and longer tones in a MELODY. Tap a rhythm pattern in "Jamaican Farewell."

So   I   left my is - land home down Ja - mai - ca   way.

Would you say this rhythm pattern is even or uneven? Why? On bongos or different kinds of drums, tap other rhythm patterns in "Jamaican Farewell." Would you say most of the rhythm patterns were even or uneven? Why?

SYNCOPATED RHYTHM PATTERNS

When a strong (accented) beat occurs in place of a weak beat, syncopation occurs. Therefore, syncopation occurs within a rhythm pattern; the pattern is then referred to as a syncopated rhythm pattern. Syncopation can be produced in the following ways:

a. Tie a portion of a strong beat to a portion of a weak beat. (Refer to p. 98 for an explanation of a *tied note.*)
b. Place a rest where a strong beat or portion of a strong beat normally would occur.

Examples:

The following syncopated rhythm pattern occurs in "Jamaican Farewell":

Down   the   bay   where the   lights were   gay,___

Can you tap other rhythm patterns in "Jamaican Farewell" and determine where the syncopation occurs?

3. Sing the entire song again to the rhythmic accompaniment of percussion instruments—bongos, maracas, guiro, claves—each instrument following a specific rhythm pattern that has been notated on the chalkboard in line duration and then transferred to actual notation:

♪ = short

♩ = long

SAMPLING OF PROCEDURES AND LESSON PLANS FOR EXPLORING MUSICAL CONCEPTS RELATED TO RHYTHM

Primary Level

The following songs and listening activities illustrate musical concepts to be explored. Each concept is related to a component of RHYTHM and is structured from simple to complex. The suggested musical activities for exploring the concepts also develop in a simple to complex procedure that is the most appropriate for children of primary school age.

Concepts are based on the following components of RHYTHM:

Steady Beat
Accented Beats–Unaccented Beats
Accented Beats—Meter
Polymeter
Even and Uneven Rhythm Patterns
Syncopated Beat–Syncopated Rhythm Pattern

Element: RHYTHM
Component: Steady Beat
Concept: Most music has a steady beat.

HICKORY, DICKORY, DOCK*

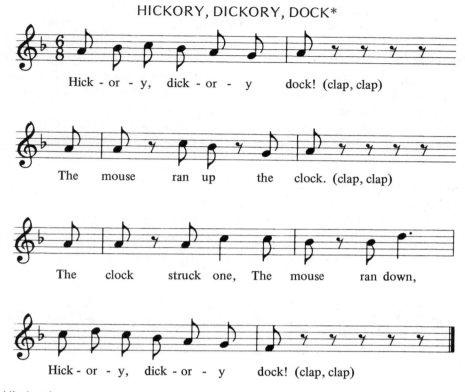

Hick - or - y, dick - or - y dock! (clap, clap)

The mouse ran up the clock. (clap, clap)

The clock struck one, The mouse ran down,

Hick - or - y, dick - or - y dock! (clap, clap)

*Public domain.

■ *Suggested Musical Class Activities for "Hickory, Dickory, Dock"*

Listening: Listen to this music. Have you ever heard it before?

Singing and Playing: Sing the music this time and tap along while you sing. What does this steady tap, tap, tap remind you of? The steady tick, tock of a clock? Tap a drumhead or tom-tom with your fingertip. Can you make the sound as steady as when raindrops fall on the roof of your house?

Creating: Make up ways to explore a steady beat, such as by tapping coconut shells in the RHYTHM of a trotting pony. Listen to the popping of corn in a popcorn popper. Does it pop steadily or does it pop up and surprise you? Compare it to the beat of your heart. Does the popping keep a steady pulse?

Reading: Draw this steady beat on the chalkboard (/ / / / / /) while your classmates make the sound of the steady beat on rhythm sticks.

Additional Music Literature for Listening Experiences on the Primary Level

Element: RHYTHM
Component: Steady Beat
Concept: Most music has a steady beat.

Ibert: Parade from *Divertissement* from *Adventures in Music*, Grade 1, Volume I

Suggestions for Presentation:

1. Listen and tap along. Is your tapping steady throughout the music?
2. Stand at your places and keep time to the music (lightly) with your feet. Does the music make you feel like walking or marching down the street?
3. Pretend you are going to a parade. The flags are flying and the bands are playing! If you were marching in a parade, how would you move?

Element: RHYTHM
Component: Accented Beats–Unaccented Beats
Concept: Some tones in music have a stronger beat than others.

ROW, ROW, ROW YOUR BOAT*

Traditional

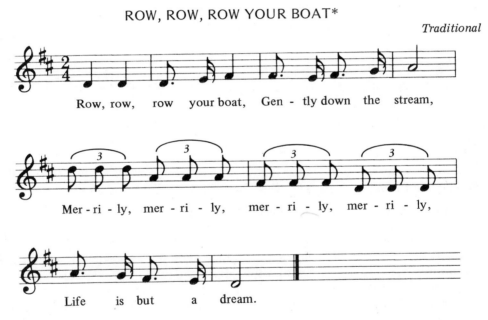

*Public domain.

■ *Suggested Musical Class Activities for "Row, Row, Row Your Boat"*

Playing: Tap the steady beat on drums, as you sing along. Tap the first beat harder as you sing the song a second time. Does it feel right? Does it seem to fit the music? Notice that some beats are stronger than others.

Singing and Playing: As you sing, clap the stronger beats and also sing with number names: 1–2–1–2–1–2, and so on. Notice that this song begins on the stronger beat, or first beat. Play cymbals on the strong beats (1s) and tap a tone block on the weaker beats that follow.

Free Movement: Pretend that you are rowing your boat. On the strong beats (1s) dip the oar; on 2s pull back on the oars as you sing and move ("row") to the music.

Creating: Make up your own music score in pictures: on white shelf paper draw a picture of your drum followed by pictures of rhythm sticks for every time they play the weaker beats.

Example:

Reading: Draw the steady beat on the chalkboard as your classmates sing and play together. Be certain to show in some way that the 1s are stronger.

Example:

$$/ \ / \ / \ / \ / \ / \ /$$

Singing and Playing: Sing several songs while you tap along and discover the strong and weak beats. Add instruments on the stronger beats.

Element: RHYTHM
Component: Accented Beats–Unaccented Beats
Concept: Music does not always begin on the strong beat.

■ *Suggested Musical Class Activities for "She'll be Comin' Round the Mountain"*

Singing: Sing "She'll Be Comin' Round the Mountain."

SHE'LL BE COMIN' ROUND THE MOUNTAIN*

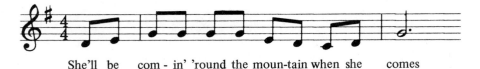

She'll be   com - in' 'round the moun-tain when she   comes

*Public domain.

Singing and Playing: Sing as you clap or tap the RHYTHM of the words. On which word of the song did you first clap louder? (Comin'.) Would you say that all the music we hear or sing begins on the accented beat? (No.)

Listening, Singing, and Playing: Listen to other familiar melodies and then, as you sing and tap along, decide on which word the first strong beat occurs.

Suggested Songs for Exploring the Unaccented Beat

1. OH WHERE HAS MY LITTLE DOG GONE?*†

Oh where, oh where has my lit - tle dog gone?

*Public domain.

†The first word of this song is "Oh." However, the accented beat does not fall on the first word, but on the second word, "where," which occurs on the strong beat (1s).

2. THE MUFFIN MAN*†

Oh, do you know the muf - fin man

the muf - fin man, the muf - fin man?

*Public domain.

†The first word of this song is "Oh." However, the accented beat does not fall on the first word, but on the second word, "do," which occurs on the strong beat (1s).

3. OH, SUSANNA*†

I come from Al - a - bam-a with my ban-jo on my knee.

*Public domain.

†The first word of the song is "I." However, accented beat does not fall on the first word, but on the second word, "come," which occurs on the strong beat (1s).

Element: RHYTHM

Components: Accented Beats—Meter

Concepts: Some tones in music have a stronger beat than others. When we discover where the strong beat falls and how many weak beats follow it, then we can group them into sets.

> Massenet: Aragonaise from *Le Cid* from *Adventures in Music*, Grade 1, Volume I

Suggestions for Presentation:

1. Listen to this music and tap the steady beat. Can you find the strong beat?

2. Clap harder on the bigger beat and tap softly on the other beats. Where does the bigger beat fall, on 1–2–3 or 4?

3. Clap on the 1s this time and swing your arms out on smaller beats, as in a clap—swing.

4. In music what do we call the strong beat? (Accented beat.)

5. Discover what body movement you could do that would fit the music while accenting the 1s.

Example:

A ball can be bounced on the 1s; a push-pull game can be played: push on the 1s; a balloon can be tapped and kept in the air only on the 1s; or the classroom instrument of your choice, the louder the instrument the better, can be played on the 1s (large drums and cymbals).

6. Play tone clusters of three black keys on a piano keyboard on the 1s (accented beat) and tone clusters of two black keys on the weaker, or unaccented, beats if it will fit the sound of the music.

7. Listen as you play tone clusters on the piano keyboard in this pattern:

What kind of music fits this RHYTHM? (Indian.)

8. Group these rhythms in sets on the chalkboard or on a wall chart.

Example:

9. Listen to another musical composition to determine the steady beat, the accented beat, and the sets of beats by grouping these sets on the chalkboard or wall chart. After grouping sets can you decide whether the music moves in sets of 2s, 3s, or 4s?

10. If the music moves in sets of 4 and the steady beat is shown by ♩ , can you draw the meter sign on the chalkboard? $\frac{4}{4}$ / ($\frac{4}{4}$)

11. Practice drawing different meter signs on the chalkboard.

Element: RHYTHM
Component: Polymeter
Concept: Music can move in different sets at the same time.

■ *Use of Classroom Instruments and Other Strategies to Explore the Concept*

1. When you go on a picnic what do you like to eat best of all? Would your list read something like this: hot dogs, watermelon, fried chicken, ice cream cones, chocolate fudge cake, hot baked potatoes, carrot sticks, and strawberry soda?

2. While the teacher plays a steady beat on a drum the class should chant the list of picnic foods one at a time, accenting the first syllable of each word.

3. After the class has been divided into eight groups, a different item should be assigned to each group.

4. All chant together specific items, accenting the first syllable of each word to the accompaniment of a steady drum beat.

5. Listen as you chant. What does it sound like?

6. Notate the rhythmic durations of the following items on the chalkboard, accenting the first syllable of each word:

hot dogs:

watermelon:

fried chicken:

7. Chant the individual rhythms in step 6 in short-long.

8. Group the rhythms in step 6 in sets of 2 by accenting the 1s as you chant 1–2, and so on.

hot dogs:

watermelon:

fried chicken:

9. Notate the rhythmic duration of the following items on the chalkboard accenting the first syllable of each word:

ice cream cones:

choc'late fudge cake:

10. Chant the individual rhythms in step 9 in short-long.

11. Group the rhythms in step 9 in sets of 3 by accenting the 1s as you chant 1–2–3, and so on.

ice cream cones: _____ _____ _____|_____ _____ _____|

choc'late fudge cake: __ __ _____ _____|__ __ _____ _____|

12. Notate the rhythmic duration of the following items on the chalkboard accenting the first syllable of each word:

apple dumplings: _____ _____ _____ _____ _____ _____ _____ _____

hot baked potatoes or
strawberry soda: _____ __ __ _____ _____ _____ __ __ _____ _____

carrot sticks: _____ _____ _____ _____ _____ _____ _____

13. Chant the individual rhythms in short-long in step 12.
14. Group the rhythms in step 12 in sets of 4 by accenting the 1s as you chant 1–2–3–4.

apple dumplings: _____ _____ _____ _____|_____ _____ _____ _____

hot baked potatoes or
strawberry soda: _____ __ __ _____ _____|_____ __ __ _____ _____

carrot sticks: _____ _____ _____ _____|_____ _____ _____ _____

15. Choose any classroom instruments and follow any of the preceding scores written in duration.
16. Transfer this blank notation to music notation using the following scale:

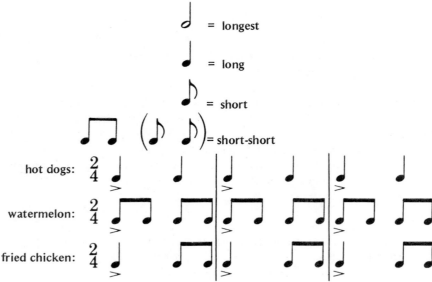

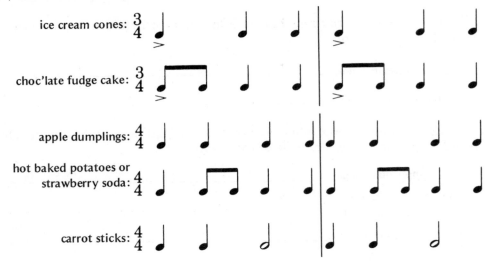

17. Choose a different item and a different classroom instrument for playing each notated item from the score. Do you think it is important for you to have a chance to play many different rhythms? Why?

18. Perform the entire score this time with all of the groups playing all of the rhythms at the same time.

19. Listen as you play together. Is it tricky to follow your score? When different meters are being performed at the same time, what do we call these meters? (Polymeters.)

20. Create free movement to accompany the rhythms being played on percussion instruments and stress the accented beat with a strong body movement.

21. Listen to musical compositions composed of different meters.

Example:

> McDonald: *Children's Symphony* First Movement from *Adventures in Music*, Grade 3, Volume II

Theme 1 has a double time signature: the MELODY moves in 2/4 time while different instruments play an accompaniment in 6/8 time, which gives a "two-against-three" effect.

22. Listen and try to determine what meters are being played.

23. Make up your own musical composition of polymeters using classroom instruments of your choice.

Note:

Advanced experiences in identifying and understanding the notation of polyrhythms should include the study of music that composers have scored by using two different meters simultaneously.

Examples:

> Copland: "Street in a Frontier Town" from *Billy the Kid, Adventures in Music*, Grade 6, Volume I
>
> Ives: "Putnam's Camp," Second Movement, *Three Places in New England*
>
> Griffes: *The White Peacock* from *Adventures in Music*, Grade 6, Volume I. (Refer to p. 174.)

Element: RHYTHM
Component: Rhythm Patterns
Concept: The groupings of shorter and longer tones in a MELODY often form a rhythmic pattern.

THIS OLD MAN (refer to p. 132)

■ *Suggested Musical Class Activities for "This Old Man"*

Listening and Playing: Listen as your teacher claps the mystery RHYTHM of a familiar song. Echo clap this RHYTHM. Tap the RHYTHM on the tom-tom or drum. Can you guess the name of the song? ("This Old Man.")

Playing: Divide the class into two groups. Have group 1 tap a steady beat while group 2 taps the mystery RHYTHM on rhythm sticks. Do these rhythms fit together?

Reading: Draw this RHYTHM on the chalkboard in blank duration as the class taps it on rhythm sticks.

Example:

"This Old Man"

— — — — — — — — — — — — — —

Chant the RHYTHM in shorts-longs or

— — — — — — — —

short short long short short long short short, etc.
   ti   ti   ta   ti   ti   ta   ti   ti   etc.

Transfer blank duration to musical notation on the chalkboard using:

♪ = short sound

♩ = long sound

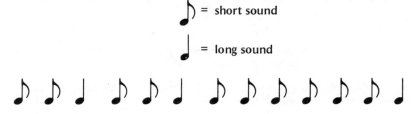

Tap a steady beat. Write it in blank duration under the notated score of a melodic rhythm as:

Is the steady beat a long or a short sound? How many short sounds in the MELODY are played while you are playing one steady beat? Therefore, can different rhythm patterns be heard in the same song?

Element: RHYTHM
Component: Even and Uneven Patterns
Concept: Some music is made up of both smooth and bouncy rhythm patterns (even and uneven).

■ *Suggested Musical Class Activities for "San Sereni"*

SAN SERENI*

Cuban folk song

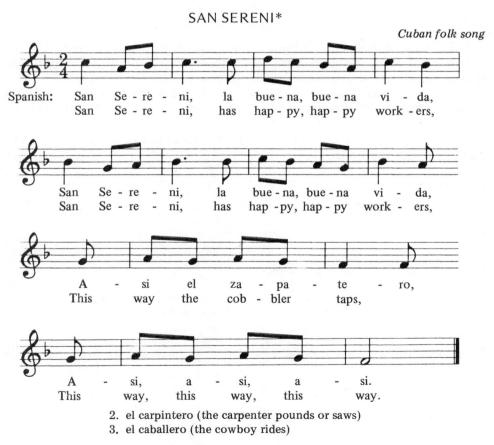

Spanish: San Se - re - ni, la bue - na, bue - na vi - da,
San Se - re - ni, has hap - py, hap - py work - ers,

San Se - re - ni, la bue - na, bue - na vi - da,
San Se - re - ni, has hap - py, hap - py work - ers,

A - si el za - pa - te - ro,
This way the cob - bler taps,

A - si, a - si, a - si.
This way, this way, this way.

2. el carpintero (the carpenter pounds or saws)
3. el caballero (the cowboy rides)

*From BIRCHARD MUSIC SERIES, Book I, Sylvesta M. Wassum, Editor, Copyright © 1962, Summy-Birchard Company, Evanston, Illinois. All rights reserved.

Singing: Sing this song as you tap the RHYTHM of the MELODY to discover for yourself the even (smooth) and uneven (bouncy) rhythm patterns.

Playing: Choose classroom instruments for a rhythm accompaniment to song.

Creating: Explore and make up rhythm patterns for each instrument to play.

Reading: Design patterns on the chalkboard using line duration and chant long-short or "ta, ti."

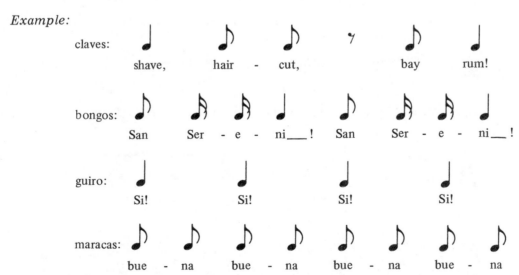

claves: long   short-short   rest   short   long

bongos: long   short-short   long

guiro: long   long   long   long

maracas: short   short   short   short   short

Playing: Play all the instruments at the same time chanting long-short or ta–ti as directed for each instrument. (This is an example of polyrhythms—many rhythms performed simultaneously.)

Reading and Creating: Transfer this blank duration to music notation and make up words to each rhythm pattern.

Example:

claves: shave,   hair - cut,   bay   rum!

bongos: San   Ser - e - ni__!   San   Ser - e - ni__!

guiro: Si!   Si!   Si!   Si!

maracas: bue - na   bue - na   bue - na   bue - na

Chant these word patterns as you read the rhythm patterns from the chalkboard. What instruments are playing even rhythm patterns? Point to them as they appear on the chalkboard. What instruments are playing uneven rhythm patterns? Point to them as they appear on the chalkboard.

Singing and Playing: Divide the class in two groups. Have group 1 sing "San Sereni" while group 2 plays a rhythm accompaniment.

Element: RHYTHM
Component: Syncopated Beat–Syncopated Rhythm Pattern
Concept: In syncopation a strong beat is used in place of a weak beat within a rhythm pattern. Hence, the pattern is termed a syncopated rhythm pattern.

TINGA LAYO*

Massie Patterson *Lionel Belasco*

Tin - ga Lay - o! Come, lit - tle don - key, come.

Tin - ga Lay - o! Come, lit - tle don - key, come.

My don - key walk, my don - key talk, my

don - key eat with a knife and fork.

Tin - ga Lay - o! Come, lit - tle don - key, come.

Tin - ga Lay - o! Come, lit - tle don - key, come.

*From *Collection of Original Calypso Songs of West Indies*, New York, N.Y., M. Baron Company, 1943.

■ *Use of Classroom Instruments and Other Strategies to Explore the Concept*

1. Listen carefully as your teacher claps the following RHYTHM:

—— —— —— —— —— —— —— —— ——

2. Echo clap your teacher.
3. Draw this RHYTHM on the chalkboard as you clap it, using blank duration this time.
4. Chant number names as you tap the RHYTHM on tom-toms accenting the 1s (1–2–3–4).
5. Listen as your teacher changes the accent of the RHYTHM by erasing these red lines and drawing them under a different rhythmic beat. When she plays it on her drum this time it may sound like this:

—— —— ══ —— —— —— ══ ——

6. Echo clap your teacher. Does the RHYTHM surprise you? Does it sound different?
7. Do you know what we call the RHYTHM when these accented beats surprise us and when they come when we expect a softer beat? (Syncopation.)
8. Sing "Tinga Layo" as you tap the steady beat.
9. Sing "Tinga Layo," again tapping a steady beat and the RHYTHM of the MELODY. Can you find the syncopated rhythm pattern in this song? (p. 164.) Can you tap it? Can you play it on a classroom instrument of your choice? What words in the song are syncopated? Tap the syncopated rhythm of these words as you sing them.

Example:

> Villa-Lobos: "The Little Train of the Caipira"
> from *Bachianas Brasileiras* no. 2 from *Adventures in Music*, Grade 3, Volume I

Teaching Guide:

1. A train chugs away from the station and then speeds on its way.
2. The MELODY, or theme, of the composition is heard.
3. Divide the class in two groups. Have group 1 tap a steady beat lightly on rhythm sticks or tone blocks. Have group 2 sing (hum) the MELODY and play the RHYTHM of the MELODY on drums, tapping loudly on the accented beats. Have several members of the class play the MELODY on resonator bells, melody bells, and at the piano keyboard.

Additional Material for Suggested Use on the Intermediate Level

Element: RHYTHM
Component: Even and Uneven Rhythm Patterns
Concept: Rhythm patterns are groupings (or combinations) of long and short
   tones of duration.

■ Use of Drumsticks and Other Strategies to Explore the Concept

1. Observe blank duration on a chalkboard and then clap or tap as you chant it in unison in longs–shorts:

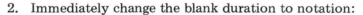

2. Immediately change the blank duration to notation:

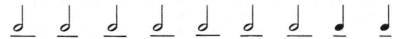

Are there any other possible combinations of notation that can be used to denote longs–shorts? (Yes.)

3. Illustrate numerous combinations of the notation characteristic of longs–shorts:

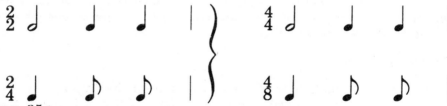

Could these same examples also serve as illustrations of different meters? (Yes.)

Example:

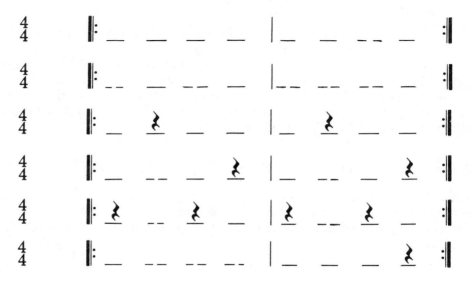

(Refer to p. 95.)

4. Create a rhythm chart of blank duration in a meter of your choice:

Note:

The chart is developed in a simple to complex approach, with each line slightly more complex than the preceding one.

5. Tap drumsticks (if drumsticks are not available, use rhythm sticks) as you read a score and chant longs-shorts to the accompaniment of a familiar march such as "Anchors Aweigh" or "The Army Goes Rolling Along."
6. Immediately transcribe the blank duration to notation and read from the score, this time observing that the various groupings of notation constitute different rhythm patterns.

7. Have every pupil in the room make up a rhythm pattern in 4/4 meter and write it on the chalkboard.
8. Have the entire class tap each of the rhythm patterns on view on the chalkboard.
9. Have everyone in the class tap a rhythm pattern of his choice simultaneously to produce polyrhythms.

■ *Use of an Overhead Projector and Transparencies to Explore the Concept*

MATERIALS

Mount a transparency that has been cut into approximately nine horizontal strips, each of which has been fastened at one end. Each strip illustrates a rhythm pattern that, when flipped over in proper position on the overhead projector, is projected on a screen. In this manner, strips can be viewed individually or simultaneously.

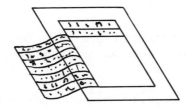

(Refer to p. 169 for a full-sized replica of a mounted transparency.

1. Choose instruments: drums, finger cymbals, triangles, tambourines, maracas, and wood blocks.
2. All tap a steady beat in unison. What kind of note can we use to signify this steady beat or pulse?

Example:

quarter note (♩) as illustrated on strip 1 on p. 169.

How can an eighth note (♪) be divided? (Refer to strip 2 on p. 169.)
3. Tap percussion instruments while reading the notation on strips 1 and 2 of the transparency that is projected on the screen.
4. Suggest, notate, and tap various groupings of beats and subdivisions of those beats. (See p. 95.)
5. Transfer the patterns from the chalkboard onto a blank transparency and perform the various patterns (which are then projected onto a screen) on different percussion instruments.
6. Look at the rhythm pattern on strip 4; do not tap it aloud, just think it. How do we designate periods of silence in music? (Rests.) Can you supply appropriate rests where they occur? Therefore, how many beats of silence are there? (Two.) Now think, count, and play this rhythm pattern on a wood block (See p. 117.)
7. Flip on a cha-cha pattern, strip 5

cha - cha   cha

1   2   3   and   4

Does this pattern look familiar? Tap the pattern; does it sound like a dance? Can you name it? (Cha-cha.)
8. Play the cha-cha pattern on various instruments; drums play all the beats, but cymbals, triangles, and tambourine play only beats 3 and 4 (cha-cha cha).
9. While continuing to use the overhead projector, flip the remaining strips of the transparency (6 through 9) one at a time onto the screen for individual performances by those students holding the designated instruments. (Those students not performing should be listening to hear whether the pattern is being performed correctly.)

10. Finally, perform all rhythm patterns simultaneously as an ensemble while listening to your own part, to the parts of others, and for the steady beat and its subdivision.

11. Listen to a cha-cha recording. Play along with it, and dance if you wish.

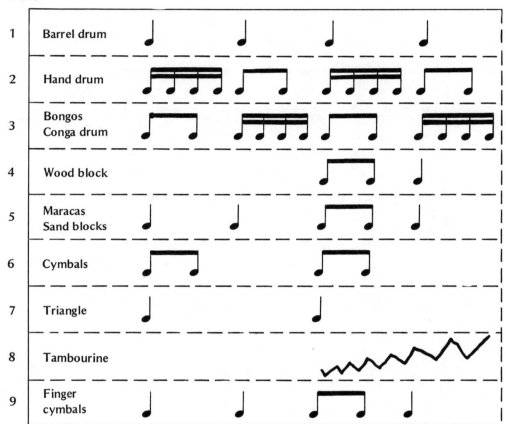

Replica of a Plastic Transparency for an Overhead Projector

Component: Meter
Concept: Music may be composed of changing meters.

■ *Use of Physical Movement (Dance) and Other Strategies to Explore the Concept*

1. Listen to

> Cailliet: Variations on the Theme "Pop! Goes The Weasel" from *Adventures in Music*, Grade 4, Volume I

and identify the change of meter by raising your hand.

2. Sing "Yankee Doodle."

3. Sing "Yankee Doodle" once more, observing the change of meter as designated in the following notated score:

YANKEE DOODLE*

U.S. folk song

*Public domain.

4. Create your own dance pattern.

Example:

a. All partners stand in line formation with arms linked, facing the front of room. Walk briskly while singing: "Yankee Doodle came to town, A-riding on a pony."

b. With the same partner, turn and walk in the opposite direction while singing: "He stuck a feather in his cap, And called it macaroni."

c. Break away from your partner and move alone freely (in 3/4 time) in any direction around the room while singing: "Yankee Doodle, keep it up, Yankee Doodle dandy; Mind the music and the step, And."

Note:

Change of meter is emphasized by the accompanying percussion instruments. They highlight the accented beats with cymbals, drums, or other instruments of choice.

d. Reach out to the person standing near you, who becomes your new partner, join arms, and walk briskly in time with beginning meter (2/4) while singing: "with the girls be handy!"

5. Create your own dance patterns to a familiar theme that has been altered by a change in meter. Accompany the dance instrumentally.

6. Create a melodic theme and incorporate variations in meter in it.

7. Listen to other compositions that are composed of changing meters:

> Griffes: *The White Peacock* from *Adventures in Music*, Grade 6, Volume I. (Refer to p. 174.)

8. Review the experiences in polyrhythms on p. 167.

Additional Music Literature for Listening Experiences on the Intermediate Level

Element: RHYTHM

Component: Syncopation

Concept: Syncopation is the unexpected placement of an accent on beats Other than the strong ones in a measure; it creates a feeling of movement and excitement.

> Chabrier: "España," *Rhapsody for Orchestra* from *Adventures in Music*, Grade 5, Volume I

■ *Use of Classroom Instruments and Other Strategies to Explore the Concept*

1. Listen to "España Rhapsodie." Does anyone know what *Espana* means? (Spain.) Did the music sound as if it is of Spanish origin? Why? What kind of music is this—a love song, a ballad, a hymn? (Dance music.)

2. Note that the composer, Chabrier, used many authentic Spanish dance melodies in writing this composition. Does anyone know what a rhapsody is? (When a composition is made up of many different melodies, *with no specific* organization, it is called a rhapsody.)

3. Listen to the composition again, raising your hands each time a distinctive new MELODY is heard. As it is identified, the teacher will flip over the notation of that theme on the transparency in its proper position on the overhead projector. How many different melodies (themes) were heard? (Seven.) (Each theme is notated in the Teachers Guide of the *Adventures in Music* series.) Was there any specific organization of when, or the number of times, each MELODY was heard? (No.)

4. Sing each MELODY, from the notation projected on the screen, keeping time with the music. Was it easy to tap along as you sang the different melodies? Did the accented beat always fall on the 1s or first beat of each measure? (No.)

5. Listen to theme 1 again while viewing the rhythmic notation of that theme on the transparency:

6. Select tambourines, maracas, high drums and castanets and read the notation until it can be played, accenting the first beat of each measure.

7. Add different accents after the teacher indicates them on the transparency of the rhythmic notation of theme 1:

8. Compare the two notated rhythm patterns:
   a. Which pattern sounded more exciting to you?
   b. Where are the strong beats in 3/8 meter? Did the accents fall on them or on the weaker beats?
   c. Listen again and try to sing along on "ta." Repeat it until it is learned.
   d. Sing the theme on "ta" again, accompanying the singing with tambourines and other instruments to emphasize the accented beats.

9. The lesson in this experience is that the musical (rhythmical) term *syncopation* is applied to the unexpected placement of an accent on a beat other than the strong ones in a measure.

Component: Rhythm Patterns
Concept: The groupings of short and long tones in a melody often form a rhythmic pattern.

> Respighi: Danza from *Brazilian Impressions*
> from *Adventures In Music*, Grade 5, Volume II

Note:

A detailed analysis of the various rhythms present in this vibrant and colorful composition are included in the Teachers Guide in the *Adventures In Music* series. However, some suggestions for exploring rhythm patterns are given here:

1. Illustrate the accompaniment pattern in line duration designating long and short tones:

—— — —— ——|— — —— ——

2. Clap or tap this pattern on any percussion instrument of your choice. If you want to project tone color characteristic of this composition, what instruments will you choose? (Maracas, bongos, claves, tambourines, and any available drumheads.)

3. Transfer the line duration to musical notation through trial-and-error procedures until this pattern results referring to the following key:

4. Listen to the music as you tap this accompaniment pattern throughout the composition. Is this easy to do? Why not? (Because of changes in TEMPO.) Did you hear any other distinctive rhythm patterns? Did you hear any syncopated rhythms? What is a syncopated rhythm? (Refer to p. 164.)

5. Tap a syncopated rhythm pattern and then, using line duration, write this same rhythm pattern on the chalkboard. Try to listen for and record on the board a syncopated rhythm pattern heard in the composition, as

— — — — — — — — — — — — — — — — — —

transferred to musical notation using the following key:

6. Divide the class into groups. Have each group make up a rhythm pattern using only one or two kinds of percussion instruments so that the pattern is easily identified aurally. Write these patterns on the chalkboard and then, after listening to each group play its respective pattern, have all of the patterns played simultaneously on all the percussion instruments. (The term *polyrhythms** is ascribed to different rhythm patterns when they are tapped simultaneously.)

*Advanced experiences in identifying and understanding the notation of polyrhythms should include the study of music that composers have scored by using two different meters simultaneously:

Examples:

Copland: "Street in a Frontier Town," from *Billy the Kid, Adventures In Music*, Grade 6, Vol. I

Ives: "Putnam's Camp," Second Movement, from *Three Places in New England*

7. Accompany a favorite MELODY of your choice using the various rhythm patterns you have explored aurally, physically, and visually.

Component: Meter
Concept: Music may be composed of changing (shifting) meters.

> Griffes: *The White Peacock* from *Adventures In Music*, Grade 6, Volume I

While listening to this composition, can you discover a steady beat? Why not? (Because a definite, regular rhythmic pulse is absent.) In this musical composition the meter shifts from 3/2 to 5/4 to 7/4 time; a definite accent is also missing, which transmits the feeling of dreaminess, or an ethereal state of unreality. Compare this music to the definite straightforward movement of the following examples:

> Bizet: "Farandole" from *L'Arlesienne Suite no. 2* from *Adventures In Music*, Grade 6, Volume I
>
> Sousa: "The Stars and Stripes Forever"
>
> *or*
>
> Coates: "Knightsbridge March" from *London Suite* from *Adventures In Music*, Grade 4, Volume II

Suggested Activity for the College or University Student

1. Devise strategies for familiarizing children with concepts related to accented beats, meter, rhythm patterns, polyrhythms (many different rhythms produced by tapping different rhythm patterns simultaneously), and polymeters (various meters experienced simultaneously).
2. Practice developmental presentations.

Example:

Have the children suggest names of current television programs or television celebrities and clap or tap them on percussion instruments of their choice:

a. Chant and tap on drums: ABC News and Weath-er Re-ports.
b. Design this rhythm pattern on a chalkboard using line duration of shorts-longs:

A	B	C	News	and	Weath-	er	Re-	ports
short	short	short	long	short	short	short	short	long- er

Then, transfer the pattern to musical notation:

𝅘𝅥 = short

𝅗𝅥 = long

𝅗𝅥. = longer

c. Clap and tap again discovering where the "feeling" for the accented beats occurs.

d. Calling the accented beats 1s, and discovering that two weak beats follow the 1s, group the beats in sets to discover that the music moves in 3s with three quarter notes (𝅘𝅥), or the equivalent, to a measure; thus, the meter of this rhythm pattern is $\frac{3}{4}$ and is notated as

As the students suggest names of people or places to tap, and after these rhythm patterns are explored, divide the class into groups. Assign each group a different RHYTHM to tap and then have all the groups tap them simultaneously; the end result will be a sudden burst of exciting rhythms (polyrhythms). Thus, accented beats, meter, rhythm patterns, polyrhythms, and polymeters can be discovered and explored in a logical procedure.

3. Plan and carry out your lesson presentation before your peer group.
4. At the conclusion of your presentation, request peer-group evaluation and discussion of your performance.

Chapter 8

Harmony–
An Element of Music

ANALYSIS OF COMPONENTS OF HARMONY

Chords Defined and Illustrated

It is the vertical arrangement of tones (chordal structure) that, when sounded simultaneously, produces HARMONY. This vertical arrangement is in

contrast to the linear, or horizontal, arrangement of tones (melodic structure) that, when played or sung, produces a melodic line, or contour. However, HARMONY often can be heard as an accompaniment to a MELODY; similarly, the MELODY may be composed of the same tones as the chord providing the harmonic accompaniment.

Example:

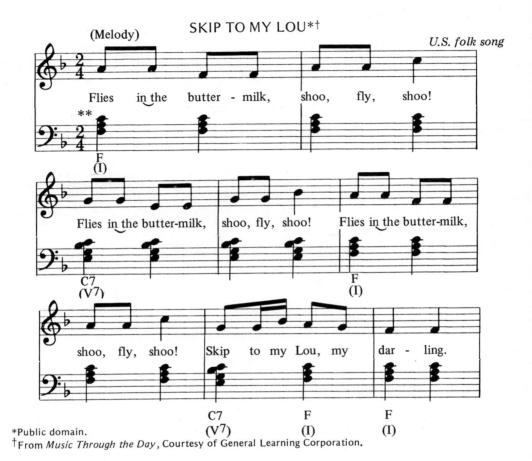

SKIP TO MY LOU*†

(Melody)

U.S. folk song

Flies in the butter - milk, shoo, fly, shoo!

F
(I)

Flies in the butter-milk, shoo, fly, shoo! Flies in the butter-milk,

C7
(V7)

F
(I)

shoo, fly, shoo! Skip to my Lou, my dar - ling.

C7   F   F
(V7)   (I)   (I)

*Public domain.
†From *Music Through the Day*, Courtesy of General Learning Corporation.

Thus, it is easy to recognize aurally as well as visually (reading the musical notation on the staff) that when the structure of the MELODY changes, the harmonic structure of the chord that provides the accompaniment also changes. Changing the traditional harmonic accompaniment to a familiar song also can change the general character, or mood, of the song.

Example:

Cailliet: Variations on the Theme "Pop! Goes the Weasel" from *Adventures in Music*, Grade 4, Volume I

**Harmonic accompaniment including chord name. *Note*: Melodic tones are also present in the accompanying chord. This type of HARMONY—a single melodic line supported by chords—is termed *homophony*.

Polyphony

HARMONY of polyphonic texture (many voiced) may result when the structure of a MELODY warrants performance as a round or canon; that is, when the same MELODY is sung by two or more groups starting in time at different points. A round or canon can be classified more definitely when groups perform as follows:

round: each group repeats the song two or three times, or an indefinite number of times

canon: each group sings the entire song through once only, in strict imitation

Some familiar rounds are "Are You Sleeping?" "White Coral Bells," and "Dona Nobis Pacem." Any song classified as a round can be labeled a canon if each group sings the entire song once only. (Also refer to a specific MELODY written in canon form, "Easter Bells," p. 207.)

Polyphonic HARMONY also results when two or more different melodies are performed simultaneously, such as "Three Blind Mice" with "Are You Sleeping?" The source of this suggested harmony can be found in William R. Sur, et al., *This Is Music 4* (Boston: Allyn, 1967). The suggested harmony of "Home on the Range" with "My Home's in Montana" can be found in Frederick Beckman. Arr., *Partner Songs* (Boston: Ginn, 1958).

In general, therefore, the harmonic structure of chords and melodic structure are related and may be dependent on one another provided the effect sought by the composer is one of *consonance* or *dissonance.**

Home Chord (Key)

Music often moves around a home chord—that is, around the final chord in a musical composition—or a chord that when strummed or played sounds as if it has reached home, or is at rest. (Refer to pp. 182–184 for further illustration and a lesson procedure for discovering the home chord in a musical composition.)

SAMPLING AND PROCEDURES AND LESSON PLANS FOR EXPLORING MUSICAL CONCEPTS RELATED TO HARMONY

Primary Level

The following songs and listening activities illustrate the musical concepts to be explored. Each concept is related to a component of HARMONY and is

---

*Consonance is a normal sound (agreeable to the listener) that results when two or more tones blend well when sounded or played together. (Refer to the illustration on p. 180.) Dissonance is a disturbing sound, or a sound that creates a feeling of tension. It results when two or more tones are sounded or played together.

structured developmentally. The suggested musical activities for exploring the concepts also are developed in a simple-to-complex procedure most appropriate for children of primary age.

Concepts are based on the following components of HARMONY:

Chords
Polyphony (Counterpoint)
Home Chord (Key)

Element: HARMONY
Component: Chords
Concept: Two or more tones sounded together is called HARMONY.

ROW, ROW, ROW YOUR BOAT (refer to p. 154)

■ *Suggested Musical Class Activities for "Row, Row, Row Your Boat"*

Singing: Sing "Row, Row, Row Your Boat."

Singing and Playing: Play an accompaniment on an autoharp, pushing down on the button. Is the autoharp playing the same MELODY that we are singing? If not, why does it sound right? Do the musical tones seem to blend together? Did you ever watch mother mix or blend sugar and butter together for making a cake? Did you ever mix or blend your water colors? When musical tones blend well together what do we call the sound? (HARMONY.) Sing other songs to the accompaniment of an autoharp, piano, and bells. Do all the musical tones seem to fit together? Is there a blend of musical tones? Is HARMONY present in this music? These tones sounding together form chords.

Listening and Playing: Look at the piano keyboard. How are the black keys grouped? (In 2s and 3s.) If you played a group of 3s at the same time, would it sound louder than a group of 2s? Play a tone cluster of the groups of three black keys as you count 1–2–3–4. Play this tone cluster only on 1 this time and accent this first beat. What could you do on beats 2–3–4? Play this pattern:

/	////
1	2 – 3 – 4
tone cluster	tone cluster
of 3-black-key	of 2-black-key
group	group

Which tone cluster is playing the accented beat? How does it sound? Would you say that the sound of the chords does not seem to fit the MELODY as well? Which tone cluster is playing the unaccented beat? How does it sound? Would you say that the sound is one of consonance or dissonance? Play this pattern on the piano keyboard repeatedly. What kind of music does it make you think of? (Indian music.) Play a large drum on the accented beat this time together with a 3-note cluster as directed. Play a small drum on the unaccented beats this time together with a 2-note tone cluster as directed.

<table>
<tr><td>/</td><td></td><td>/ / /</td></tr>
<tr><td>1</td><td></td><td>2 – 3 – 4</td></tr>
<tr><td>3-note</td><td></td><td>2-note</td></tr>
<tr><td>tone cluster</td><td></td><td>tone cluster</td></tr>
<tr><td>large drum</td><td></td><td>small drum or tambourines</td></tr>
</table>

Singing: Sing "Indian Song" on p. 58 to this accompaniment.

Creating: Make up your own Indian song to this accompaniment pattern as it is played on a piano keyboard and on classroom instruments. Make up your own Indian dance as you sing the song. Would you make a strong or weak movement on the accented beat? (1s.) Why? Would you make a strong or weak movement on the unaccented beats? (2–3–4.) Why? Could you make up many different Indian dances? Play, sing, and dance to this Indian music.

Element: POLYPHONY (Counterpoint)
Component: Simultaneous Sounding of Two or More Melodies
Concept: Polyphony is heard when two or more melodies are sung at the same time.

ARE YOU SLEEPING?*

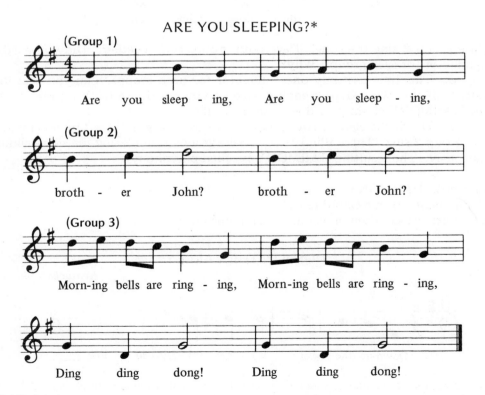

(Group 1)
Are you sleep - ing, Are you sleep - ing,

(Group 2)
broth - er John? broth - er John?

(Group 3)
Morn-ing bells are ring - ing, Morn-ing bells are ring - ing,

Ding ding dong! Ding ding dong!

*Public domain.

■ *Use of Classroom Instruments and Other Strategies to Explore the Concept*

1. All sing "Are You Sleeping?"

2. Divide the class into three groups and all sing the song again, only this time have each group begin to sing the entire song once starting at different times. Be certain to hold on to the last note until each group catches up so that all the groups can end the song together. When you hear a MELODY sung by many voices at the same time, but the voices begin to sing the MELODY at different times, would you say HARMONY is present?

3. Play a "do-sol-do" pattern on resonator bells:

What does it sound like? A doorbell? Church bells? A school bell?

4. Sing a "do-sol-do" pattern as you play on the bells.

5. Divide the class into two groups. Have group 1 sing "ding, dong, ding, dong" on a "do-sol-do" pattern throughout the song.

Have group 2 sing the song. Have both groups sing together. Did you need a conductor for each group? Why?

6. This time use only one conductor for both groups. Can you hear the sounds of the two groups blending? Would you say HARMONY is present? Is the HARMONY clashing or does it seem to fit?

7. Divide the class in two groups. Have group 1 sing "Are You Sleeping?" and group 2 sing "Three Blind Mice." Have groups 1 and 2 sing the songs simultaneously. The resulting HARMONY is called polyphony.

Element: HARMONY
Component: Home Chord (Key)
Concept: Music often moves around a home chord.

DOWN IN THE VALLEY*

Kentucky folk song

*Public domain. This version of the song is from Robert W. Winslow and Leon Dallin, *Music Skills for Classroom Teachers* (Dubuque, Ia.: Brown, 1970), p. 148.

Hang your head   o - ver,   hear the wind   blow. ___

Hear the wind   blow,   dear,   hear the wind   blow, ___

Hang your head   o - ver,   hear the wind   blow.

■ Use of Classroom Instruments and Other Strategies to Explore the Concept

1. Sing "Down in the Valley."
2. While your teacher plays the song on the autoharp, close your eyes and hum as you listen. Did you hear the chord change in the accompaniment?
3. Sing along this time and raise your hand every time your ears tell you that a chord has changed. How many different chords were played?
4. Strum a pretend autoharp in the air as you hum along, but sing the word "change" whenever you hear the need for a change in chord.
5. Play the autoharp and sing along. Did you change to another chord whenever your ears told you to? When the song ended, did the final chord you were strumming sound as if it had reached home? Did it sound at rest? This is called the home chord.
6. Sing and play a different song starting on the home chord and listen for the home chord throughout the song.
7. Raise your hand whenever you hear the home chord being played.

WHEN JOHNNY COMES MARCHING HOME*

L. Lambert

When   John - ny comes march - ing   home   a - gain,   Hur -

rah! ___   Hur - rah! ___   We'll   give him   a   heart - y

wel - come then, Hur - rah! _____   Hur - rah! _____   The _

*Public domain. This version of the song is from Robert W. Winslow and Leon Dallin, *Music for Class-room Teachers* (Dubuque, Ia.: Brown, 1970), p. 70.

men will cheer, the boys will shout, The

la - dies they will all turn out, And we'll all feel

gay when John - ny comes march - ing home! ___

8. Sing "When Johnny Comes Marching Home." Does the song end on the home chord? Does this home chord sound different from the home chord in "Down in the Valley"?

9. Strum the home chord in "Down in the Valley" on the autoharp (G major). Now, strum the home chord in "When Johnny Comes Marching Home" (g minor on the autoharp). Alternate strumming these two chords. Raise your hand each time you hear the G major chord and bow your head whenever you hear the sound of the g minor chord.

Additional Material for Suggested Use on the Intermediate Level

Element: HARMONY
Component: Chords
Concept: Experience in playing all MELODY and chording instruments strengthens aural perception of chord progressions I–V^7–I and, later, I–IV–V^7–I.

■ *Use of Chording Instruments and Other Strategies to Explore the Concept*

1. Use an overhead projector (if a screen is not available, make one by taping white shelf paper to a chalkboard) to cast a piano keyboard (from a transparency) onto a screen. Use transparent, colored bingo discs, available at variety stores, to build the chord pictorially by moving the desired keys pictured on the transparency. In this way, students can view the specific keys to be played singly or in chord formation and, by means of the overhead projector and keyboard transparency, see how the teacher builds triads in root position as well as in their respective inversions. Building these same triads on the musical staff while viewing them pictorially on the keyboard motivates the student immediately to find and play the triads on melody bells, resonator bells, and piano keyboards. (Resonator bells can be removed from their case and placed in chord boxes for ease in playing chords that require triple- or quadruple-headed mallets.)

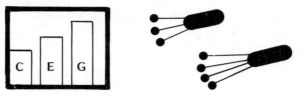

Example:

The following illustrations are of a C major triad on a screen from a keyboard transparency and from a staff on a chalkboard:

○ = red transparent discs highlighting a C major chord in root position

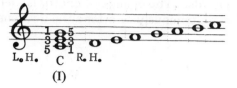

Note:

The C major scale is written in its entirety for ease in relating to chord building; also, fingering for the right and left hands, respectively, is indicated by finger numbers on the staff. It corresponds to the finger numbers on the visual aid:

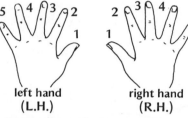

left hand
(L.H.)

right hand
(R.H.)

● = green transparent discs highlighting a G⁷ chord in root position, showing the relation to the C major chord

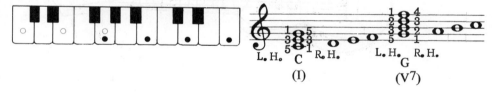

● = green transparent discs highlighting a G⁷ chord in an inversion showing its relation to the C major chord

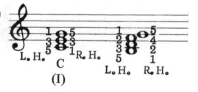

2. Sing some of the familiar songs listed on p. 187 while playing your own accompaniment and aurally identify when the chord should change from I-V⁷-I, playing in the key of C major. Four or five students can play on one keyboard with either their left or right hands, using middle C as point of reference, but building the C major chord on any C (high or low) on the keyboard. Do the same with all the other chords built on any tone of the keyboard. This will allow several students to play simultaneously. Also, play the chords on an autoharp, on melody bells, tuned water jugs, and on jars or soda pop bottles. (See pp. 54-55 in Chapter 3.) If ukuleles are available for strumming chords,

consult the fingering chart illustrated on p. 187. Chord boxes provide an effective receptacle for building chords from individual bells in a set of resonator bells. Those remaining students not playing instruments can sing and, by means of one (I) and five-finger (V^7) hand gestures, signal the performers to change chords. (The change of chords is identified aurally; visual perception may occur simultaneously or after aural awareness is experienced.)

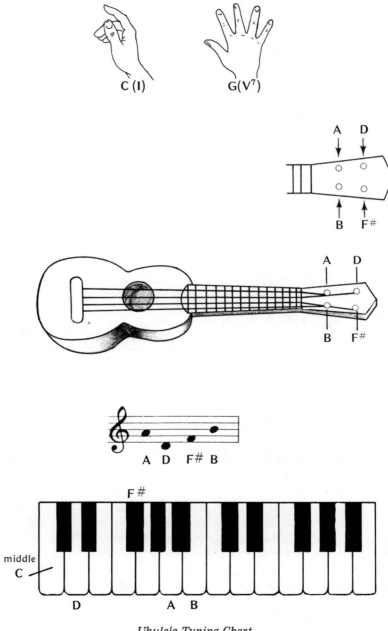

Ukulele Tuning Chart

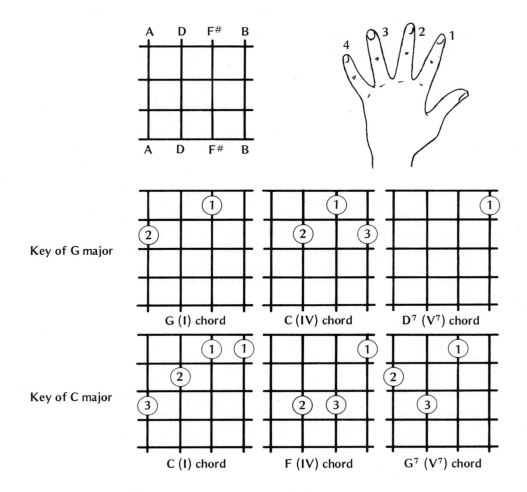

Key of G major

G (I) chord   C (IV) chord   D⁷ (V⁷) chord

Key of C major

C (I) chord   F (IV) chord   G⁷ (V⁷) chord

Ukulele fingering chart for most common chords used in this book.
(Refer to any ukulele instruction book for additional chords.)

Familiar songs using simple harmonic background of I–V^7 chords:

Clementine
Down in the Valley
Hail, Hail the Gang's All Here
Lightly Row
London Bridge
Polly Wolly Doodle
Shoo Fly, Don't Bother Me
Skip to My Lou
Ten Little Indians
Three Blind Mice
Row, Row, Row Your Boat

Are You Sleeping? (Brother John)
Joshua Fit de Battle of Jericho
Oh, Dear, What Can the Matter Be?
Billy Boy

3. Have these same chords played on melody flutes, recorders, and melody bells in whichever tone of the two chords (I–V[7]) the performers want to use while other class members sing and play the chords on autoharps, resonator bells, and piano keyboards.

4. Divide the class into three groups. Have group 1 play the chords on chording instruments (autoharp, piano, resonator bells, and ukulele). Have group 2 sing and design the contour of a simple MELODY in the air using hand levels to determine the approximate movement of the MELODY in steps and chords. Then, play it by ear on melody instruments—flutes, recorders, melody bells, resonator bells, or piano. When groups 1 and 2 play and sing together homophony will occur (the resulting HARMONY when a chord accompanies a MELODY). Group 3 can notate the simple melody line on the musical staff on the chalkboard or chart. Indicate where chord changes occur.

Example:

LIGHTLY ROW*

German folk song

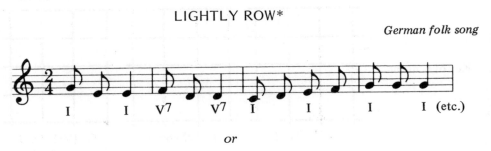

or

Notate the complete chord structure on a bass staff as follows, which is also a notated illustration of homophony:

*From The Golden Book of Favorite Songs © Schmitt, Hall & McCreary Co., Minneapolis, Minnesota, 1951.

5. Everyone play and sing together reading the notation from the chalkboard or chart.

6. Play, sing, and notate other familiar songs for reinforcement of the concept and to strengthen physical dexterity in moving smoothly from one chord to another in the I–V^7 progression while performing on chording instruments.

7. Sing songs that require the chord progression I–IV–V^7–I, notating them on the chalkboard and performing them on all melody and chording instruments.

Familiar songs using simple harmonic background of I–IV–V^7 chords:

Auld Lang Syne
Away in a Manger
Sweet Betsy from Pike
For He's a Jolly Good Fellow
Home on the Range
Happy Wanderer
Michael Row the Boat Ashore
Happy Birthday
O Christmas Tree
Oh, Susanna
She'll Be Comin' 'Round the Mountain
Silent Night
Swing Low, Sweet Chariot
Yankee Doodle
When the Saints Go Marching In
Marines' Hymn
Joy to the World
The First Noel

8. Sing, play, and notate the same songs in different keys building the chords from the tones of each new scale that is written on the musical staff on the chalkboard.

9. Identify the chord progressions used by composers in other favorite songs of yours and sing, notate, and play them on all the instruments available to you.

10. In building chords (triads) on the tones of the scale, identify aurally the major and minor sounds of the chords and reproduce them on melody and chording instruments. In building a minor chord on the staff, what tone of the major chord is altered? (The third tone of a major chord is lowered a half step):

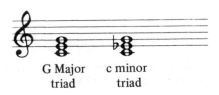

G Major   c minor
triad   triad

Additional Music Literature for Listening Experiences
on the Intermediate Level

Element: HARMONY
Component: Counterpoint (Polyphony)
Concept: When two melodies are heard simultaneously, the resulting HAR-
MONY is termed *counterpoint*.

> J. S. Bach: "Jesu, Joy of Man's Desiring" from
> Cantata no. 147 from *Adventures in Music*,
> Grade 5, Volume I

The chorale MELODY is easily recognized as moving slowly and with great dignity as compared to the flowing melody line of the introduction. Later in the composition, the flowing melody line of the introduction becomes the accompaniment of the chorale MELODY, and the resulting HARMONY is counterpoint.

Because this chorale MELODY moves on a scale, it can be played by half the class on melody bells, resonator bells, melody flutes, recorders, or a piano while the remaining half sings the flowing MELODY of the accompaniment.

Suggested Activity for the College or University Student

1. Divide the class into groups. After becoming familiar with the procedures in this chapter for chord building on chording instruments—
   autoharp, resonator bells, piano keyboard* and ukuleles and guitars,
   if available—practice gaining facility in performing on these instruments
   in groups. (Refer to the fingering charts for changing hand and finger
   positions from I–V^7 chords in only one key of your choice until you
   are able to perform with ease.)
2. Choose familiar songs that only demand the chord change of I–V^7 and
   sing and play them together. (Refer to the list of songs on p. 187.)
3. Having achieved satisfactory dexterity in performing a chordal accompaniment to several songs, have the groups perform individually in a
   brief "sing along" during the methods class.
4. Rotate performing on instruments so everyone receives an opportunity
   to play various instruments.

---

*As many as four or five adults can perform a chordal accompaniment simultaneously at one piano keyboard, each person using only one hand.

Chapter 9

Form–
An Element of Music

COMPONENTS OF FORM DEFINED
WITH SUGGESTED REFERENCES

The arrangement, or organization, of the elements in music results in the structure or design of the music that is referred to as its FORM. The FORM of music is dependent on the use of unity and contrast within the composition.

The musician can use numerous devices to achieve unity and contrast: recurring melodic or rhythmic patterns; repetition of like phrases; repetition of dissimilar phrases; differences in dynamic reproduction of the same phrases or entire sections of the music; melody patterns repeated higher or lower; and different harmonic progressions to accompany the same melody line. This list could be extended indefinitely.

Thus, one can see that a composer must utilize his powers of musical understanding of the interrelationship of the elements of music to create compositions that will reflect originality of design.

The purpose of this chapter is to encourage children to explore and discover the FORM (design) of music and thereby become aware of the balance that can be achieved through unity and variety in the structure of both a major orchestral composition and a simple folk song.

SAMPLING OF PROCEDURES AND LESSON PLANS
FOR EXPLORING MUSICAL CONCEPTS RELATED TO FORM

Primary Level

The following songs and listening activities illustrate the musical concepts to be explored. Each concept is related to a component of FORM (as listed here and is structured developmentally.

Concepts are based on the following components of form:

Unity and Variety
Phrase
Question and Answer
Two- or Three-Part Sections
Rondo FROM

Element: FORM
Component: Unity and Variety
Concept: Music is usually made up of sections, or parts.

TWINKLE, TWINKLE, LITTLE STAR*

Folk song

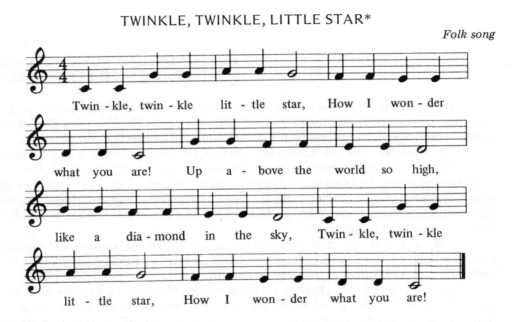

Twin - kle, twin - kle   lit - tle   star,   How I   won - der

what you   are!   Up a - bove the   world so   high,

like a   dia - mond in   the   sky,   Twin - kle, twin - kle

lit - tle   star,   How I   won - der   what you   are!

*Public domain.

■ *Suggested Musical Class Activities for "Twinkle, Twinkle, Little Star"*

Listening: Listen to "Twinkle, Twinkle, Little Star" and raise your hand if you hear parts that sound alike. Did you hear parts of the music that sounded different? Even though there were parts in the music that sounded different and parts that sounded alike, did the parts seem to fit together in a musical design?

Listening and Free Movement: Design "Twinkle, Twinkle, Little Star," at the chalkboard and label each part with a letter name:

TWINKLE, TWINKLE, LITTLE STAR

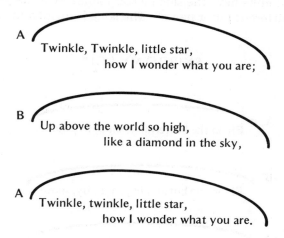

A

Twinkle, Twinkle, little star,
    how I wonder what you are;

B

Up above the world so high,
    like a diamond in the sky,

A

Twinkle, twinkle, little star,
    how I wonder what you are.

Notice that section A is repeated, which gives unity to the song. Section B is like a new MELODY within the song and, therefore, gives the song variety. Design a free body movement for each section. Will the same movement be used when section A is repeated? (Yes.)

Creating: Make up your own music or song with parts that are alike and parts that are different. Can you make the parts fit in a musical design that sounds good? How many parts of the music are different? How many parts of the music are alike?

Element: FORM
Component: Phrase
Concept: The sections, or parts, of a song usually contain a musical thought called a phrase.

SKIP TO MY LOU (refer to p. 178)

■ *Suggested Musical Class Activities to "Skip to My Lou"*

Listening: Have you ever seen a family group of puppies? Have you ever seen a family group of kittens? They are both families, but different families. How many people are in your family group at home? In music we hear family groups of words and tones. Some family groups are alike and some are different. In music all of these families are called musical phrases. When you are learning how to read stories in school do you group your words in phrases? In music when we sing a song can we group the words and music of the song into phrases?

Singing and Listening: Listen as you sing "Skip to My Lou" and raise your hands at the end of each phrase. Do these phrases sound like a musical thought or idea? Do these musical phrases sound alike or different? Design the phrases in the air and on the chalkboard as you sing the song again. (Use an arm movement to form an arc ⌒.)

Reading: Write letter names on the chalkboard for each phrase. Will the phrases that sound alike have the same letter name? Will the phrases that sound different have a different letter name? The song is divided into phrases here:

SKIP TO MY LOU

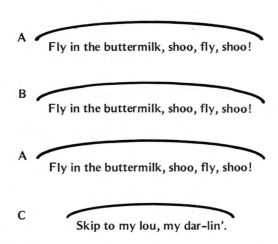

A   Fly in the buttermilk, shoo, fly, shoo!

B   Fly in the buttermilk, shoo, fly, shoo!

A   Fly in the buttermilk, shoo, fly, shoo!

C   Skip to my lou, my dar–lin'.

From this design can you tell (a) How many phrases are in the song? (b) Which phrases are alike? (c) Which phrases are different?

Singing and Listening: Sing the song again and use colored chalk on the chalkboard to design the phrases this time. Will you use the same color for the phrases that sound alike? What colors will you use for the phrases that sound different?

Element: FORM
Component: Question and Answer
Concept: Two phrases often appear as question and answer.

LITTLE JACK HORNER*

Lit - tle Jack Hor - ner   sat   in   a   cor - ner,

Eat - ing   his   Christ - mas   pie, _____   He

*Public domain.

put in his thumb, And pull'd out a plum,

And said "What a good boy am I!"_____

■ *Suggested Musical Class Activities for "Little Jack Horner"*

Singing: Sing "Little Jack Horner."

Singing and Listening: Sing the song again, but this time raise your hand when you come to the end of a "family group of words," or a phrase. When you talk to each other, do you emphasize each word as you speak? Do you talk like this, *"The sun is shining bright-ly"*? Try talking like this to your friend. Would people like to hear you talk like this? Do you like to talk like this or do you talk smoothly like this, "The sun is shining brightly"? Notice that the words are under a curved line or an arc, which reminds you to speak smoothly as you group your words. When you read in school, does your teacher tell you to emphasize your words or to read your words smoothly and group them together in families or phrases?

Singing and Listening: Sing the song again. Design the phrases of the song in the air with your arm.

LITTLE JACK HORNER

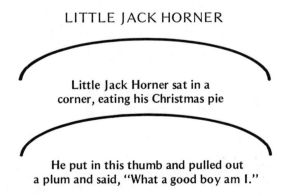

Little Jack Horner sat in a
corner, eating his Christmas pie

He put in this thumb and pulled out
a plum and said, "What a good boy am I."

How many phrases did you design? Sing other songs and design the phrases in the air as you sing. Design the phrases on the chalkboard as you sing the song.

Listening and Playing: Choose any classroom instrument to play as you accompany the song. Do you think the instruments you chose should be heard throughout the song? If the song is divided into two phrases, give the phrases number names and divide the class into two groups. Group 1 designs and sings the first phrase, and Group 2 design and sings the second phrase. Choose classroom instruments to play on the first phrase and to play on the second phrase. Would you choose the same instruments to play on both phrases? Are both phrases alike? Is each phrase different? If both phrases are alike, would you choose the same instruments to play for both phrases? If each phrase is different, would you choose different instruments for each phrase?

Creating: Make up your own sentence songs or question-and-answer songs of two phrase groups. Example: (Question-and-answer songs based on everyday questions Mother might ask you.)

(1) Did you brush your teeth today? Yes! And I am on my way.

(2) Do you have your books for school? Yes! I have my lunch box too!

(3) Take your sweater, too, it's cold!! Yes, I'll do as I am told.

Listening and Singing: Invite classmates to listen to the song you made up as you play it on the resonator bells and then sing it all together. Divide the class into two groups; Group 1 sings the question, and Group 2 sings the answer.

Reading: Write your own question-and-answer songs on the chalkboard, using blank notation that shows when the song goes up, down, or stays the same.

Listening: Listen to other music and discover how many sections or phrases are present.

Element: FORM
Component: Two Sections
Concept: Phrases may join to form a larger section, or part. Sometimes two or three parts are joined.
Presentation: Two Parts (A B)

BAA, BAA, BLACK SHEEP*

*Public domain.

■ *Use of Classroom Instruments and Other Strategies to Explore the Concept*

1. Listen to your teacher sing "Baa, Baa, Black Sheep." Does the song tell a story? If the song tells a story, is it longer than many songs you have sung before?

2. Listen as you sing the song. In how many parts is the song divided? As you sing the song again raise your hand where the two parts are joined together. Is part 2 different from part 1?

3. Using the letter names of the alphabet for the two parts of the song, what would you call part 1? (A.) What would you call part 2? (B.)

4. Write the letters on the chalkboard as the parts are heard in the song. (A B.)

BAA, BAA, BLACK SHEEP

A | Baa, Baa, Black Sheep, have you any wool?
"Yes, sir, yes, sir, three bags full:

B | One for my master and one for my dame
And one for the little boy that lives in the lane."

5. Divide the class into two groups. Have group 1 choose classroom instruments to play the steady beat in part A. Have group 2 choose classroom instruments to play the steady beat in part B. Will you choose different sounding instruments to play in part B? Why?

Example:

Group 1 plays tambourines and taps drums lightly in part A.
Group 2 plays rhythm sticks and jingle bells in part B.

6. Discover other songs that are divided in A B FORM, explore the sound, and then choose classroom instruments to play for each part.

Presentation: Three Sections or Parts (A B A)

SHOO FLY*

B. Reeves   F. Campbell

Shoo fly don't both-er me,
Shoo fly don't both-er me, Shoo fly don't
both-er me for I be-long to some-bod-y.

*Public domain.

I feel, I feel, I feel, I

feel like a morn - ing star. I feel, I feel, I

D. C. al Fine

feel, I feel like a morn - ing star.

■ *Use of Classroom Instruments and Other Strategies to Explore the Concept*

1. Listen to the familiar music of "Shoo Fly" and raise your hand if you have heard it before. (Teacher: hum or play the song by ear.)

2. All sing the song.

3. Listen as you sing the song again. In how many parts is the song divided? As you sing the song again raise your hand when you hear the end of the first part. Raise your hand when you hear the end of the second part and the return of the first part. How could you tell when the first part ended? Is the second part different? In what ways?

4. Use the letter names of the alphabet to label the parts of the song as you hear them. (A B A.)

SHOO FLY

A | Shoo fly, don't bother me, shoo fly, don't bother me,
Shoo fly, don't bother me for I belong to somebody.

B | I feel, I feel, I feel, I feel like a morning star
I feel, I feel, I feel, I feel like a morning star.

A | Shoo fly, don't bother me, shoo fly, don't bother me,
Shoo fly, don't bother me for I belong to somebody.

5. Make up your own song written in A B A FORM.

6. Design the FORM of the music using geometric shapes.

Example:

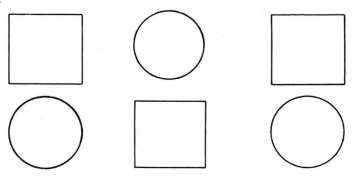

7. Listen to this composition.

> Meyerbeer: Waltz from *Les Patineurs* from *Adventures in Music*, Grade 2, Volume I

The introduction to this composition consists of two long chords. The first section (section A) is repeated. Therefore, the outline of the FORM of this composition can be illustrated as follows:

> Introduction
> Section A
> Section B
> Section A
> Coda

This listening activity is recommended for easy aural recognition of parts. Punctuate the ending of the section by having the children shake tambourines, or encourage them to choose instruments to play at the end or beginning of each section.

Suggested Listening Activity for Discovering the Rondo Form on the Primary Level

Element: FORM
Component: Rondo FORM
Concept: The first section, or section A, often reappears between new sections (A B A C A).

> Prokofieff: "Waltz on the Ice" from *Winter Holiday*, *Adventures in Music*, Grade 3, Volume II

Suggestions for Presentation:

1. Listen to this musical composition. Is the music divided into sections?
2. Listen to the first MELODY you heard.
3. Sing the first MELODY you heard while you design it in the air and on the chalkboard.
4. Listen to this music and raise your hand every time you hear the sound of the first MELODY. What do we call the MELODY in a musical composition? (A theme.) Can there be different themes in the same composition? Is the first theme we hear ever repeated?
5. Listen to this music again and raise your hand every time you hear the first theme.
6. List the orchestral instruments playing theme 1 on the chalkboard.
7. Choose classroom instruments that will best accompany theme 1 and play along every time you hear theme 1 in the composition. How many times was theme 1 announced? What letter name would you give theme 1? (A.)

8. Listen for the other different sections that are played. How many different sections did you hear? What letter names would you give those sections? Were those different sections ever repeated in the composition?

9. Diagram on the board the order in which themes 1, 2, and 3 appear in the composition, using letter names in your diagram.

Example:

A B A C A

In a musical composition do you know what we call this FORM when section A keeps returning? (Rondo.) Can you think of a way to remember the name of this FORM?

Example:

Theme A keeps coming around and around and around again.

Did you hear smaller sections in between the large sections that seem to join them all together? In music what do we call these smaller sections? (Interludes.) Spell the word and write or print it on the chalkboard.

Additional Material for Suggested Use on the Intermediate Level

Element: FORM
Component: Phrase
Concept: The sections, or parts, of a song usually contain a musical thought or idea called a phrase. Some phrases within a song are different and some phrases are alike.

SING FOR THE WIDE, WIDE FIELDS* (National 4–H Club song)
Fannie Buchanan   *Rena M. Parish*

Sing for the wide, wide fields,___ Sing for the

wide, wide sky,___ Sing for the good, glad earth, __

___ For the sun on hill-tops high. ___ Sing for the

*© 1933 Assigned to National 4-H Service Committee, Published by National 4-H Service Committee, Chicago, Ill. 1968.

com - rade   true,_____   Sing   for the   friend - ship

sweet;_____   Sing   as   to - geth - er   we   swing   a -

long, With the   turf   be - neath our   feet._____

■ *Use of Classroom Instruments, Movement, and Other Strategies to Explore the Concept (Grades 4 or 5)*

1. Listen to the National 4-H Club song "Sing for the Wide, Wide Fields" while visually following the score as projected on a screen or notated on a chart or chalkboard.

2. Sing the song in unison, keeping a steady beat by clapping, tapping, or marching in place.

3. Listen and design phrasing, such as an arc ⌒ in the air and on the chalkboard. Crash cymbals at the end of each phrase.

4. Determine that this song is composed of four phrases. Ascribe letter names to the phrases, design them on the chalkboard, and identify the like and unlike phrases:

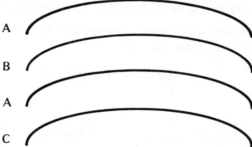

A

B

A

C

5. Divide the class into three groups (A B C). Have each group choose a combination of different sounding classroom instruments.

Example:

    Group A: tambourines, rhythm sticks, tone blocks
    Group B: poinciana pods, tom-toms, triangles
    Group C: instruments from both groups A and B, plus cymbals and bells

6. Design the phrases of the song through physical movement; that is, have group members march in pairs as a drill team *after* jointly deciding on a floor plan of activity. Aural recognition of the phrases—like and unlike—is the cue for movement and for playing classroom instruments by the specific groups as they literally "come alive" in response to the phrases. The following illustra-

tion is an example of an actual floor plan of movement designed by boys and girls in grade 5[1] after having identified the phrase pattern of "Sing for the Wide, Wide Fields."

Floor plan.

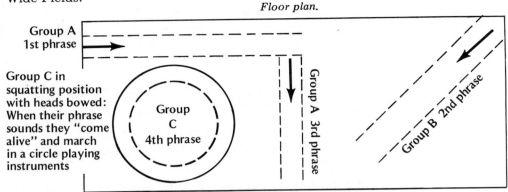

Group A
1st phrase

Group C in
squatting position
with heads bowed:
When their phrase
sounds they "come
alive" and march
in a circle playing
instruments

Group
C
4th phrase

Group A 3rd phrase

Group B 2nd phrase

At end of the last phrase—on fermata (⌒ which is the musical sign for a pause or hold)—everyone plays his own instrument and calls out "yea!" in unison while punctuating the ending with arms thrust upward.

Component: Theme and Variations
Concept: The subject of a theme and variations is a MELODY. The variations are a modified version of that MELODY.

■ *Use of Classroom Instruments and Other Strategies to Explore the Concept*

1. Play and sing the original version of "Hot Cross Buns" on recorders, melody flutes, bells, and piano keyboard.

HOT CROSS BUNS*

Sylvesta M. Wassum   *Traditional*

Hot   cross   buns!   Hot   cross   buns!

One - a - pen - ny,   two - a - pen - ny

Hot   cross   buns!

*From BIRCHARD MUSIC SERIES, Book I, Sylvesta M. Wassum, Editor. Copyright © 1962, Summy-Birchard Company, Evanston, Illinois. All rights reserved.

[1] Grade 5 in Blume Elementary School, Wapakoneta, Ohio.

2. Write "Hot Cross Buns" in 3/4 meter (with creative embellishments, if desired) as a variation of the original version in 4/4 meter and perform it as a solo on a melody instrument of your choice.

Example:

3. Sing and play "Hot Cross Buns" in round or canon form determining (by means of trial and error) the instrumental and vocal entrances. Can you think of other possible variations of "Hot Cross Buns" to include in this musical design of *theme* and *variations*?

4. Choose any familiar song and develop it into a theme-and-variations design, or FORM.

5. Listen to

> Gould: *American Salute*, Grade 5, Volume I
>
> and
>
> Gailliet: Variations on the Theme "Pop! Goes The Weasel" from *Adventures in Music*, Grade 4, Volume I

Component: Three Sections or Parts

Concept: A B A FORM is the design of a composition with two contrasting sections in which the first section is repeated after the second section is heard once.

■ *Use of Electronic Equipment to Explore the Concept (Tape Recorders)*

1. Receive instructions and a demonstration from an authority for operating a tape recorder. Be sure you understand the threading technique, what the position of the reels on the tape deck must be to record; how to identify and manipulate the controls for playing and for recording; the techniques for producing sound effects—such as, decrease and increase of speed, playing forward or backward, and splicing tape; and the technique for making a tape loop.

2. Encourage the students to learn how to operate the tape recorder.

3. Make a tape loop of environmental sounds.

4. Using classroom instruments, make up an original composition consisting of several phrases and record it on tape.

5. Play the tape loop and the original composition in that order and identify the sections with letter names: tape loop, A; original composition, B; and tape loop, A. You have made up your own composition in A B A (ternary) FORM.

6. By operating tape recorders, discover other ways of combining or isolating sounds at various speeds to produce organized sound compositions that are representative of various forms of musical compositions, such as binary FORM (A B); rondo FORM (A B A C A); and theme and variations.

Component: Rondo FORM
Concept: The first section, or section A, often reappears between new sections (A B A C A).

■ *Use of Classroom Instruments and Other Strategies to Explore the Concept*

1. Distribute boxes of crayons and shelf paper cut in 6-foot lengths.
2. Listen to three musical compositions and interpret the broad, over-all sound of each composition on paper with crayons in an unrestrained manner. (The titles of the compositions should not be announced to the class. Select three distinctly different qualities or textures of sound. Use a third of the paper for each interpretation.)
3. Learn or review the definitions of legato, staccato, and marcato and ascribe them to appropriate interpretations.

Example:

Label legato (smooth and connected) pictures A ("Wheat Dance").

Label staccato (disconnected) pictures B ("Ballet of the Unhatched Chicks").

Label marcato (emphatic) pictures C ("Parade").

4. Place the legato pictures on the front wall as follows, leaving a space between each one:

A　　A　　A　　A　　A

Place the staccato and marcato pictures alternately between the As as follows:

A　B　A　C　A　B　A　C　A

and discover rondo FORM.

5. Divide the class into three groups. Have group 1 choose classroom instruments (including the piano) that can be played legato; have group 2 choose classroom instruments that can best interpret staccato; and have group 3 choose classroom instruments that can best interpret marcato. Assign a leader to each group and have them adjourn to a corner of the room to improvise a rhythmic pattern over a steady beat. (Limit the time for this activity to two to five minutes.)

6. Reassemble in groups to perform from the score: A B A C A B A C A what might later be entitled "Percussion Rondo."

7. Add a coda to the composition, with all instruments playing various rhythm patterns simultaneously for a polyrhythmic texture.

Example:

Ginastera: "Wheat Dance" from *Estancia, Adventures in Music*, Grade 4, Volume I

Possible interpretation of the smooth, flowing sound of the passages in this composition.

Moussorgsky: "Ballet of the Unhatched Chicks" from *Pictures at an Exhibition, Adventures in Music*, Grade 1, Volume I

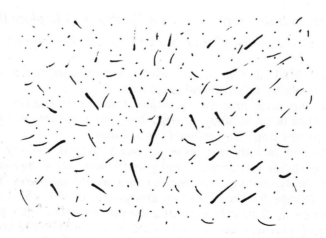

Possible interpretation of baby chickens pecking and scratching.

Ibert: "Parade" from *Divertissement, Adventures in Music*, Grade 1, Volume I

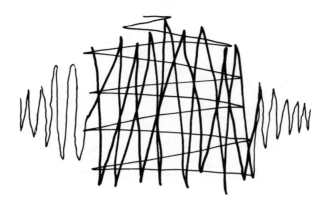

Possible interpretation of the DYNAMICS of a parade approaching, passing in review, and moving away.

8. Use this activity as an exploration of all the elements of music through the use of classroom instruments to underscore the lesson that a combination of all of these elements determines the mood of the musical composition.

Component: Canon (Refer to HARMONY p. 179)
Concept: A canon results when the same MELODY is sung by two or more groups starting in time at different points; each group sings the entire song through only once.

■ *Use of Classroom Instruments and Other Strategies to Explore the Concept*

1. Listen to the entire MELODY of "Easter Bells" played through once only.
2. Sing the MELODY in unison while reading from the score, which has been cast on a screen by an overhead projector.
3. Divide the class into two groups. Observe the entire score, noting that group 2 should begin to sing the MELODY one measure later than group 1.
4. Both groups sing "Easter Bells" as a canon.
5. Choose any melody instrument—resonator bells, melody bells, melody flutes, recorders—divide into groups, and play "Easter Bells" as a canon.
6. Design body movements (dance) that would interpret the joy of the Easter season. Divide the class into two groups and perform this interpretation as a canon, with group 2 strictly imitating the movements of group 1.
7. Sing and perform this canon using body movements and melody instruments, rotating the groups involved so that every class member has the experience of exploring a canon through the various media. Can you list the elements of music that could be represented in the presentation of this canon?

EASTER BELLS* Canon† by M. Lament

Al - le - lu - ia!

East - er glad - ness Al - le - lu - ia!

*Original.
†This is an example of a canon score. If the use of songs with a religious text is restricted in your school, substitute your own words to this canon score.

MELODY: moves by step and skip
RHYTHM: steady 4/4 meter
HARMONY: polyphonic texture (many voiced)
FORM: A B A' (over-all FORM of the canon)
TEMPO: steady, moderate
DYNAMICS: expressive quality of the music achieved through interpretive ideas of loud and soft passages
TONE COLOR: performance on various melody instruments

After the MELODY has been sung well in unison, could more than two groups perform it as a canon? (Yes.)

Additional Music Literature for Listening Experiences
on the Intermediate Level

Focus: Free Form

> Grofé: "Desert Water Hole" from *Death Valley Suite* from *Adventures in Music*, Grade 4, Volume I

1. This composition lends itself to storytelling about the Forty-niners (the California gold rush of 1849) through creative movement. After identifying the three familiar melodies (by Stephen Foster) as "Oh, Susanna," "Old Folks at Home," and "I'm Comin'," divide class into three groups. Have each group choose one of the melodies and, with a designated leader, listen intently for its presentation.
2. Upon aural identification of the chosen MELODY, design a movement or series of creative dance patterns that identify the activity presumably occurring in the music.

3. The contrasting moods of the Forty-niners—hopelessness, solemnity, and joy—as they plod courageously onward in their search for dreams come true can also be interpreted and enacted through creative (nonverbal) movement that will also project the free form of this musical composition.

> The simple fact that stories are written in words and that dance is expressed in nonverbal movements tells us that we cannot merely translate from one form to another. What distinguishes dance from other art forms is the unique use of space-time-force as aesthetic elements. Explored in innumerable combinations and in varying intensities, these elements give expressive qualities to a child's interpretation of movement, which transforms imagery from storytelling to dance. [2]

In this statement Miss Dimondstein has reference to space-time-force as aesthetic elements of the dance. *Space* is the area covered by the movement; *time* is the duration of the movement; and *force* is the intensity of the movement.

Component: A B A FORM
Concept: This composition is divided into two different sections (A B) with section A repeated. It also includes an Introduction that is repeated.

Vaughan Williams: Fantasia on "Greensleeves"
from *Adventures in Music*, Grade 6, Volume II

1. Do you know of any current popular melodies whose forms are easily recognized as A B A and that have an Introduction and an extended ending that could be termed a coda?
2. Bring in recordings of the compositions for the entire class to enjoy as a listening activity for analyzing FORM or design.

Suggested Activity for the College or University Student

1. Divide the class into groups. Listen to a selected number of musical compositions and, after determining the FORM or design of the composition, devise strategies for guiding the children to explore and discover for themselves the FORM of the same compositions through listening, singing, free movement, creating, playing, and reading.
2. Record the developmental activities used for this purpose. Include questioning techniques that will provide a smooth transition from one activity to another. This record is now a lesson plan.
3. As a culminating activity, present the lesson before the entire class. At the conclusion of the lesson initiate a class discussion for the purpose of evaluating the effectiveness of the lesson.

---

[2] Geraldine Dimondstein, *Children Dance in the Classroom* (New York: Macmillan, 1971), pp. 217–218.

Chapter 10

Tempo, Dynamics, and Tone Color– Expressive Elements of Music

TEMPO—AN ELEMENT OF MUSIC

COMPONENT (FAST–SLOW) OF TEMPO DEFINED

TEMPO—the speed of movement, or the speed experienced by the student while involved in listening, singing, playing, creating, and dancing (free movement)—is relative rather than absolute. For the purpose of comparison, it might be well to consider the musical terms and definitions as listed here in approximate order of TEMPO variation—slow to fast. The terms are relative to moderato—moderate rate of speed, or TEMPO (performance not in excess of fast or slow).

To indicate the TEMPO of a piece, a number of Italian terms are used, the most important of which are given here, in order of slowest to quickest:

largo: broad
lento: slow
adagio: slow; literally, at ease
andante: walking
moderato: moderate
allegretto, allegro: fast; literally, cheerful
presto: very fast
prestissimo: as fast as possible

In addition to these are terms calling for gradual change of speed, mainly

ritardando: slackening
accelerando: quickening
rubato: a deliberate unsteadiness of TEMPO.[1]

There are gradations of TEMPO in addition to, and within, this listing. The definitions of these terms can also be found in the *Harvard Dictionary of Music.*

The following suggestions for discovering and exploring TEMPO are made for the primary and intermediate levels. It must be remembered that the complex details of terminology, definitions, and differentiations must be reserved for pupils who display a readiness for advanced study and experiences. The alert teacher should determine the expanding needs of her pupils as they become increasingly involved in the developmental growth process.

The component of TEMPO explored in this text is:

Component: Fast–Slow

SAMPLING OF PROCEDURES AND LESSON PLANS FOR EXPLORING MUSICAL CONCEPTS RELATED TO TEMPO

Primary Level

Element: TEMPO
Component: Fast–Slow
Concept: Music may move fast or slow.

TWINKLE, TWINKLE, LITTLE STAR (refer to p. 192)

■ *Suggested Musical Class Activities for This Presentation*

Singing: Sing "Twinkle, Twinkle, Little Star." Did you sing it fast? Did you sing it slowly? Did you sing it somewhere in between fast and slow? In music, what do we call the "in-between" speed? (Moderato.) Sing the same song fast. Does it sound right? Why not? Sing the same song very, very slowly. Does it sound right? Why not? Sing the song at a moderate TEMPO. Does it sound right? Why?

Playing: Play triangles and finger cymbals as you sing to make the stars "twinkle." Would you play them steadily in time with the music?

---

[1] Willi Apel, *Harvard Dictionary of Music*, 2nd ed. (Cambridge, Mass.: The Belknap Press of Harvard, 1969), p. 837.

Creating: Pretend you are a star in the sky and can twinkle when you want to. Would you like to watch a conductor direct you? Why? Do stars twinkle fast and steadily like the flashing red light on a police car or fire truck? Choose other familiar songs to sing and then decide how fast or slow you think they should go.

Reading: List these three words on the chalkboard that tell you how fast or slowly to play and sing your song. The words are

Largo: slow speed
Moderato: medium speed
Allegro: fast speed

What is another word for speed of the song? (TEMPO.)

Singing: Sing your songs at different tempos and then discover which one you think fits the words and music best.

Dancing (Free Movement): Associate these terms with a body movement that would act out the TEMPO.

Largo: In your places move feet slowly as if you were climbing a high hill.
Moderato: In your places move your feet as if you were the postman delivering the mail. Would you move fast, slowly, or inbetween? How would he move if it were raining?
Allegro: In your places run briskly or quickly on tiptoes as you do when you are late for school.

Show me by clapping your hands (a) how he would move if he were very tired at the end of the day and (b) how he would move if he were starting out on a beautiful sunshiny day and his load were not too heavy?

■ *Additional Material and Teaching Guides for Exploring the Concept*

Songs pertaining to modes of transportation are ideal examples for applying changes in TEMPO or maintaining a steady TEMPO.

Additional Music Literature for Listening Experiences on the Primary Level

Element: TEMPO
Component: Fast–Slow
Concept: Music may move fast or slow.

Massenet: "Aragonaise" from *Le Cid* from *Adventures in Music*, Grade 1, Volume I

Suggestions for Presentation:

1. Listen to this music. Can you find the steady beat and tap along, or does it move too fast?

2. Stand anywhere in the room and move your arms and hands the way the music is moving. Is it whirling fast or rocking slowly?

3. Listen to the music and raise your hand when you hear it slow down. What is the musical term for slowing down? (Ritard.) Did you ever watch a spinning top? Did it ever slow down? When? Does music ever slow down when it is about to stop? Were you ever on a merry-go-round that slowed down before the ride was over and then went fast again? In this music where did you hear a ritard taking place? Does a ritard *only* take place at the end of the music?

Additional Material for Suggested Use on the Intermediate Level

Element: TEMPO
Component: Fast–Slow
Concept: Some musical compositions move faster than others. The speed of a composition is referred to as the TEMPO.
Concept: Sometimes the TEMPO remains steady; sometimes it gradually becomes faster or slower.

■ *Use of Song Materials and Other Strategies to Explore the Concepts*

1. Study the text of a song for clues as to probable TEMPO.
2. Listen to the MELODY of the song.
3. Sing the song at various tempos.
4. Decide which TEMPO is most satisfying after observing the ritards and sudden changes of TEMPO as determined by members of the class.
5. Observe the printed notation of a song as originally scored by the composer and perform it, comparing differences in interpretation at the conclusion of the performance.
6. Sing familiar songs at various tempos identifying each TEMPO with its corresponding term.
7. After the repeated performances of a song at contrasting tempos, decide which TEMPO was the most satisfying and then compare it with the composer's original interpretation or, in the event that the song is folk material, compare it to a specific arrangement. Can you think of other activities in which TEMPO can be explored by all members of the class while singing?

■ *Use of Folk Dancing and Other Strategies to Explore the Concepts*

A recommended source for definitions, directions, and recordings of the following folk dances is Edna Doll and Mary J. Nelson, *Rhythms Today* (Morristown, N.J.: Silver Burdett, 1965). The dances should be learned and performed in a large room such as a gymnasium or all-purpose room that has been cleared.

I Hora (Middle Eastern)

1. Sit on the floor and listen to the music as you clap or tap along. Did the TEMPO vary? Did the music begin fast or slowly? Did the TEMPO change gradually or suddenly?

2. Learn the basic dance steps of the hora standing in horizontal line formation behind a leader.

3. Dance the hora in circle formation to the accompaniment of a recording, noting the gradual change in TEMPO with which the dance steps are executed. If the physical characteristics of the room warrant performance by only a small group of dancers, those remaining can furnish an accompaniment on drums and tambourines of varying sizes. Because it is advisable for all members of the class to have an opportunity to perform the dance, alternate the dance groups with those providing a percussive accompaniment.

II The Sponge Diver (Greek)

1. The technique for learning this dance is the same as that outlined for the hora.

2. Note that the TEMPO is steady and moderate throughout, whereas in the hora, it moves gradually from slow to fast.

III Uba (African, pronounced: $\overline{oo}'$ -ba)

1. The technique for learning this simple but effective dance is the same as that outlined for the hora.

2. Note that the TEMPO begins moderato, increases to allegro, and moves to vivace for the final movements.

3. Drum beats on varying sizes of tom-toms, congas and bongos and tambourines can be used to provide exciting accompaniments, especially when different rhythm patterns are repeated simultaneously.

■ Use of Recorders, Melody Flutes, and Other Melody Instruments (Melody Bells, Resonator Bells, Xylophones) to Explore the Concepts

1. Listen to a short melody fragment or passage played by a leader on any melody instrument and repeated (echoed) by class members who also are playing instruments. (If sufficient melody instruments are not available, the remaining class members can sing or hum the repeated passage and then alternate this activity with those who are playing instruments.)

2. Play the melody fragments at various tempos, identifying them with the musical term that most accurately describes the TEMPO.

3. A leader chooses familiar songs (keeping the titles of the songs a secret) and plays fragments of their melodies out of context at various tempos as his classmates echo play the fragments. Then, the leader plays the entire song as it was written while the members of the class listen to identify the song title and TEMPO marking.

4. After first identifying the song title and TEMPO marking by ear and then by correct musical terminology, the entire class plays and sings the song at the most appropriate TEMPO. The notated score is simultaneously cast on a screen (by an overhead projector), chalkboard, or chart.

■ Use of an Audiovisual Aid to Perceive a Concept Related to TEMPO

The song "Boa Constrictor" is from a record album entitled *Peter, Paul and Mommy* written by Peter, Paul, and Mary, a Seven Arts Records' release by Warner Brothers (WS 1785).

Such current recordings that are pertinent to a concept of an element of music—"Boa Constrictor" specifically relates to TEMPO—often are conducive also to pictorial representation.

The lyrics and MELODY of the song slowly increase in TEMPO as the victim in the song falls prey to the boa constrictor and is gradually consumed. While listening to and singing the song young students can be looking at representations of the lyrics that they each drew earlier on individual sheets of paper. The motion of flipping over the pictures will increase in speed as the lyrics relate the story, thereby making students cognizant of the steady increase in TEMPO.

Sample illustrations (as interpreted by a young student) of the action occurring in the "Boa Constrictor" are presented here in chronological order:

Oh no . . . . . toe

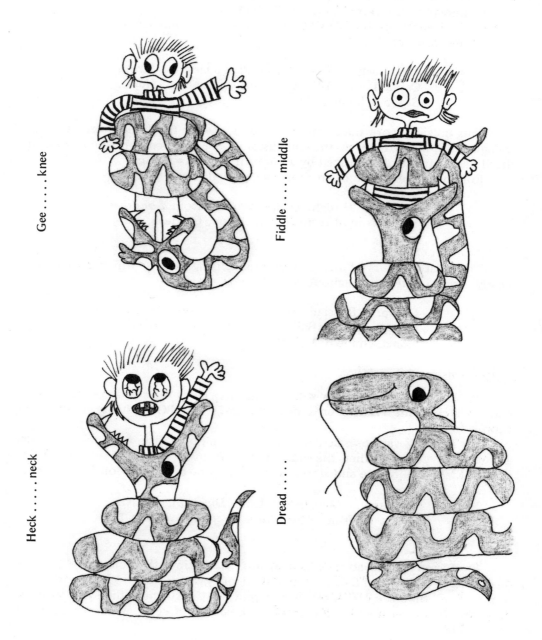

Gee . . . . . knee

Fiddle . . . . . . middle

Heck . . . . . neck

Dread . . . . . .

Additional Music Literature for Listening Experiences
on the Intermediate Level

Element: TEMPO
Component: Fast–Slow
Concept: Some musical compositions move faster than others. The speed of a composition is referred to as the TEMPO.
Concept: Sometimes the TEMPO remains steady; sometimes it gradually becomes faster or slower.

> J. S. Bach: "Jesu, Joy Of Man's Desiring" from Cantata no. 147 from *Adventures in Music*, Grade 5, Volume I

This musical work maintains a constant, steady rhythmic pulse at an unchanging TEMPO, except at the conclusion of the composition when a definite ritard occurs that is emphasized by a choir of brass instruments.

For another example of an easily recognized ritard, refer to

> Coates: "Knightsbridge March" from *London Suite* from *Adventures in Music*, Grade 5, Volume II

The ritard occurs at the end of this rousing March, which maintains a steady, brisk TEMPO throughout, *until* the ritard.

> Glière: "Russian Sailors' Dance" from *The Red Poppy*, op. 70 (Ballet Suite) from *Adventures in Music*, Grade 6, Volume II

Suggestions for Presentation:

1. Listen and keep time with the music. Does the steady pulse of 2s remain at a constant TEMPO or does it change? (TEMPO gradually moves from slow to fast.)

2. Tapping various sized drumheads or tapping fists on knees or desks discover for yourself when the music moves from fast to slow and vice versa. Is the TEMPO deliberate and stately as it is in Mozart compositions?

> Mozart: "Menuetto" from *Divertimento No. 17 in D* from *Adventures in Music*, Grade 5, Volume II

3. Listen to the composition again. Each time the folk melody is repeated at a different TEMPO, can you identify some of the instruments you hear? Each time the MELODY is repeated, is it performed the same way, or does the theme seem to be decorated with special effects? What are some of the effects?

Suggested Activity for the College or University Student

Divide into groups and have each group devise strategies for guiding children through exploring the TEMPO of music. Some of these strategies should be included:

1. Investigate current elementary textbooks for songs that are the most applicable to the exploration of concepts related to TEMPO.
2. Listen to musical compositions that reflect historical periods in the development of music—classical, romantic, impressionistic, and so forth. (Include current and contemporary instrumental compositions as well.) Choose those selections that are the most pertinent to the exploration of TEMPO.
3. Compile a list of songs and listening activities in a log or a form suitable to future reference. The list should include annotated or descriptive notes about each musical work with suggestions for how children can be guided through exploratory experiences that will lead to self-discovery of the TEMPO or changes in TEMPO in the composition.
4. Have more than one group participate in this project so that ideas and materials can be exchanged. In that way, maximum benefits resulting from the undertaking are assured.
5. Become aware of the many different sounds of your environment and sounds associated with the classroom and the home that move fast and slow or gradually move from slow to fast, and so forth. By exploring these sounds and their origin, discover for yourself how you can implement them into a further understanding of TEMPO.

Example:

a. View an electric or hand-manipulated cornpopper that has just been prepared for popping corn by addition of oil, grains of popcorn, and application of electrical heat or flame. Notice that there is no sound or movement of the corn popping as yet.

b. As the popper slowly becomes hot, the popcorn likewise *slowly* starts to pop. (This may be termed an example of LENTO. See p. 211.)

c. Over a short period of time gradually more and more corn begins to pop. The speed or tempo of the corn popping becomes faster and faster and can be associated with TEMPO as it moves from ALLEGRO to PRESTO to PRESTISSIMO. (See p. 211.)

d. As almost all of the corn is popped, one may be aware of the TEMPO slowly diminishing until just a very few "late-comers" pop intermittently, creating a return to LENTO.

DYNAMICS—AN ELEMENT OF MUSIC

COMPONENT (LOUD–SOFT) OF DYNAMICS DEFINED

The comparative loudness and softness of musical tones or of entire musical passages within an orchestral composition are generally referred to as DYNAMICS.

DYNAMICS add variety to a musical performance and can be explored by children in numerous ways. For instance, children can be guided skillfully to discover the monotony of singing or playing instruments on only one dynamic level and then to compare their emotional responses when gradations of dynamic intensities are incorporated in a repeated performance of the same work.

Dynamic levels are relative and are indicated by certain terms and markings (signs), which are listed here in order of gradation of intensity:

Term	Sign	Meaning
pianissimo	pp	very soft
piano	p	soft
mezzo-piano	mp	medium-soft
mezzo-forte	mf	medium-loud
forte	f	loud
fortissimo	ff	very loud
crescendo (cresc.)		gradually louder
decrescendo (decresc.) diminuendo (dim.)		gradually softer
sforzando, sforzato	sf	sudden loudness
forte-piano	fp	sudden softness

Various levels of DYNAMICS can be explored and experienced through the musical activities of listening, singing, playing, dancing, and creating.

Listening: Identify the loudness and softness of musical passages in choral, band, and orchestral recordings and, through repeated listening experiences if necessary, determine the techniques the composer used to achieve the desired dynamic effects:

Example:

1. Various combinations of instruments or voices
2. Increase or decrease in the number of instruments or voices used in specific passages

3. Recognition of the contour of various melodic passages, which may suggest the increase or decrease of DYNAMICS

Singing: Sing the same song at different dynamic levels and, after making comparisons, study the original score to be aware of the composer's intent.

Playing: Maintain a music laboratory using instruments (classroom, band, and orchestral) for experimental purposes in producing sounds of varying dynamic intensities.

Example:

By actually bowing or plucking a string instrument, children can discover the intensity in sound for themselves. Also, by actually making the louder or softer sound, children can be encouraged to associate the dynamic sound with the corresponding musical term or marking: beating a large drum might be designated as *ff* (fortissimo) in comparison to tapping a small drum, which might correspondingly be represented by *pp* (pianissimo).

Dancing: Encourage the expression of free body response to a loud or soft musical passage to identify varying dynamic intensities. Also, participate in the folk dances of ethnic groups to explore the dynamic characteristics inherent in dances of various cultures.

Creating: Relate various experiences in self-expression to the DYNAMICS present in musical compositions: use dramatization, choral speech, poetry, or fine arts, which, in itself, provides eclectic media for encouraging creativity.

Numerous ideas for initiating experiences in concepts related to DYNAMICS seem to grow and develop over a period of time when children, under skillful leadership, are permitted freedom to explore and thus discover for themselves. The presentation of specific lessons (examples) in this chapter, projects this philosophy.

The component of DYNAMICS explored in this text is

Component: Loud–Soft

SAMPLING OF PROCEDURES AND LESSON PLANS FOR EXPLORING MUSICAL CONCEPTS RELATED TO DYNAMICS

Primary Level

Element: DYNAMICS
Component: Loud–Soft
Concept: Some music is loud and some music is soft.

MY ROCKET SHIP (refer to p. 137)

■ *Suggested Musical Class Activities for This Presentation*

Singing: Sing the scale song "My Rocket Ship" with the same level of loudness throughout. Sing the song again, but slowly becoming louder as you zoom closer to the moon. As your rocket ship zooms downward away from the moon, slowly become softer. Which way of singing did you like best? As you sing draw this sign on the chalkboard showing a soft-to-loud tone and then a loud-to-soft or faraway sound.

Explore other ways of singing the same song and then choose the way you like best. How could you use classroom instruments to show the difference in soft and loud sounds?

Playing: Discover the different ways of playing loudly and softly on different rhythm and melody instruments in the classroom, including the piano.

Reading: Sing other songs you know and use these musical signs as signals for singing loudly or softly; for singing loudly gradually to singing softly gradually:

Example:

  p = soft
 pp = very soft
  f = loud
 ff = very loud

 ⟨ gradually loud

 ⟩ gradually soft

Creating, Free Movement, and Reading: Make up any body movement that will suggest sounds gradually growing louder or bigger to growing softer or smaller. What movement would you use to show sudden loud or soft sounds? Choose proper classroom instruments to accompany this movement.

Example:

  p or pp: finger cymbals or triangles
  f or ff: drums, cymbals

Teaching Suggestion:

Songs pertaining to modes of transportation are ideal examples for applying DYNAMICS. Children can dramatize the intensity of sound as a vehicle gradually comes closer and then gradually moves away.

Massenet: "Aragonaise" from *Le Cid* from *Adventures in Music*, Grade 1, Volume I

This composition is a recommended listening activity for identifying music that is sometimes loud and that then is echoed softly. Children can demonstrate aural recognition by playing one set of classroom instruments on the soft music (the echo) and another set on the loud music. (See the Suggested Activity section on p. 229.)

Grétry: Gigue from *Céphale et Procris*

Compare this music with Massenet's. In the Gigue there are no specific echoes, even though a question-and-answer effect is achieved by a statement of loud music answered by soft music. This composition also contains passages that gradually build in DYNAMICS from soft to loud or loud to soft. Children can be encouraged to identify these sections in numerous ways: by raising hands, playing various classroom instruments, executing physical body movement, and so on.

Additional Material for Suggested Use on the Intermediate Level

Element: DYNAMICS
Component: Loud–Soft
Concept: Sometimes music is loud; sometimes it is soft.
Concept: The loud and soft characteristics present within a musical composition can change gradually or suddenly.

AFRICAN NOEL*

Adapted from a Liberian folk song by Aden G. Lewis

Sing No - el,   Sing No - el,   No - el, No - el. _____

Sing No - el,   Sing No - el,   No - el, No - el. ____   ___

Sing we all No - el,   Sing we all No - el,

Sing we all No - el,   Sing we all No - el,

*From *Growing with Music*, Book 7, p. 178. Courtesy Prentice-Hall, Inc., Englewood Cliffs, N.J.

Sing we all No - el.   Sing we all No - el!

Sing No - el,   Sing No - el,   No - el, No - el. _____

Sing No - el,   Sing No - el,   No - el, No - el. _____

■ *Use of Classroom Instruments and Other Strategies to Explore the Concepts*

1. Listen to the MELODY of "African Noel," noticing that the repeated words "Sing we all Noel" constitute the lyrics of the entire song.

2. Sing the song in unison. What vocal technique could be employed to make this song more exciting, especially because the words are repeated many times? (Gradually sing the song louder—crescendo—and then, at the appropriate time, observe a gradual decrescendo or diminuendo—that is, gradually become softer.)

3. Sing the song, observing a gradual increase and decrease of DYNAMICS, and identify those sections with the appropriate dynamic markings:

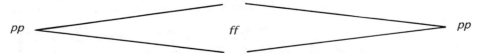

pp   *ff*   *pp*

4. Practice conducting "African Noel," experimenting with the use of DYNAMICS in various ways suggested by classmates. Choose the performance that sounds the most appropriate. What hand gestures or signals will you use to designate loud and soft or crescendo and decrescendo passages?

5. Choose any drums available—kaluba drums, tom-toms, bongos, conga drums—and make up a rhythm pattern or patterns to be tapped throughout the performance also to observe DYNAMICS. (Experiment until the most satisfying arrangement is achieved.) Notate these rhythm patterns on the chalkboard.

6. Play the MELODY on melody bells and make up a second part (harmony part) on other melody bells or melody instruments, thereby providing a melodic accompaniment to the vocal rendition. Add a percussion accompaniment using tambourines, shakers, and other instruments of your choice.

7. Notate the melody with the second part on the musical staff on the chalkboard.

8. Create dance movements dramatizing the rise and fall of the MELODY (melodic contour) as well as the gradual increase and decrease of DYNAMICS.

9. Sing, dance, and play instruments to perform "African Noel" as a class project.

O the Grand Old Duke of York*

O the grand old Duke of York,
He had ten thousand men;
He marched them up a great high hill,
And he marched them down again!
When they were up, they were up,
And when they were down, they were down,
And when they were neither down nor up,
They were neither up nor down!

■ *Use of Vocal Inflection and Body Sounds to Explore the Concepts*

1. Chant the poem "O the Grand Old Duke of York" in unison.
2. A leader should chant one line at a time, incorporating dynamic effects, while the class members echo chant† him or her. The rhythmical flow of the chant should be maintained by clapping or tapping a steady beat.
3. Write the poem on the chalkboard, including dynamic markings:

mf O the grand old Duke of York

f He had ten thousand men;

He marched them up a great high hill,

And he marched them down again!

When they were up, they were up,

And when they were down, they were down,

mp And when they were neither down nor up,

ff *p*
mf They were neither up nor down!

*This nursery rhyme appears in Lawrence Wheeler and Lois Raebeck, *Orff and Kodály Adapted for the Elementary School* (Dubuque, Ia.: Brown, 1972), p. 292.
†The leader chants a vocal passage that is then repeated by the group.

4. Chant the poem again, changing the dynamic markings as suggested by classmates and notating the markings on the chalkboard over the words of the poem.

5. Chant the poem again, and, if you have not previously done so, use higher and lower voice inflections that seem to occur the most naturally with dynamic control.

Key to Voice Inflection:

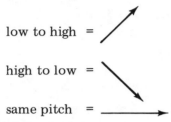

low to high =

high to low =

same pitch =

Example:

mf O the grand old Duke of York,

f He had ten thousand men;

He marched them up a great high hill,

And he marched them down again!

When they were up, they were up,

And when they were down they were down,

And when they were neither down nor up,

up, nor

they were neither

down!

6. Choose a partner and, facing your partner, devise an accompanying routine of body sounds to the chant: clap, snap fingers, slap knees, and stamp feet, staying cognizant of the DYNAMICS involved.

Example:

| | | (slap knees) | | (slap hands) | | (snap fingers) | |
| O | the | grand | old | Duke · | of | York | (etc.) |

7. Create your own poem related to your interests in subject matter at school or in your afterschool activities.

8. Experiment with the dynamic production of your poem involving your classmates and using classroom instruments, body sounds, and other devices of your choice to improvise a "dynamic ditty."

■ *Use of Additional Suggested Strategies to Explore the Concepts*

1. Listen to a current popular recording noticing the dynamic effects; then, listen to the same MELODY recorded by a different soloist or ensemble, noting the variation in dynamic effects. List the different dynamic effects on the chalkboard.

2. Listen to a musical composition by a noted composer as performed by a specific symphony orchestra; then, listen to the same composition as performed by a different symphony orchestra with a different conductor, noticing the similar or contrasting dynamic effects that are the result of the conductor's musical interpretation.

3. Listen to recordings of the *Brandenburg concertos* (especially nos. 2, 4, and 5) by J. S. Bach, which employ a group of solo instruments against a string orchestra. This technique, characteristic of the baroque period, is termed *concerti grossi*. It results in dynamic effects termed *terraced dynamics*, or, the dynamic effect of suddenly loud to suddenly soft.

4. Sing call-and-response spirituals, a type of folk music in which the answer, or response, to the initial call lends itself to dramatic dynamic effects. Examples of songs in this category that can be found in most community song books are "Swing Low, Sweet Chariot"; "I Got Shoes"; "Rock-a-My Soul"; and "Roll, Jordan, Roll." Examples of familiar songs that are appropriate for implementing an echo as an effective dynamic technique are

a. "Sing for the Wide, Wide Fields" (refer to p. 200), in which each line of the song can be echoed:

Group 1: "Sing for the wide, wide fields"
Group 2: (echo) "Sing for the wide, wide fields."

(This technique can be utilized throughout the song except for the last line, which is sung forte, *f*, by both groups in unison: "Sing as together we march along, with the turf beneath our feet."

b. "Happy Wanderer" (Chorus)

Group 1: "fol di ri"
Group 2: (echo) "fol di ri" (etc.)

c. "I'm Going' to Leave Old Texas Now"

Group 1: "I'm goin' to leave"
Group 2: (echo) "I'm goin' to leave (etc.)"

5. Review and reinforce your knowledge of dynamic terms and markings by singing a fragment or section of a new song at different dynamic levels while identifying the DYNAMICS with the correct term, sign, or marking. Tape record these performances for immediate playback in order to choose the most satisfying rendition. Finally, check the composer's original dynamic markings to compare and contrast musical interpretations.

6. Play recorders, melody flutes, and other classroom instruments as accompaniment for vocal groups in order to produce various and complete dynamic effects.

Additional Music Literature for Listening Experiences
on the Intermediate Level

Element: DYNAMICS
Component: Loud–Soft
Concept: Sometimes music is loud; sometimes it is soft.
Concept: The loud and soft characteristics present within a musical composition can change gradually or suddenly.

>Tchaikovsky: Waltz from *The Sleeping Beauty*
>from *Adventures in Music*, Grade 4, Volume I

The contrast in this music in dynamic levels is attributed to be (1) controlling the volume of the same instruments, such as the strings performing

and (2) adding other instruments that provide contrast from *pp* (very soft) to *ff* (very loud). A suggested strategy for interpreting these dynamic effects is creative dance, employing heavy and light body movements.

>Gottschalk–Kay: "Grand Walkaround" from
>"*Cakewalk*" Ballet Suite from *Adventures In*
>*Music*, Grade 5, Volume I

Salient Features Relative to DYNAMICS:

1. Introduction of special interest

2. Gradations of DYNAMICS achieved through solo instrumental passages and various combinations of brass instruments, muted and otherwise.

3. A gradual swelling of tone or sudden bursts of tone from various orchestral families of instruments: strings, brass, woodwinds or percussion.

■ *Suggested Strategy for Interpreting These Dynamic Effects*

Chart pictorially or symbolically the contrasts in DYNAMICS and then translate the symbols into actual dynamic markings. After viewing the completed score of dynamic markings for a composition, make up your own interpretation of the chart using body sounds, unconventional sounds, and classroom instruments. Could you create your own title for the completed composition, relating your title to DYNAMICS, such as, "Subtlety in Sound"? Or, was the gradation or contrast in DYNAMICS not always aurally subtle?

Suggested Activity for the College or University Student

Divide the class into groups and have each group devise strategies for guiding children through exploring the DYNAMICS of music. Some of these strategies should be included:

1. Investigate current elementary textbooks to find songs most applicable for exploring concepts related to DYNAMICS.
2. Listen to musical compositions that reflect historical periods in the development of music—classical, romantic, impressionistic, and so forth. (Include current and contemporary instrumental compositions as well). Then, choose those selections that are most pertinent to exploring DYNAMICS.
3. Compile a list of songs and listening activities in a log suitable to future reference. The list should include annotated or descriptive notes about each musical work with suggestions for how children can be guided through exploratory experiences that will lead to self-discovery of the DYNAMICS employed in the composition.
4. Have more than one group participate in this project so that ideas and materials can be exchanged. In that way maximum benefits resulting from the undertaking are assured.

TONE COLOR—AN ELEMENT OF MUSIC

COMPONENT (INSTRUMENTAL) OF TONE COLOR DEFINED

TONE COLOR is an element of music that relates to the quality of sound produced by the various types of vocal or instrumental groups or soloists. It also relates to the different tonal effects that techniques can achieve on an instrument.

Examples:

plucking and bowing string instruments
beating a drumhead and tapping the rim of the same drum
lightly sliding the fingertips across the head of a tambourine; or, tapping
while vigorously shaking the same tambourine

A variety of tonal effects also can be produced by tapping different rhythm patterns on percussion instruments and repeating the same patterns on melody instruments (improvising a MELODY), thus transferring the nonmelodic tonal sounds to melodic pitches. Current recordings of popular songs that mix children's voices with adult voices or an adult soloist provide interesting TONE COLOR.

The ways and means of testing for TONE COLOR and identifying it are innumerable and can be developed by children if they are permitted to express ideas freely and to experiment with music.

In this chapter developmental procedures related to concepts of TONE COLOR are offered as examples to motivate the reader to utilize his creative ability in preparing other new and diversified teaching techniques. The objective is to prepare children to recognize and identify the element of TONE COLOR in musical works.

The component of TONE COLOR explored in this text is

Component: Instrumental

SAMPLING OF PROCEDURES AND LESSON PLANS FOR EXPLORING MUSICAL CONCEPTS RELATED TO TONE COLOR

Primary Level

Element: TONE COLOR
Component: Instrumental
Concept: Music has a different sound when played on different instruments.

HOT CROSS BUNS (refer to p. 202)

■ *Suggested Musical Class Activities for This Presentation*

Singing: Sing "Hot Cross Buns."
Singing and Playing: Sing this same song and accompany yourself on an autoharp. How does it sound? Do you like it? Why? Play "Hot Cross Buns" on the piano keyboard and resonator bells. Play the MELODY on the piano and resonator bells while you sing along, also to the accompaniment of the autoharp. Did the song sound the same as when you first sang it alone? Did the sounds of the tones you heard seem to blend or go together well? Did you ever choose colors (water colors or crayons) in making a design that blended well? Did you ever choose colors that seem to "clash"? Would you say that the tone colors in this music clash or blend well? Do you think differences in tone color when we sing or play the same song add interest to the music? Choose the proper rhythm instruments to add to the song you are playing and singing. Do the words of the song call for a sharp or brittle sound? A smooth sound? A jingly sound? Do you think that the words of a song help you to decide which instruments to use?

Listening: Listen to this music and raise your hand if you know it or have ever heard it before.

>McDonald: *Children's Symphony* Third Movement from *Adventures in Music*, Grade 2, Volume II

>or

>McDonald: *Children's Symphony* Third Movement from *Adventures in Music*, Grade 3, Volume II

Singing and Listening: Sing the songs you heard played in the composition. How many familiar songs did you hear? Which orchestral instruments played these songs?

Listening (Recall): List the orchestral instruments you heard. Point to the pictures of the instruments you heard in the recording. Can you name them?

Playing and Creating: Play classroom instruments in different ways and discover new sounds.

Example:

tambourines:	Shake, tap, rap, rub the head with your fingertips, tap the wooden rim.
autoharp:	Strum with felt pads, paper clips, plastic picks, and the wooden handles of mallets; rapidly strum back and forth with quadruple mallets; or strike the wooden part of the autoharp alternately as you strum.

Creating: Make your own instruments and discover how many different sounds they can produce. Write your own musical scores for playing these instruments. Use signs or symbols for creating the score at first.

Example:

$$\xi = \text{shaking instruments}$$

$$\textit{llllll} = \text{jingling instruments}$$

$$//// = \text{tapping instruments}$$

Draw your own pictures of the instruments you are playing and do a musical score using pictures instead of signs or symbols.

Playing: Tape record the composition you wrote and play it back immediately to hear the sound effects you created. Did you like the sound of your composition? Would you like to play it a different way? Make a new score and play it.

Additional Music Literature for Listening Experiences on the Primary Level

Element: TONE COLOR
Component: Instrumental
Concept: Music has a different sound when played on different instruments.

1. Listen to this band music.

> Copland: "Circus Music" from *The Red Pony*
> from *Adventures in Music*, Grade 3, Volume I

Does it sound different from the orchestral music we have been hearing? What makes it different? What family of instruments do you hear playing in an orchestra that does not play in a band?
2. Name the families of classroom instruments according to sound: clicking sounds, ringing sounds, tapping sounds, scraping sounds, jingling sounds, rattling sounds, and thudding sounds.
3. Listen to the sounds of classroom instruments and then print their names on the chalkboard according to the families to which they belong.
4. Make up your own musical composition, dividing it into sections. Discover which sounding instruments you want to hear in the different sections.
5. Listen to other musical compositions, paying special attention to the instruments you hear. Can you name the instruments you heard? Why do you think the composer chose to have those particular instruments play? Did you like the sound effects you heard? Why?

> McDonald: *Children's Symphony* First Movement from *Adventures in Music*, Grade 3, Volume II

6. The following orchestral instruments were recognized in sequence in the composition by McDonald:

a. Brass and crashing cymbals
b. Flutes playing the MELODY of "London Bridge"
c. Strings playing a variation of the MELODY
d. Interludes
e. Full orchestra playing the MELODY
f. Drum interlude
g. Contrast of strings playing softly "Baa, Baa, Black Sheep"
h. French horns followed by trumpets playing a segment of the MELODY
i. Drum interlude
j. Full orchestra on "London Bridge"

7. The listening sequence outlined here is an obvious one. A child could recall it as a storytelling experience.
8. Children can identify the instruments heard in this composition from pictorial charts as the instruments are being played.

9. To reinforce concepts of instruments that jingle and rattle, or that can be tapped, shaken, rapped, or scratched, the children can make a pictorial score of those appropriate classroom instruments that they have chosen to play along with the recording.

Additional Material for Suggested Use on the Intermediate Level

Element: TONE COLOR
Component: Instrumental
Concept: Music has a different sound when played on different instruments.

JAMAICAN FAREWELL*

Words by M. A. Dufay   *Caribbean folk melody*

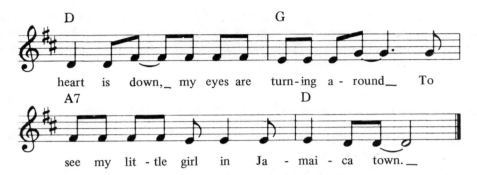

heart is down,_ my eyes are turn-ing a - round_ To
see my lit - tle girl in Ja - mai - ca town. _

*From *Growing with Music,* Related Arts Edition Book 7 by Harry R. Wilson, Walter Ehret, Alice M. Knuth, Edward J. Hermann, and Albert A. Renna © 1972 by Prentice-Hall, Inc., Englewood Cliffs, N.J. Reprinted by permission.

■ Use of Classroom Instruments and Other Strategies to Explore the Concept

1. Listen and then sing "Jamaican Farewell" as written here in the key of D major.

2. View the score of the song on a chart or by means of an overhead projector and identify song as being written in D major. Write the D major scale on the chalkboard and build I–IV–V^7 chords on the scale:

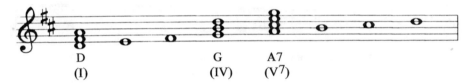

Sing the song again with an autoharp accompaniment and determine the sequence of the chords used as accompaniment:

$$I \qquad IV \qquad V^7 \qquad I$$
$$(D) \qquad (G) \qquad (A^7) \qquad (D)$$

As you listen to the chords while singing, identify when the chord should be changed by raising your hand. What other instruments can be used for playing this chordal accompaniment?

3. Build chords from resonator bells; also place the bells in chord boxes to be played with triple- and quadruple-headed mallets.

4. Strum the chords on ukuleles and autoharps, noting the difference in TONE COLOR. Also, pluck the open strings of the string bass, which are also the roots of the $\frac{I}{(D)} - \frac{IV}{(G)} - \frac{V^7}{(A^7)}$ chords in D major. (See the D major scale built on the staff in step 2 here.)

5. Play and sing the MELODY of "Jamaican Farewell" on melody bells and a piano keyboard to the chordal accompaniment of ukuleles, autoharps, resonator bells (in chord boxes), and a string bass. (Refer to p. 236 for an illustration of a string bass, including the names of the open strings and corresponding pitches for the tuning notated on the musical staff.)

6. Add TONE COLOR to this calypso folk song with the appropriate percussion instruments. Create your own rhythm patterns while repeatedly chanting the rhythm patterns of specific words in the song; then, transfer marks of duration to notation.

Example:

7. Create your own dance movements while singing and playing "Jamaican Farewell" on melody, chording, and percussion instruments; be aware of the differences in TONE COLOR among all the instruments used in your performance.

8. Make up (compose) other verses to this calypso song and rotate the instruments so that everyone can have an opportunity to perform on percussion, melody, and chording instruments as well as on the string bass.

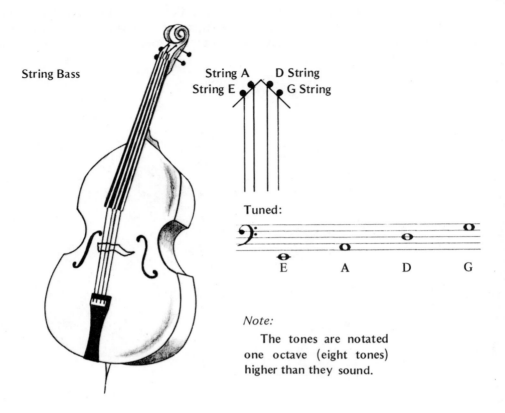

String Bass

String A D String
String E G String

Tuned:

E   A   D   G

Note:

The tones are notated one octave (eight tones) higher than they sound.

■ *Additional Suggestions for Exploring the Concept*

1. Periodically make all classroom instruments available to young students—melody and percussion—for exploratory experiences in determining sound and pitch qualities. For these experiences the classroom could be converted (temporarily) into a sound laboratory. With guidance, these experiences can materialize into organized sound productions, with a "Symphony of Sound" the culmination of the experiment.

2. Construct the seating plans of various symphony orchestras as determined as being the most satisfactory by current distinguished conductors. Listen to recordings of these same orchestras and discuss why the seating arrangements may vary.

3. Listen to recordings or live performances of various instrumental soloists and ensembles: string, brass, woodwind, and percussion.

4. Listen to recordings or live performances of musical works (current popular melodies included) that are distinctive for combining two or more instruments of different or similar TONE COLOR—such as guitar and banjo; and flute and piccolo. Also, encourage children to be aware aurally of repeated themes played by different instruments. Have them strive to identify the instruments. (Refer to Gary, Charles, ed., *The Study of Music in the Elementary School—A Conceptual Approach*. Washington, D.C.: Music Educators National Conference, 1967, for a listing of suggested recorded compositions to play

when exploring TONE COLOR. Also, consult any current music education textbook that has accompanying records for possible examples of instrumental ensembles.)

Additional Music Literature for Listening Experiences
on the Intermediate Level

Element: TONE COLOR
Component: Instrumental
Concept: Music has a different sound when played on different instruments.

> Cailliet: Variations on the Theme "Pop! Goes
> the Weasel" from *Adventures in Music*, Grade 4,
> Volume I

■ *Use of Classroom Instruments and Other Strategies to Explore the Concept*

1. Listen to the Cailliet composition and discuss the changes and contrast in TONE COLOR.

2. Write all or as many names of different instruments as you can hear in the work on the chalkboard or on paper. (A detailed analysis of the instruments used throughout each variation is presented in the Teachers Guide of the *Adventures In Music* record series.) Because in some sections of the music the same instruments can be heard, contrast is provided by the different ways the same instruments are played, such as the wa, wa mutes of the trumpet and various ensemble groupings of the instruments.

3. Divide the class into groups and experiment with producing TONE COLOR: (a) discover different ways to tap or beat a drum (with drumsticks, with the open hand, by tapping the wood and rim of drum); (b) discover ways to elicit unconventional sounds from objects in the classroom and also experiment with body sounds, vocal sounds, and the sounds of available classroom instruments; (c) choose a familiar melody or make up your own to be accompanied with percussion instruments, melody instruments, voice, body, or room sounds and experiment with the different ways to produce sound; and (d) have each group perform and record on tape their individual composition for instant replay and then have the class discuss the various sounds they heard and how they are produced.

Suggested Activity for the College or University Student

1. Divide the class into groups and listen to numerous musical compositions (current as well) identifying the instruments by ear.

2. Compare your notes with other members of the group and, if possible, check with the Teacher's Guides to the compositions. (Teacher's Guides are available in the *Adventures in Music* series.)

3. As a group, discuss strategies for introducing orchestral instruments to children; include ideas for incorporating audiovisual aids into your lessons or presentations.
4. Record these strategies, ideas, and suggestions for future reference. If possible, specify musical compositions that are suitable for classroom presentations.

Chapter 11

Integrating Music into the Total School Program

MUSIC OF ETHNIC GROUPS EXPLORED CONCEPTUALLY

An ethnic group is one whose members are racially or historically related and claim a common and distinctive culture. Ethnic groups can be found living in sections or divisions of every American city or town. Just as each ethnic group boasts of a distinctive culture of beloved traditions and customs, so also do these groups proudly convey the spirit of their people through song and dance.

In this chapter percussion and melody instruments are used to accompany the folk music of particular cultures. Preceding each song is a concept or musical idea to serve as the focal point for a meaningful learning experience. After a song has been learned, numerous concepts for the same song may appear obvious as relating to one or more of the elements of music: MELODY, RHYTHM, HARMONY, FORM, DYNAMICS, TEMPO, and TONE COLOR. After listening to the music, try to structure a concept that you think would be feasible for exploration. Think of different ways children might be guided to explore a concept and thereby discover its musical value for themselves.

A sampling of a suggested developmental procedure for exploring the stated concept (including questioning techniques) follows each song and serves as an example of the explore-and-discover technique set in motion.

Element: MELODY
Component: Direction
Concept 1: The pitches in the MELODY of this song move up and down and sometimes stay the same.

and

Element: RHYTHM
Component: Accented Beat
Concept 2: In this song, some tones have a stronger beat than others.

MA BELLA BIMBA*

Italian folk song

Refrain:

Ma   co - me bal - li   bel - la   bim - ba,   bel - la
Pron. mah   ko' may bah lee   bay lah   beem bah,   bay lah

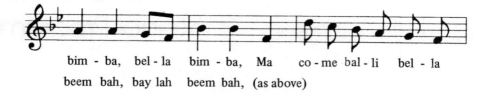

bim - ba, bel - la bim - ba,   Ma   co - me bal - li   bel - la
beem bah, bay lah   beem bah,   (as above)

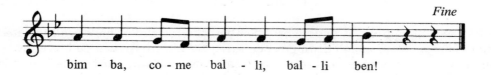

Fine

bim - ba, co - me   bal - li,   bal - li   ben!

Verse:

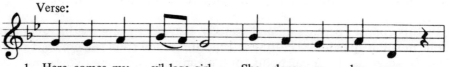

1. Here comes my   vil-lage girl,   She danc - es   by   you
2. Morn-ings she   loves to dance, Noon -day   or   eve - ning

†*D. C.*

All   must ad - mire her,   Grace - ful de - light.
Light as   a   swal-low's wing, She seems to   fly.

*Reprinted with permission from *Work and Sing* an International Songbook, Cooperative Recreation Service, Inc. (Delaware, Ohio: 1948).
†Back to the beginning and, after the second verse, play until *fine* (end).

■ *Use of Classroom Instruments and Other Strategies to Explore the Concepts*

1. Listen and sing "Ma Bella Bimba."

2. Sing the song using hand levels or arm movements to design its shape. Did the song move from low to high or high to low? On what words did the song move from low to high? Can you play those tones on the melody bells? On what words did the song move from high to low? Did those tones move by step or skip? Sing them as you play them on the melody bells or piano keyboard. Did the MELODY ever stay the same? On what words? Can you play the words on the melody bells?

3. Play the entire song by ear as the class sings. Can you think of a classroom instrument that would be appropriate for accompanying this song? Would you choose the tambourine? finger cymbals? Why?

4. Sing and tap along with the music. Do you feel as if you would like to tap and shake the tambourine too?

5. Sing and play the tambourine this time, but rap or tap the tambourine whenever it feels right to do so and shake it whenever you wish. Did you tap the head of the tambourine on a strong beat of the music? When did you shake the tambourine?

6. Sing the song using number names this time, and call the strong beat number 1. How many weak beats follow number 1? (Two.) Will you shake the tambourines on these weak beats?

7. Make up your own pictorial score for reading the tambourine accompaniment on the refrain.

Example:

8. Transfer this pictorial score to the musical score, placing the accented mark (>) over the proper note on the staff.

When would you play the finger cymbals? On the strong beats? (Pulse.) On the weak beats? Why? What is the musical term for strong beat? (Accented beat.) Would you play the same instruments on both the refrain and the verse or would you rather explore and discover the sounds of different instruments before making your choice?

9. Make up a dance pattern to the refrain. What kind of movement would you perform on the accented beat—a strong or a weak movement?

10. Sing, dance, and play this Italian folk song.

11. Design your own costumes for a colorful rendition of this folk song. The girls can wear colorful peasant skirts made of crepe paper or bright, printed cotton with white blouses and wide peasant belts made of glossy black oil cloth. They can use artificial flowers for headdresses fashioned as wreaths. The boys can wear jeans (any color) with white or colored shirts. Those students who are the dancers can use tambourines decorated with colored ribbons or they can tie crepe paper streamers to their wrists. Do you have your own ideas that might add to the enrichment of the performance of this music?

Example:

Older children can provide an instrumental accompaniment playing I–V^7 chords in the key of G major on guitars or ukuleles on the refrain and recorders on the MELODY of the verse. (Refer to p. 187 for the fingering of chord progressions for ukulele.)

Element: RHYTHM
Component: Syncopation
Concept: When a strong beat is used in place of a weak beat within a rhythm pattern syncopation results. Hence, the pattern is termed a syncopated rhythm pattern.

SATURDAY NIGHT*

Nigerian folk song

ev-'ry-bod-y,   ev-'ry-bod-y,   loves Sat-ur-day   night.____

2. Ev-'ry-bod-y loves Af-ri-ca (etc. as above)

*Reprinted with permission from *East–West Songs,* (Delaware, Ohio: Cooperative Recreation Service, Inc. 1960).

■ Use of Classroom Instruments and Other Strategies to Explore the Concept

1. When listening to this African folk song, what instrumental sounds would you choose for an accompaniment? Would you limit your choice to the instrumental sounds that reflect the culture of the African people? Would the mood of the song influence your choice?

2. These instruments are suggested for your use: conga drums, bongos, kalimba (a thumb piano; if one is not available, melody bells are an excellent substitute), claves, and tambourines.

3. Sing and keep time to the music by tapping the drums.

4. Accent the strong beat, which is the first beat in each measure.

Example:

If you change the accent to another beat, will it sound different?

Example:

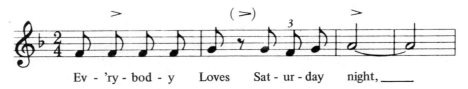

Ev - 'ry - bod - y   Loves   Sat - ur - day   night,____

5. Sing as you play the MELODY on the bells. Can you explore and discover the many different kinds of rhythm patterns that can provide an exciting accompaniment to this song? Remember to observe the syncopated RHYTHM and highlight it by means of a contrasting sound.

Examples:

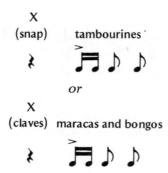

X
(snap)   tambourines

or

X
(claves) maracas and bongos

Element: MELODY
Component: Repeated Pattern
Concept: Several tones in this MELODY group themselves into units or patterns. When a pattern is repeated on the same tones it is called a repeated pattern.

KUM BA YAH (Come by Here)*

African folk song

2. Someone's cryin', Lord, Kum ba yah etc.
3. Someon's prayin', Lord, Kum ba yah etc.

*Reprinted with permission from *Song Sampler No. 1*, January, 1956 (Delaware, Ohio: Cooperative Recreation Service, Inc.).

■ *Use of Classroom Instruments and Other Strategies to Explore the Concept*

1. Refer to steps 1 and 2 of "Saturday Night" p. 242.

2. Sing and design the MELODY using hand levels or arm movements. Did the first three tones of the MELODY move by step or skip? Can you play them on the bells and kalimba? On the words "my Lord," did the tones stay the same or did they move up or down? Can you play them on the bells? How many times is "Kum ba yah, my Lord" sung? What do we call this grouping of tones in music? (Pattern.) If the pattern is sung more than once what do we call it? (Repeated pattern.)

3. Could you tap Kaluba drums ("talking" drums) on the different melody patterns?

Examples:

First drum: ⎯⎯ ⎯⎯ ⎯⎯ ⎯ ⎯⎯

Kum ba yah, my Lord

Second drum: ⎯⎯ ⎯⎯ ⎯⎯

Kum ba yah

Listen as each pattern is tapped individually on a different drum. Can all of the patterns be sounded at the same time? Do you hear the various tonal effects produced by this type of drum? The percussive sounds of the Kaluba "rain forest" drum are achieved because there is water inside the drum. Could you now improvise a melodic RHYTHM on the drums in a question-and-answer sequence?

Example:

    "question"   *"answer"*

⎯ ⎯ ⎯⎯ ⎯⎯ ⎯ ⎯ ⎯ ⎯⎯   ⎯ ⎯ ⎯⎯ ⎯ ⎯ ⎯ ⎯ ⎯

4. If you do not have a Kaluba drum, can you improvise tonal effects in other ways?

Examples:

a. Tap bongo and conga drums on the rims of the drums as well as on the drumheads.
b. Tap various shapes and sizes of sealed cardboard cartons.
c. Tap various sizes of coffee cans that are sealed with plastic lids on both ends.

5. Make up your own verses to this song; sing them, play them, and accompany them on the drums.

Element: FORM
Component: Two Sections
Concept: The phrases in this music join to form a larger section, or part. This music is divided into two sections, or parts.

IRISH WASHERWOMAN*

Part A

Part B

*Reprinted with permission from *English Country Dances of Today* (Delaware, Ohio: Cooperative Recreation Service, Inc., 1948).

■ *Use of Classroom Instruments and Other Strategies to Explore the Concept*

1. As you listen to this music played on the bells or piano keyboard, does it make you want to sing or dance? Why? Is it bouncy? The Irish people have a special name for their kind of dancing. It is called an Irish jig. Have you ever seen people dance an Irish jig, perhaps on television? Can you make up your own jig to this music? Remember to keep your arms down at your sides while dancing as the Irish dancers do.

2. Listen to the music again and raise your hand when you come to the end of the first part. What helps you to hear when the first section is completed? Did the last few tones of the MELODY give you a feeling of rest, or the feeling that you had reached home?

3. How is the MELODY different in the second part? Is it higher or lower? What helps you to hear when this second section is completed? Is the last measure in this section the same as the last measure in the first section?

4. If we were to give these two sections of the music letter names, what could we call them? (Part A and Part B.)

5. What classroom instruments would you choose to accompany this Irish jig?

Suggestion:

Part A: melody flutes or recorders. Children learn to read the music as cast on a screen by an overhead projector.

Part B: recorders, melody bells, rhythm sticks, and drums. Divide the class into four groups: Have group 1 play the MELODY on recorders or melody bells and group 2 tap the RHYTHM of the MELODY on rhythm sticks. Group 3 can tap a steady beat on small drums, and group 4, the "Irish dancers," can perform the Irish jig.

Example:

Group 2: sticks 2 — — — — — —   — — — — — —
Group 3: drums 4 ___   ___   ___   ___

Element: MELODY
Component: Sequence
Concept: Several tones of a MELODY may group themselves into units, or patterns. When a pattern is repeated higher or lower, it is called a sequence.

HIMMEL UND ERDE (Music Alone Shall Live)*

German folk song

All things shall per - ish un - der the sky,
German: Him - mel Und Er - de Muss - en ver - gehn,
Pron.: Him - mel Und Air - dah mee - sen fair - gain,

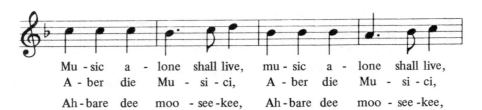

Mu - sic a - lone shall live, mu - sic a - lone shall live,
A - ber die Mu - si - ci, A - ber die Mu - si - ci,
Ah - bare dee moo - see - kee, Ah - bare dee moo - see - kee,

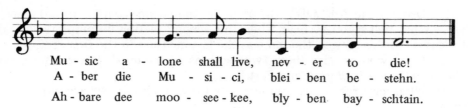

Mu - sic a - lone shall live, nev - er to die!
A - ber die Mu - si - ci, blei - ben be - stehn.
Ah - bare dee moo - see - kee, bly - ben bay - schtain.

*Reprinted with permission from *Song Sampler No. 1,* January, 1956. (Delaware, Ohio: Cooperative Recreation Service, Inc.).

■ Use of Classroom Instruments and Other Strategies to Explore the Concept

1. Listen to this song as played on the piano.

2. Sing the song in German (using the tone syllables for correct pronunciation) or in English.

3. Sing and design the direction of the song using hand levels. On what words in the song do the tones move in the same direction—up, down, and straight ahead—but sound higher or lower? ("Music alone shall live.")

4. Play this pattern of tones on the melody bells as you sing it. How many times is this pattern repeated? Is it repeated higher or lower? This pattern has now become a sequence.

5. Sing and play the entire song on the melody bells and recorder.

Element: DYNAMICS
Component: Loud–Soft
Concept: Several parts of this MELODY are loud and several parts are soft.

WHEN THE SAINTS GO MARCHING IN*

Spiritual
(American folk song)

1. Oh, when the saints go march-ing in, Oh, when the

saints go march-ing in; Oh, Lord, I want to be in that

num-ber,____ When the saints go march - ing in.____

*Public domain.

■ *Use of Classroom Instruments and Other Strategies to Explore the Concept*

1. Listen and sing this familiar song. As you sing it do you feel as if you want to tap along with the music? Why?

2. Sing and keep time with the music by clapping your hands and tapping your feet. What kind of instrumental group would play this music? (Jazz.) When? (Celebration.) If a band were marching down the street playing this spirited song, would you think a parade was passing by? How can we imitate the sound of a parade as it begins far down the street, moves closer, passes in review, and then moves steadily away from us?

3. Describe the sound of the music when it is far away. (Soft.) What happens to the sound of the music as the band gradually moves closer? (It becomes louder.) In music, what do we call the changes from soft to loud or loud to soft? (DYNAMICS.)

4. Sing this song and tap percussion instruments of your choice (including drums) to imitate a parade. Be certain to observe the DYNAMICS of a parade as these crescendo and descrescendo signs illustrate:

soft — loud   loud — soft

Can you make up other verses to this song that would convey a jubilant feeling?

Element: HARMONY
Component: Ostinato
Concept: A phrase on the same pitch is repeated steadily throughout this song and is termed an ostinato.

ZUM GALI GALI*

Israeli work song

Zum   ga - li, ga - li, ga - li,   Zum   ga - li, ga - li,   - li,

*Reprinted with permission from Kit V.—*Joyful Singing* (Delaware, Ohio: Cooperative Recreation Service, Inc., n.d.)

†Divide the class into two groups. When the first group reaches here, the second group begins stanza one. The first group continues the chant, repeating the first line throughout the song. As the second group is completing stanza 2, the first group should still be chanting the first line in diminishing degrees of softness.

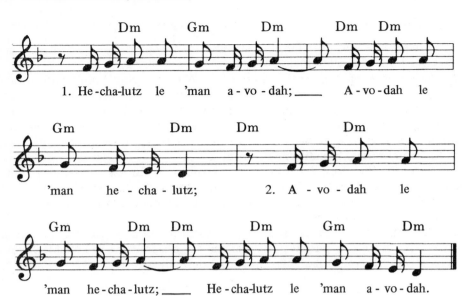

1. He-cha-lutz le 'man a-vo-dah; _____ A-vo-dah le
   'man he-cha-lutz; 2. A-vo-dah le
   'man he-cha-lutz; _____ He-cha-lutz le 'man a-vo-dah.

3. He-cha-lutz le 'man hab-b'tulah;   4. Ha-sha-lom le 'man ha'a-mim;
   Ha-b'tulah le 'man he-cha-lutz.   Ha'a-mim le 'man ha-sha-lom.

Pronounce: a as in father   i as in machine

                   he like hay   o as in come

                   le with very short e   u as in rule

                   ch as in German ach*

■ *Use of Classroom Instruments and Other Strategies to Explore the Concept*

   1. Listen to the MELODY and hum along.
   2. Sing the words of the MELODY. Is the MELODY easy to learn? Why?
(It is repeated.)
   3. Sing and play the work chant on the melody bells. ("Zum gali gali
gali, Zum gali, gali," etc.)
   4. Divide the class into two groups. Have group 1 sing the work chant
as an introduction and continue it throughout the song. Have group 2 sing the
MELODY while several classmates play it on recorders. How many times did
group 1 sing the work chant? If you cannot remember, sing the entire song
again and count the number of times chant is repeated. Because this work
chant, or phrase, is repeated persistently throughout the song on the same
pitch, it is called an ostinato. Does the simultaneous sound of the ostinato
blending with the MELODY line result in HARMONY? What other classroom
instrument would provide harmonic enrichment by accompanying this song?
(Autoharp.)

*The approximate translation of the various Hebrew phrases is provided by Eugene J.
Lipman, Hebrew Union College, Cincinnati, Ohio: Stanzas 1 and 2: The pioneer's purpose
is labor; labor is for the pioneer. Stanza 3: The pioneer is for his girl; his girl is for the pioneer. Stanza 4: Peace for all the nations; all the nations are for peace.

5. Sing and perform this folk song using melody bells, recorders, and an autoharp (the two chords to strum on the autoharp are notated on the music above the staff.)

6. Refer to the English translation of the various stanzas as it appears here and then compose your own verses to sing in English.

Element: TEMPO
Component: Fast–Slow
Concept: This song moves at a steady TEMPO.

NAVAJO HAPPY SONG*

Navajo Indian song

Hai yo, hai yo ip si nai yah,

Hai yo, hai yo ip si nai ___ yah,

Hai ___ yo, hai yo ip si nai yah,

Hai ___ yo, hai yo ip si nai yah!

Hay nah yay nah yo. Hai - i - i - i!

*Public domain.

■ *Use of Classroom Instruments and Other Strategies to Explore the Concept*

1. Listen to this music and tap along on tom-toms or drums. Would you tap your drum with a drumstick or your hand? Why would you use your hand? Did you tap your drum steadily? Would you say this music has a steady beat? Did the speed, or TEMPO, of this steady beat change? Did it ever move faster or slower? If the speed of the steady beat remained the same, would you say the TEMPO is steady throughout?

2. Sing the "Navajo Happy Song" as you tap a steady RHYTHM throughout. What other instruments would the Indian people choose to add to the gaiety of this song?

3. Choose shakers (maracas), various sizes of drums, and Indian dancing bells to keep time to the music.

4. In performing this song tap a steady beat on tom-toms for the Introduction. Sing the song to the steady accompaniment of drums. Make up your own Indian dance. Use maracas and wear dancing bells on your arms or ankles in addition to tapping the tom-toms. Keep an even and steady RHYTHM throughout the performance of this music.

Element: MELODY
Component: Direction
Concept: This MELODY moves up and down by step and skip.

CHERRY BLOSSOMS (Sakura)*

Japanese folk song

Sa - ku - ra! sa - ku - ra! Ya - yo - i no
Cher - ry trees, cher - ry trees Bloom so bright in

so - ra wa, Mi - wa - ta - su ka - ghi - ri
A - pril breeze Like a mist or float - ing cloud;

Ka - su - mi ka? ku - mo ka? Ni - o - i - zo
Fra - grance fills the air a - round, Shad - ows flit a -

i - zu - ru I - za ya! i - za ya!
long the ground. Come, oh, come! come, oh, come!

Mi - ni yu - ka - n.
Come, see cher - ry blos - soms!

*Reprinted with permission from *Song Sampler No. 3.* July, 1956. Folk Songs of Asia. Delaware, Ohio: Cooperative Recreation Service, Inc.

■ *Use of Classroom Instruments and Other Strategies to Explore the Concept*

1. Listen to this music.
2. Sing the MELODY on a neutral syllable ("la") as you design it in the air using hand levels. How does the MELODY move? Up? Down?
3. View the song from a wall chart or on a screen by means of overhead projector and sing the words of the song as you design it again in the air using hand levels. Does the MELODY ever move by steps? On what words? On what words does it move by skip?
4. Find the first tone of the MELODY on the melody bells and play it as you sing along. Can you play this MELODY on your melody flute or recorder?

Element: RHYTHM
Component: Meter
Concept: This song moves in 3s.

LA SPAGNOLA*

Words by F. B.   *Vincenzo Di Chiara*

La Spa-gno-la, Beau-ti-ful Span-ish maid.___
Pron. Lah Span-yo-lah,

Soft gui-tars in the dis-tance strum

As she danc-es be-neath the sun.

La Spa-gno-la, Ev-'ry-thing she ex-alts. ___

Spar-kling eyes ca-bal-le-ros prize As they

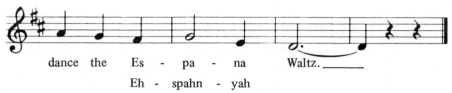

dance the   Es - pa - na   Waltz._____
           Eh - spahn - yah

*Public domain.

■ Use of Classroom Instruments and Other Strategies to Explore the Concept

1. As you listen to this MELODY would you say that it moves along smoothly? Does the rhythmic movement of the music make you feel like dancing? Why? Is it because you feel and hear an accented beat that produces a rhythmic flow to the music?

2. Sing the song and play finger cymbals on the accented beats.

3. Sing the song again using number names and giving the accented (strong) beat the number name 1. How many unaccented (weak) beats follow? What are their number names? (2 and 3.) Therefore, would you say that this music moves in 3s? A ballroom dance that moves in 3s is called a waltz.

4. Play the song on melody bells and sing the song again, choosing appropriate sounding instruments to accompany your singing. Be certain to emphasize the rhythmic flow of the music moving in 3s by accenting the first beat. Choose different sounding instruments for the accented and unaccented beats.

Examples:

             1   2   3
        castanets   tambourines

or

             1   2   3
   finger cymbals   wood block + maracas

or combine any instruments of your choice that will produce satisfactory tonal effects while highlighting the accented beat.

Element: TONE COLOR
Component: Instrumental
Concept: Different sounding instruments create oriental tonal effects distinctive of the music of the Far East.

THE NARCISSUS (Sui Sin Fa)*

Chinese folk tune

*Public domain.

■ Use of Classroom Instruments and Other Strategies to Explore the Concept

1. Listen to this music played on the melody bells. Would you describe it as gentle? What is a narcissus? Is this flower fragile? Does this music describe the delicate nature of the narcissus?

2. Listen to the music again and raise your hand when you hear a section that is repeated. How many phrases are in this song? What phrases sound alike? What phrases sound different?

3. Hum or sing this Chinese folk MELODY on a neutral syllable ("la"). Will you sing it lightly? Why?

4. Refer to an encyclopedia and study the qualities of the narcissus. Make up a poem about this delicate flower. Does your poem fit the RHYTHM of this Chinese MELODY?

5. Sing your poem to this oriental MELODY.

6. Choose instruments of oriental tonality to accompany this song and play it by ear or notate it in score FORM.

Example:

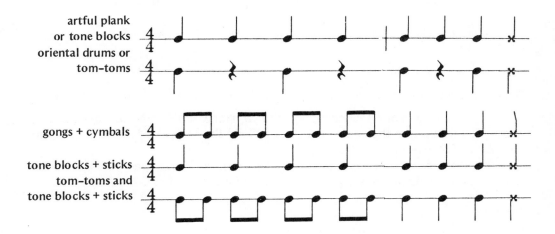

7. Choose your own combination of instrumental sounds to enrich the tonal effect of this oriental folk song.

Element: RHYTHM
Component: Rhythm Pattern
Concept: The groupings of shorter and longer tones in a MELODY often form a rhythmic pattern.

COMIN' THRO' THE RYE*

Robert Burns   *Scotch air*

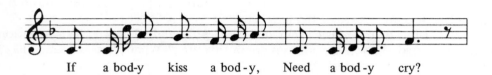

If   a bod-y   meet   a bod-y,   Com-in' thro' the Rye,

If   a bod-y   kiss   a bod-y,   Need   a bod-y   cry?

Ev - 'ry las-sie   has   her lad-die,   Nane, they say, ha'e   I;

Yet   a' the lads they smile on me, When com - in' thro' the Rye.

*From The Golden Book of Favorite Songs, © Schmitt, Hall & McCreary Co., Minneapolis, Minnesota, 1951.

■ *Use of Classroom Instruments and Other Strategies to Explore the Concept*

1. Listen as your teacher claps the mystery RHYTHM of this familiar song. Can you name the song? ("Comin' Thro' the Rye.") If so, sing it as you clap the RHYTHM of the Melody.

2. Take turns clapping parts of the song for your classmates to echo clap. Which words of the song fit the rhythm pattern just clapped?

Example:

While a student taps this RHYTHM on a drum

— — — — —

his classmates echo clap the rhythm pattern and guess the words of the song that fit the RHYTHM. ("Comin' Thro' the Rye" or "Need a body cry?")

3. Sing the entire song as you tap the RHYTHM of the MELODY on small drums. How many times was this rhythm pattern heard? Why do you think this rhythm pattern was called the Scotch snap? Can you match the blank notation of this pattern to the musical notation of the same pattern on a wall chart of "Comin' Thro' the Rye"?

4. Listen as you sing the words to the MELODY that fits this rhythm pattern. Can you play this pattern on the bells? From a wall chart of this folk song try to play the entire MELODY on the bells, being careful to observe the Scotch snap every time you see it.

5. All sing the song while some tap the RHYTHM of this Scotch air on small drums and tone blocks and others play it on the melody bells. What accompanying instrument do the Scotch people play while singing the melodies of their nation? Can some of you imitate the sound of the bagpipe? Explore and discover for yourself on the piano keyboard how the drone of the bagpipe can be imitated.

Example:

The piano keyboard is illustrated and marked (x) to show which keys, when played simultaneously, simulate the sound of the bagpipe.

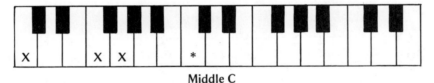

Middle C

These same tones are illustrated on the musical staff:

F G

6. Bagpipes play a steady beat throughout this folk song while other percussion instruments tap the RHYTHM of the MELODY as it is played on the bells.

Example:

Bells, small drums, and tone blocks tap the

RHYTHM of the
  MELODY: __ _ __ __ __ __ __ | __ __ __ _ __
                4
Bagpipes play 4
a steady beat: ___   ___   ___   ___ | ___   ___   ___   ___

Element: HARMONY
Component: Chords
Concept: When two or more tones are sounded together, HARMONY results.

ALOHA OE*

Queen Liliuokalani

Proud - ly   sweeps   the __   rain - cloud by   the
Ha - a - heo   e   ka   u - a   i   na
Pron. Hah - ah - ha-oh   a   kah oo - ah ee   nah

cliffs ____   As   on - ward   it   glides   thru the
pa - li   Ke   ni - hi   a - e   la - i ka - na -
pah - lee   ka - nee - hee   ah - a   lah - ee kah - nah -

trees ____   It __   seems   to be fol - low - ing   the
he   le   E   u - hai   a - na pa - ha - i   ka
ha   la   A   oo - hah - ee ah - nah pah - hah - ee   kah

Li - ko   The __   a - hi - hi le - hu - a   of the
Li - ko   Pu - a   a - hi - hi le - hu - a   o __
Lee - koh   Poo - ah   ah - hee - hee la - hoo - ah   oh __

vale. __   Fare - well   to   thee, fare - well to thee, thou __
u - ka.   A - lo - ha   oe   a - lo - ha   oe   E ka
oo - kah.   Ah - loh - hah   oa   ah - loh - hah   oa   A kah

*Reprinted with permission from *Aloha Sings*. Delaware, Ohio: Cooperative Recreation Service, Inc., 1948.

■ Use of Classroom Instruments and Other Strategies to Explore the Concept

1. Listen to the MELODY of "Aloha Oe" (pronounced "Ah-loh-hah Oh-ā")

2. Sing the MELODY while it is accompanied on an autoharp. (Chord symbols are above the staff.) Is the autoharp playing the MELODY that we are singing? If not, why does it sound pleasing to the ear? Do the musical tones seem to blend well together? Would you say HARMONY is present in the music?

3. Play the autoharp again, but instead of strumming it, use a quadruple-headed mallet and brush it swiftly back and forth across the strings with the right hand as the fingers of the left hand press down firmly on the button for the chord changes: the index finger (or "pointer" finger) falls on the G button (I); the third finger falls naturally on the D^7 button (V^7); and the fourth finger falls naturally on the C button (IV).

4. Build the G, D^7, and C chords in chord boxes from a set of resonator bells and play them with triple- and quadruple-headed mallets to reproduce the chord sounds.

5. Play a guitar* and ukulele, strumming the same chords (G, D^7, and C) as were played on the autoharp and bells. (Consult the following chord symbols and fingering chart.)

---

*Those children who study guitar privately should be encouraged to bring their instruments to school.

Key of G major:

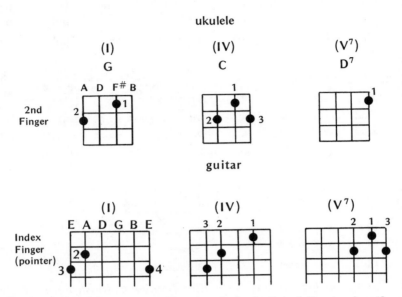

ukulele

(I)   (IV)   (V⁷)

G   C   D⁷

guitar

(I)   (IV)   (V⁷)

6. Sing and play "Aloha Oe" on melody bells while viewing the song on a wall chart or on a screen as cast from an overhead projector. Add harmonic accompaniment by playing an autoharp, guitar, and ukulele, as directed.

7. Make up your own Hawaiian dance using hand gestures to pantomime the words of the refrain as it is sung by the choral group. Because there are four steady beats to a measure, they would be interpreted by the basic hula step as follows:

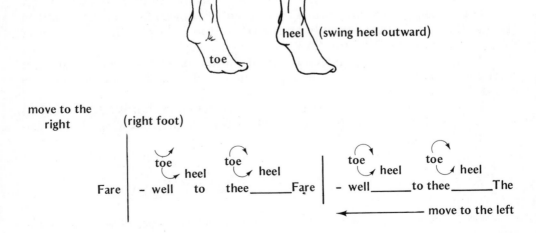

heel   (swing heel outward)

toe

move to the right   (right foot)

toe   heel   toe   heel   toe   heel   toe   heel

Fare | - well   to   thee_____Fare | - well_____to thee_____The

⟵——————— move to the left

MUSIC IN RELATED ARTS PROGRAMS

In referring to related arts in the modern educational curriculum, educators emphasize "the need to draw relationships from several different areas to free children to understand the interrelated world in which they live."[1]

There are numerous ways of relating to other areas in the curriculum through the music education program. However, regarding the area of social studies, Ralph C. Preston states that integration should never be forced: "A class which is studying Switzerland, for example is under no obligation, during music periods to learn Swiss folk songs—unless other circumstances justify doing this."[2]

From this statement music educators might consider "justifying circumstances" to mean that definite musical learnings will be projected through the teaching of specific Swiss folk songs.

Example:

WEGGIS SONG*

Swiss folk song

From Lu - cerne to_ Weg - gis fair, Hol - di - ri - di - a,
Pron. vay - gis

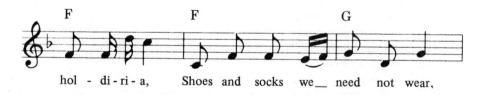

hol - di - ri - a, Shoes and socks we_ need not wear,

Hol - di - ri - di - a, hol - di - a. Hol di

*Reprinted with permission from *Manitowoc Sings* (Delaware, Ohio: Cooperative Recreation Service, Inc., n.d.).

[1] Robert Nye and Vernice Nye, *Music in the Elementary School* (Englewood Cliffs, N. J.: Prentice-Hall, 1970), p. 587.

[2] Ralph C. Preston, *Teaching Social Studies in the Elementary School* (New York: Holt, 1958), p. 8.

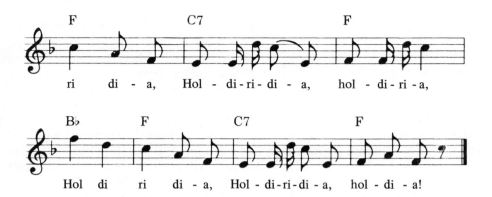

ri - di - a, Hol - di - ri - di - a, hol - di - ri - a,

Hol - di - ri - di - a, Hol - di - ri - di - a, hol - di - a!

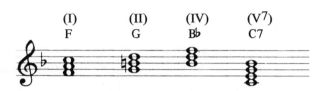

Chords that provide harmonic accompaniment and can be played on autoharp, resonator bells, and piano keyboard.

After the class has become familiar with this Swiss folk song, the teacher can check it for those musical characteristics from which valuable musical learnings or concepts will evolve. The following elements of music are found in this Swiss hiking song:

MELODY: repeated melody patterns
RHYTHM: steady beat throughout; an accented beat occurs on the first beat of every measure
HARMONY: melody line supported by I, II, IV, V^7 chords played on an autoharp, resonator bells, and piano keyboard
FORM: verse and refrain
TEMPO: steady
DYNAMICS: echo effects in the refrain, distinctive of a Swiss folk song
TONE COLOR: melody bells, rhythm sticks, and tone blocks; high and low drum

Through repeated experiences of actively becoming involved in singing, dancing, playing instruments, listening, and creating dramatic interpretations of the lyrics, the children will recognize the musical value of this specific folk song. Consequently, the song is not merely of value for the purpose of enrichment, but also for its own integrity. William C. Hartshorn notes that "Music will serve other subject fields best when its own integrity as an art is maintained."[3]

[3] William C. Hartshorn, "The Role of Listening," in *Basic Concepts in Music Education*, Nelson B. Henry, ed. (Chicago: U. of Chicago, 1958), p. 285.

The following examples of related arts projects are illustrative of creative ventures for children in the elementary grades. The projects are arranged in approximate developmental order; however, because classroom situations, interests, and curriculum content usually vary among school systems, the sequence of activities will be modified as conditions warrant.

Example 1: Life of the American Indian

SOCIAL STUDIES

In the early elementary grades, children are introduced to the American Indian in social studies classes. Authentic stories of the life, traditional customs, and habits of the various tribes of Indians who inhabited America many years ago are of vital interest to most children.

Figure 3. Marriage.

Figure 4. Sun dance.

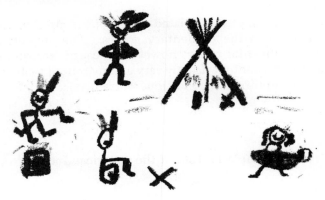

Figure 5. Celebrating the birth of a child.

Figure 6. Soon the warriors will return with the necessary food and supplies needed for the long winter months ahead. The tom-tom announces the hunt.

Figure 7. Sad news has arrived of the death of a warrior.

ART

A sample of an Indian mural (Figures 3, 4, 5, 6, and 7) depicts events that occur within the life span of the Indian. American Indian arts and crafts (pots, robes, baskets, and beaded jewelry) also can be engaging and artistic activities.

MUSIC AND DANCE

Rhythm instruments—especially drums, rattles, shakers, and bells—were made and used by Indians. In fact, the drum played such a vital role in the life of the American Indian, that it is represented in each scene of the mural. The events portrayed in the mural also can be interpreted through creative dance movements to the accompaniment of drums and rhythm instruments.

LANGUAGE ARTS

If the children have studied the free verse style associated with the American Indian they can write a script in that form to describe the events portrayed in the mural.

Example 2: Islands of the Caribbean

SOCIAL STUDIES

Studying the islands in the Caribbean Sea, including the West Indies (of which Trinidad is the largest island), can be enhanced by learning about the customs, everyday work habits, and music of the natives.

Figure 8. Linstead Market: boxes covered with colored paper create little shops.

Figure 9. Dancers form a circle floor pattern in front of the market place.

Figure 10. Dancers move to the calypso music of the islands.

Reproduced here are scenes in a market place in Trinidad as portrayed by children in the fifth grade in Pike Central Elementary Grade School, Pike Metropolitan School District, Indianapolis, Indiana. The scenes represent a program written, planned, and performed by these children that evolved from their study of the islands in the Caribbean Sea.

Figure 11: A little Caribbean boy in a pose looking for the "Yellow Bird."

Figure 12.   A little Caribbean boy responds to the Latin American sounds of calypso music by playing the bongos.

ART

The children designed the programs. They also designed the stage scenery and costumes.

Pike Central Elementary School
John R. Kerr — Principal
Wm. E. Dickerson — Asst. Principal

The Music Program

"CARIBBEAN CARIOCA"

Linstead Market. . . . . Calypso from Jamaica
Yellow Bird . . . . Norman Luboff
    (Stroller: Robert Bivens)
Dancing the Merengue. . . . . Puerto Rican Folk Song
Tinga Layo . . . . Calypso from the West Indies
    (A Pal and His Donkey: Steve Taylor & Larry Adams)
Mary Ann. . . . . Island Song
    (Island Dancer: Tammy Willits)
Hosanna. . . . . Calypso from Jamaica
    Brick-Masons: Eddie Mankus & David Soper)
Jamaican Farewell . . . . Lord Burgess

Program Presented by

Mrs. Deborah Blake's Fifth Grade Class
Program Designed By Student — Robert Bivens
Art Instructor — Mrs. Leonora Galloway
Music Supervisor — Mrs. Mary Louise Jones

1971 Room Program

MUSIC

All musical activities (listening, singing, dancing, playing, and creating) were represented in the production. Children made up such calypso verses to the folk songs of the islands as

My Cat

My cat he got in a fight, all right
My cat came home all hurt last night
My cat is funny—just like a bunny
—and doesn't like honey!

Folk songs selected from various music education textbooks as well as from the numerous folk songs of the islands available in sheet music were studied and performed in different ways.

A typical listing of songs representative of the Islands might include

Lindstead Market
Dancing the Merengue
Tinga Layo
Mary Ann
Jamaican Farewell
Yellow Bird

Vibrant rhythm instruments used to accompany the music of the islands include guiro, bongos, claves, maracas, and castanets.

LANGUAGE ARTS

New vocabulary, or word study, in the project included calypso music, Latin instruments, improvise, accompany, and Trinidad. The script and dialogue written by the children for this project also were considered integral parts of the classes in language arts because they included calypso verses. The class used the following sources of information: various encyclopedias; "Isles of the Caribbees," published by the National Geographic Society; American Automobile Association (AAA) maps and travel guides; and songbooks containing reference material pertinent to the Caribbean Islands and to calypso music.

Example 3: The Origin of Christmas Symbols

SOCIAL STUDIES

Studying the traditions and customs of celebrating Christmas in many different lands is an ideal project for small-group activity that will culminate in group reports shared by the class.

Divide the class into groups. Have the groups decide which country or countries they will investigate: group 1, Holland; group 2, Germany; group 3, France; group 4, Italy (and so on).

LANGUAGE ARTS

Each group is responsible for composing a narration of their research and presenting it before the class at a designated time.

MUSIC

Each group chooses a Christmas carol or song of the season that will correlate with their specific narration. Melody bells and other classroom instruments provide interesting tonal effects for the musical performance.

Example:

Group 3, France, might choose "The First Noel" to sing in conjunction with a description of the significance of the yule log in that country.

ART

Song sheets that include all the songs in the class program can be designed by the class or by a committee and distributed to each class member. Providing everyone with a song sheet will encourage group participation, which is necessary to the success of the singing.

The symbols of Christmas—tree, star, yule log, mistletoe, and so on—are the theme of the project and should be in evidence in the room.

Note:

This project can be modified or expanded to include any grade in an elementary school and, through the combined efforts of children and faculty, can culminate in an all-school holiday program.

Example 4: Haiku

SOCIAL STUDIES

Studying the country of Japan (or any country), the Japanese people, and their way of life can provide many opportunities for related arts activities.

LANGUAGE ARTS

The Japanese haiku is a form of poetry composed of only three lines of five, seven, and five syllables each. After investigating and discussing the strict rules for composing a haiku, the children can become involved in writing haiku. These haiku were composed by elementary school children:

Roads

From Heaven to earth
and far beyond a road goes
on and on; wailing.

Wintertime

In the wintertime
In the lovely fluffy snow,
A bird sits and waits

Autumn

Sounds of Hallow'een
Rust'ling cornstalks, crunchy leaves,
October! don't go . . .

Winter

Icy fingertips—
Snow drips down over rooftops
King Winter holds on!

Summer

The sounds of summer—
Crickets chirp, birds sing, bees buzz,
Lazy, happy days.

MUSIC AND MOVEMENT

Through free creative movement, small groups of children can pantomime the haiku while it is being read by a narrator. In her book *Children Dance in the Classroom*, Geraldine Dimondstein states, "Poems sometimes give us feelings that we can express in movement."[4] She illustrates this statement with photographs of children creating through movement. Appropriate classroom instruments can provide tonal effects to enhance the performance.

Example:

Spring

Raindrops on rooftops
on sidewalk, on windowpane
Smile! There's a rainbow.

Classroom instruments can be used to achieve various tonal effects for raindrops: Lightly tap finger cymbals or triangles or play two different melody bells or resonator bells repeatedly throughout the reading to imitate the steady pitter, patter of raindrops. Tap various sized drumheads with the fingertips to explore and discover the most satisfactory sound effect for the rain on rooftops. Whisper the words "pitter, patter" rhythmically throughout recitation of the haiku. For greater TONE COLOR play a slow glissando on bells on the words "Smile! There's a rainbow."

[4] Geraldine Dimondstein, *Children Dance in the Classroom* (New York: Macmillan, 1971), pp. 243-245.

ART

A pictorial representation of the haiku can be sketched and displayed as a combined class mural.

Example 5: Folklore of American Heroes

SOCIAL STUDIES

The study of American folklore, which is reflective of a mixture of cultures and deals with history, legend, and geographical localities, stimulates elementary school children to study the history of the United States of America.

LANGUAGE ARTS

The "tall tales" and "yarns" of Pecos Bill, John Henry, Paul Bunyan (with his giant blue ox, Babe), Davy Crockett, and Mike Fink can be used to motivate young children to compose their own tall tales and convey those tales orally or in a written project assigned as a language arts activity.

MUSIC AND DRAMA

Composing a short MELODY for a tall tale is a challenging activity for small-group work guided by a teacher, or as a joint effort by the entire class. Dramatizing or pantomiming a tall tale using the appropriate sound effects from classroom instruments is also a stimulating activity.

ART

Folklore characters can be interpreted in charcoal sketches by children in their art class. (Refer to Figure 13.)

Example 6: Geometric Designs

MATHEMATICS

A concentrated study of geometric figures (triangle, square, and rectangle), by an elementary class on the intermediate level resulted in the following designs (refer to Plates 1, 2, 3, 4, and 5). The musical activity proceeded in the following manner. The class was divided into five groups. Each group chose a design to interpret musically with classroom instruments. Each group displayed and performed its musical interpretation.

The following verbal analyses correspond to Plates 1 through 5.

PLATE 1 HARMONY

The blending of colors appearing in sustained movement was interpreted by slowly strumming various chords on the autoharp. As members of the class listened to the tones of each chord being sounded, they intoned the sounds they heard vocally. Thus, by incorporating explore-and-discovery techniques, they created their own harmonious chord progressions.

PLATE 1: HARMONY

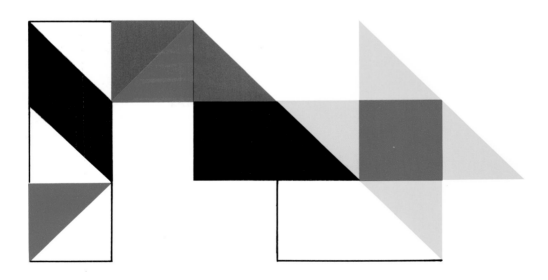

PLATE 2: MELODY

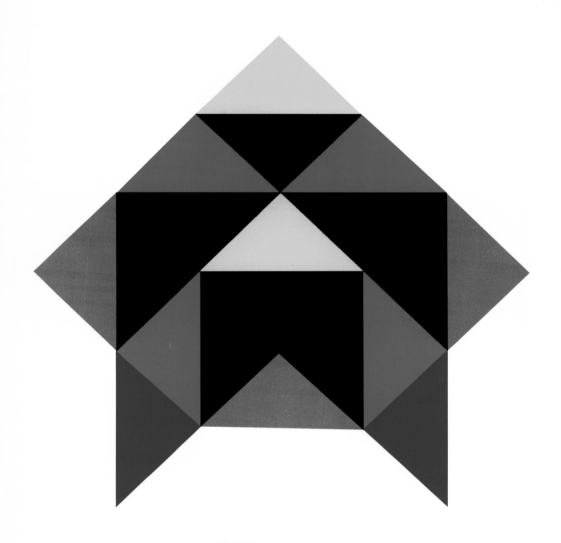

PLATE 3: DYNAMICS

PLATE 4: FORM

PLATE 5: ALEATORIC MUSIC

Figure 13. John Henry as sketched by Bruce B., grade 6, Pike Central Elementary School, Pike Metropolitan School District, Indianapolis, Indiana.

PLATE 2   MELODY

A hidden melody line was observed in this design. It culminated in a cluster of tones that is represented by a blending of color. Therefore, an improvised MELODY played on melody bells was ended climactically by a chord strummed on autoharp.

PLATE 3   DYNAMICS

This design was described as resembling a kite at rest. The slow ascent of the kite into the sky, its sudden soaring upward with the wind, like a great bird in flight, and its gentle descent, far too soon, was compared to gradual DYNAMICS in music signified by:

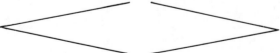

The effective use of percussion instruments to interpret the design through sound was demonstrated while observing

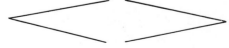

PLATE 4   FORM

A group of students agreed to the interpretation of this design as comparable to the canon FORM in music. The outside circle of color was thought of as a single melody line and, as illustrated by additional lines of color, succeeding melodic entrances were superimposed on it, creating a harmonious blend of sound. Melody bells, autoharps, and percussion instruments were chosen to aurally demonstrate the design.

PLATE 5   ALEATORIC MUSIC

The theme of this geometric design was determined by the group as reflecting aleatoric or "chance" music. For an aural interpretation of the colorful design, each member of the group chose different classroom instruments to correspond with a color.

Example:

> red = tambourines, jingle bells, and large cymbals
> blue = finger cymbals and autoharp
> black = wood blocks and large drums
> yellow = castanets and maracas
> green = triangle and glissando on resonator bells and melody bells

As the leader pointed simultaneously to two colors on the design, the resultant sounds could be distinctly classified as aleatoric in texture.

Chapter 12

Music in Special Education in the Regular Classroom

INTRODUCTION: THE NEED FOR CONSIDERATION

Music in special education and music therapy are specialized areas of concentration that should be reserved for music educators and classroom teachers who are professionally equipped and certified. Unfortunately, in-service workshops conducted periodically within a school system cannot provide sufficient training experiences for trainees. Donald E. Michel concludes that

> it is wrong to assume that they (music educators) can become competent music therapists by attending a workshop or taking a few courses. Music therapy curriculums, at both undergraduate and graduate levels, differ greatly from music education; that is, more foundational behavioral science courses and special professional courses in the psychology of music and in music therapy are required.[1]

However, many college students who are preparing to become elementary classroom teachers or music educators in a regular classroom situation, as well as numerous teachers presently "on the job," are aware that they will have little or no opportunity for future professional training to become certified teachers in the area of music in special education and music therapy. They are also aware that throughout the world, children who suffer fundamentally from

[1] Donald E. Michel, "Filling a Special Need," *Music Educators Journal* 58: 7 (April 1972).

the inability to learn as a result of a lack of normal abilities or because of behavioral disorders are thrust into regular classroom situations where they are in
need of special consideration on the part of the teacher. Hence, the need for
providing teachers with some basic knowledge of the physical and mental characteristics of these children is recognized as essential by this writer.

CHARACTERISTICS OF CHILDREN IN NEED
OF SPECIAL ATTENTION WHO ARE MAINSTREAMED
INTO A REGULAR CLASSROOM SITUATION

Throughout this section, devoted to the needs of special education, it must
be remembered that: "In therapy, music is the means, or medium; in music
education, music is the end goal."[2]

Contrary to the philosophy expressed in the preceding chapter, in which
the use of classroom instruments is emphasized in a conceptual approach, the
emphasis here will be on the use of a concrete approach to music. Not only do
mentally retarded children have limited ability for conceptualizing, but they
also exhibit behavior problems. "Mentally retarded children experience difficulty in conceptualizing and find success in 'learning by doing,' the educational
philosophy of Jerome Bruner."[3]

The explore-and-discovery techniques of education that should be in evidence in educational institutions today offer all children (including those in
special education) enrolled in the classroom the opportunity to learn how to
learn. Boys and girls explore and discover for themselves numerous strategies
for problem solving and in this way continued growth and development in attitudes, abilities, judgments, and skills is fostered.

In considering the use of classroom instruments in special education it is
well to remember that music is a means of self-expression and children love to
accompany music with their instruments. What could be more fun than music
provided by instruments they make themselves?[4]

■ *Suggestions for Making Instruments*

GONG AND MALLET

A cowbell or a large metal lid from a potato chip can or a can of house
paint can be used as a gong. A mallet can be made by tying a woolen mitten
stuffed with cotton to one end of a wooden dowel or drumstick.

---

[2] Ibid., p. 7.

[3] Abraham J. Tannenbaum, ed., *Special Education and Programs for Disadvantaged
Children and Youth* (Washington, D.C.: The Council For Exceptional Children, 1968),
p. 88.

[4] Artelia Moore Cox, *Arts and Crafts Are More Than Fun in Special Education* (Danville, Ill.: Interstate Printers and Publishers, 1970), p. 50.

TRIANGLE

Draw a long shoelace through a piece of lead pipe and tie its ends together to form a triangle. A large nail, a screw driver, or various discarded kitchen utensils can be used to tap the triangle.

HORNS

Decorate paper towel tubes. Hair combs wrapped in tissue paper produce a resonant humming effect.

DRUMS

Use large coffee or shortening cans or any of the various types of cartons found in markets and grocery stores as drums.

TAMBOURINES

Lace aluminum pie pans together after punching holes around the rim of the pans. Before securing the lace, pour rice, sand, or corn into the interior of the pans. Tie jingle bells to the rim for added tonal effect.

MARACAS

Pierce the bottom of a salt carton with a wooden skewer. Pour rice or sand through the spout on the box top. Decorate the boxes. Large drinking cups of styrofoam or heavy cardboard will produce comparable TONE COLOR if the open end is covered securely. Spikes or nails tied together or suspended from a wooden dowel or rhythm stick produce a tinkling sound.

Can you and your pupils explore and discover other ways to make musical instruments?

The areas of special education are numerous and complex, because each individual within a given category is usually a modified entity from the norm of that specific category. Therefore, we will limit our study to the three main areas of special education that concern us as educators in a regular classroom situation: the mentally retarded, the brain injured, and the emotionally disturbed.[5]

The characteristics of the aforementioned handicapped children have been grouped and defined by Ernest Siegel. (Siegel terms these characteristics "nine basic problems.") They are listed here and are followed by detailed examples of musical experiences that can be implemented in the curriculum of the regular classroom to provide meaningful experiences to all pupils.

[5] Ernest Siegel, *Special Education in the Regular Classroom* (New York: Day, 1969), p. 13.

NINE BASIC PROBLEMS

Poor Self-Concept

Handicapped children possess a poor self-image because learning is frustrating for them, they lack the ability to perform given tasks, and/or they feel unaccepted by their peer group and, at times, by their teachers.

> The negative self-image, often anxiety provoking, is self-defeating, thereby creating a downward spiral: Difficulty in perceiving and utilizing sensory data leads to inadequate performance (learning as well as behavior), resulting in non-acceptance; anxiety and feelings of inadequacy and self-reproach ensue, resulting in even poorer performance; scorn, rebuffs, and hostility accrue in ever-increasing frequency.[6]

Siegel also notes that

> All children need acceptance, but the normal child, having more positive self-concept is better able to cope with defeat. Thus, a good mental hygiene approach on the part of the classroom teacher, one that is supportive and accepting is, for the handicapped child, a curricular priority.[7]

Suggestions for incorporating a positive approach:

A. Develop success-assured activities.

■ *Suggested musical activities for the primary level:*

1. Make classroom instruments (refer to pp. 53, 54, 55, Chapter 3; also refer to p. 276).

   a. Play these instruments as an accompaniment to favorite songs.
   b. Make a pictorial score of the instruments used in the accompaniment.

   Example:

   Tape a long sheet of white shelf paper to the chalkboard and encourage the children to draw a picture or facsimile of their instrument at their seat. (Be available for assistance and support.) When the drawing activity is completed, permit the children to cut out their pictures and to paste or tape them on the shelf paper in the spaces provided for the verse the instrument accompanied in the song. Figure 21 illustrates the song "Sing and Play," which is classified as easy because both the MELODY and words are, for the most part, repetitious.

---

[6] Ibid., p. 46.
[7] Ibid., p. 40.

SING AND PLAY*

M. Lament

1. Lis - ten to the tam - bour - ines; ching - a - ching - a - ching - a

Tell - ing us to dance and sing, ching - a - ching - a - ching, ching, ching.

2. Hear my drum go boom! boom! boom!
   As we march a-round the room;
   Hear my drum go boom! boom! boom!
   Boom-Da-Boom-Da-Boom-Da-Boom.

3. Rick-ey tick-ey click, click, click
   Hear me rap and tap my sticks.
   Rick-ey tick-ey go my sticks
   Rick-ey ticke-ey rick-ey o!

4. Hear my bells ring ting-a-ling
   Ting-a-ling-a-lay-o.
   Hear my bells ring jing-le jing
   Ting-a-ling-a-jing-le-o!

5. Hear us play our instruments
   in a ring—as we sing;
   Hear us play our instruments
   Listen to us play and sing!

*Original.

Shelf Paper

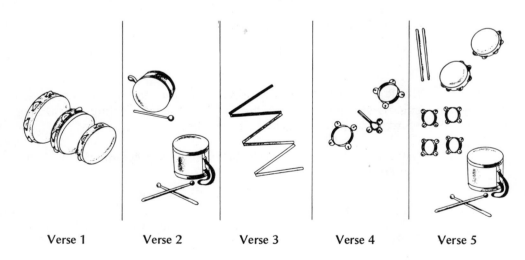

| Verse 1 | Verse 2 | Verse 3 | Verse 4 | Verse 5 |

Figure 14. Pictorial instrumental score for "Sing and Play," illustrating the instrumental accompaniment for each of the five verses.

2. Use singing games as an activity.

    a. Pretend you are toasting marshmallows over a campfire, then join hands with your neighbor and back away to form a circle.

    b. Choose a boy or girl to be the leader in the center of the circle as everyone sings a simple song to a familiar tune. To the tune of "London Bridge Is Falling Down" you might sing these words, using the name of the leader:

> Johnny, show us what to do,
> What to do, what to do.
> Johnny, show us what to do,
> What to do today.

    c. Have the leader pantomime rowing a boat, ice skating, batting a ball, painting a wall, or some such activity.

    d. Have the entire class follow the leader by performing the same motions while singing:

> This is what we'll do today,
> Do today, do today.
> This is what we'll do today,
> We'll have lots of fun.

    e. Have the leader choose someone to take his place and repeat the game.

    f. Repeat this circle game as often as desired, keeping a record of the names of the children who play the leader so that, over a period of time, everyone has a turn.

Note:

Can you think of other ways all children can have fun with some aspect of music and experience enjoyment? They will appreciate feeling acceptance for what they contribute to the musical experience.

3. Chant familiar poems in RHYTHM emphasizing enunciation (clarity of speech).

    a. Choose a favorite poem, such as "Pease Porridge Hot."
    b. Teacher and children sit in a circle on the floor.
    c. Echo chant* the poem together rhythmically until it is learned.
    d. Chant the entire poem rhythmically:

*The teacher chants the first line of the poem in RHYTHM and the children echo it.

> Pease porridge hot,
> Pease porridge cold,
> Pease porridge in the pot
> Nine days old.
>
> Some like it hot,
> Some like it cold,
> Some like it in the pot
> Nine days old.

e. Clap hands or tap the RHYTHM of the poem on coffee-can drums while chanting the words in unison.

f. Sit Indian style and make up a rhythmic movement while chanting the poem:

Bend Over and Slap Floor	Clap Hands	Clap Hands
Pease	porridge	hot
Pease	porridge	cold
Pease	porridge	in the pot
Nine	days	old.

g. Add one new movement to the same poem to create a new challenge. However, if the children are not ready for a new challenge, avoid creating the tension that results in frustration.

Bend Over and Slap Floor	Clap Hands	Snap Fingers
Pease	porridge	hot
Pease	porridge	cold
Pease	porridge	in the pot
Nine	days	old.

h. On another day, instead of sitting in a circle, sit on the floor and face a partner to perform the activity.

Note:

Can you think of other entertaining ways to perform "Pease Porridge Hot," perhaps using classroom instruments? Consider chanting words using various levels of DYNAMICS, remembering to enunciate clearly even though you might be chanting in a whisper (*pppp*) or observing a crescendo ⟨ or speaking moderately loud (*mf*).

■ *Suggested Musical Activities for the Intermediate Level:*

4. Use classroom instruments or unconventional sounds as a group activity.

    A. Choose symbols to represent the instruments that are available and jot these symbols on the chalkboard:

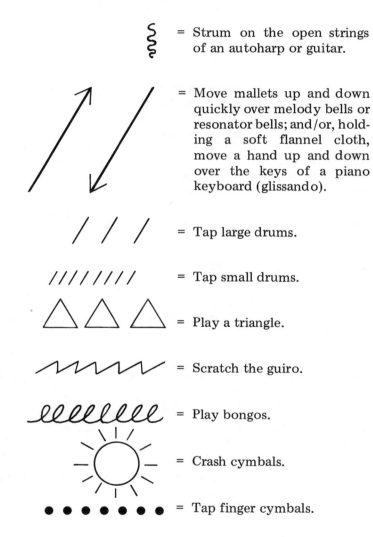

= Strum on the open strings of an autoharp or guitar.

= Move mallets up and down quickly over melody bells or resonator bells; and/or, holding a soft flannel cloth, move a hand up and down over the keys of a piano keyboard (glissando).

= Tap large drums.

= Tap small drums.

= Play a triangle.

= Scratch the guiro.

= Play bongos.

= Crash cymbals.

= Tap finger cymbals.

Suggestions to the class:

What other instruments or sounds would you like to add to this list? After you have exhausted the kinds of sounds you would like represented in your "Portrait in Percussion" and have scored them all symbolically, record each sound individually on a tape recorder. Play back the tape and then, as a group, decide how you would like to score the instrumental sounds on a nine- or ten-foot sheet of white shelf paper that has been taped to chalkboard for easy viewing. (Use colored felt-tipped markers for easy reading.)

Example:

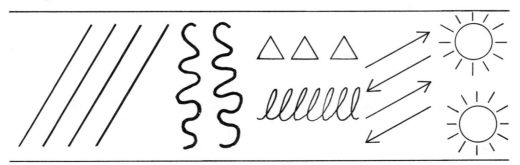

Now, can you compose your own "Portrait in Percussion" and record it on tape using your own ideas? A more complex activity would be to transfer these symbols to notation, thereby introducing actual score reading.

B. Assign special tasks to display your confidence in the ability of individuals or groups of individuals to accept responsibility.

Suggested activities in which music classes can participate:

1. Distribute classroom instruments carefully or place them on a designated table or desk. Exert extreme care when gathering instruments, shelving them, or packing them in boxes at end of the music period.
2. Handle music books with care while distributing or collecting them.
3. Rotate the task and responsibility of keeping the music bulletin board a current center of interest among groups of children. Every group should have an opportunity within the nine-month academic year.

General suggestions:

Encourage the children to maintain a bulletin board of current interest and to be certain to remove obsolete program announcements.

Aid the children in keeping the bulletin boards attractive by suggesting that they use splashes of color. Check with the art teacher on the use of collage and other techniques for displaying materials. By choosing collage as a technique for bulletin boards, the children can bring together all types of materials (both flat and dimensional) to create pictures and designs. Suggested materials are pebbles, sand, buttons, twigs, shells, macaroni, rice, seeds, various qualities of paper (all colors), yarn, and cloth. Choose a heavy background paper—manila tag board or construction paper. After cutting and arranging the materials in a desired design, paste or glue them to the background paper.

The musical staff can be made of strips of black felt or crepe paper to be stapled across a bulletin board that has been covered with white shelf paper. The first phrase of a favorite song of the season or holiday can be notated easily on this staff using black construction paper for notes. The children will become involved totally in the project if they are permitted to add colorful designs symbolic of the season.

SHAMROCK*

Helen Hart Whitaker

Say   it   with   a   sham - rock, _____

That's   the   I - rish   way, _____

*From *Sing and Celebrate* by Helen Hart Whitaker © 1961 Silver Burdett Company. Reprinted by permission of General Learning Corporation.

Note:

Each child can make several shamrocks to paste on the bulletin board and around the musical staff. The remaining shamrocks can be dangled from the ceiling lights from threads of various lengths for a mobile effect.

■ *Ideas for Bulletin Board Themes*

Title: "Name That Tune"

Use new songs plus old favorites: notate the first phrase of each song on a separate piece of staff paper. Place the song titles and musical phrases in helter-skelter positions on the bulletin board. Can you match the song title with the musical phrase?

Title: "Tops in Talent"

Use newspaper clippings of advanced announcements of programs or concerts to be presented live in concert halls or on television. Include announcements, pictures, and articles that appear in current periodicals. Remember to include announcements of all the musical programs in your own school system.

Title: "Sing a Song of Christmas"

or

"Here We Come a Caroling"

Divide the class into eight or ten groups and designate a leader from each group to draw the name of a Christmas song out of Frosty the snowman's hat. Each group will be responsible for a pictorial representation of its chosen song for a bulletin board display. Groups should be free to exercise a choice of collage technique, water colors, and so on.

Note:

Plans for this particular bulletin board should be completed *before* Thanksgiving so that the display can be viewed the first week of December. (Many schools dismiss early for the holidays.)

Title: "Suzy Snowflake"

Directions for making snowflakes:

1. cut plain white tissue paper or notebook paper in circles measuring approximately 5 to 6 inches in diameter;
2. fold circles in half and then continue folding in fourths, eighths, and so forth;
3. with a scissors cut numerous indentations or notches of various shapes and sizes on the folds of the paper. Example:

   Sampling of indentations or notches cut on folds of the paper.

4. unfold notched paper circle and now see a lacy design which is representative of a snowflake.

Have every child in the room make one or two snowflakes. Those children responsible for the bulletin board can add a touch of paste or tape to the back of each snowflake and, for variety, stick them on a blackboard instead of a bulletin board. The effect is quite unique. Everyone participates in this effort. Any winter song can be used, such as "Snowflakes," which is also very easy to accompany with tuned bottles or melody bells.

SNOWFLAKES*

M. Lament

See   the   snow - flakes   gen - tly   fall - ing,

See   them   fall - ing,   See   the   snow - flakes

gen - tly fall - ing   to   the   ground.   from   the   sky.

*Original.

C. Use praise when teaching music in the classroom.

1. Verbal praise for the favorable performance of a task encourages the child to continue to strive for acceptance.

Examples:

"That was fine singing, boys and girls."

"Everyone followed the conductor well and played right on cue!"

2. Through the use of prodding questioning techniques, the teacher can encourage children to think for themselves:

"You made an excellent choice of instrument to accompany this song. What are the reasons you chose it? Does your instrumental choice relate to the words or text of the song? Is the shape (contour) of the MELODY smooth and connected (legato) or jagged and even disconnected (staccato) at times?

Why did you choose to tap a wood block rather than finger cymbals in this part of the song?

Can you think of other reasons related to the TEMPO, HARMONY, RHYTHM, or DYNAMICS of the song that helped you to choose the sound of these particular instruments? How can we write down (score) the instrumentation for this music so that we can refer to it whenever we need it?"

D. Avoid negative value judgments.

Instead of saying, "That singing was awful!" say, "Were you proud of the way we just sang? Do you think we could do a better job if we tried once more? Before we sing this song again, do you think it would be wise to decide and determine why our singing needs to be improved?"

By using this kind of leadership the instructor is able to guide the children to be cognizant of their performance and simultaneously to achieve his own goals. The approach places the emphasis on the development of attitudes, ideas, skills, and abilities—on the process of education—rather than on content. It emphasizes the discovery methods of instruction and the development of problem-solving skills—learning how to learn. It rejects the notion that the main task of education is to bottle quantums of knowledge to be poured into children.[8]

Anxiety

Children with learning and/or behavior problems often are besieged with anxiety. Retarded children are plagued with doubts, with failure and rejection centering about their inability to render satisfactory performances.[9]

[8] Tannenbaum, op. cit., p. 113.
[9] Thomas E. Jordan, *The Exceptional Child* (Columbus, Ohio: Merrill, 1962), p. 159.

■ *Suggested Musical Activities for the Primary Level:*

1. Choose failure-free activities.

   a. Perform creative movement, free rhythmic movement, to a familiar song that lends itself to riding a pony to the accompaniment of coconut shells or inverted paper cups taped together or on a sounding board. "Rig-a-Jig-Jig" or "Trot, Pony, Trot."

      Suggestion to children:

      Can you make up your own pony song? Or, do you just want to walk your pony out of the barn, up the hill, across the meadow or pasture, and then down to the stream for a cool drink of water? Will your pony always move at the same speed or will he slow down and, at times, move faster? When? Does he ever stop to rest?

   b. Have the entire class explore the many different ways to walk while singing this song:

WALKING, WALKING*

M. Lament

Walk-ing, walk-ing down the street, walk-ing, walk-ing hear our feet,

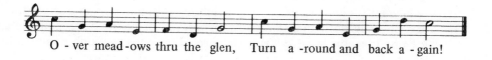

O - ver mead-ows thru the glen, Turn a -round and back a -gain!

*Original.

Can you walk to the sound of a drum? Can you walk forward? Backward? Sideways? In a circle? Straight ahead? Fast? Slow? At a regular speed? How do you walk home from school when you must tell mother you lost your new mittens? How do you walk home from school when you know mother is planning to serve your favorite dessert after dinner, chocolate fudge cake and ice cream? How do you walk to school or to the bus stop when you've overslept twenty minutes? Can you think of enjoyable ways you might walk? If you were a circus clown? If you were a tightrope walker? If you were a prancing pony? If you were a bear who performs stunts? If you were an elephant on parade?

c. Use puppets to teach music activities in the classroom.

> Puppetry is recommended for many reasons. Handicapped children in the regular classroom are painfully aware of the difference between themselves and the nonhandicapped children around them. They may become overly sensitive, fearful of reciting, avoiding eye contact and shrinking from any role that might place them in the limelight. By means of puppets, such children are able, without fear, to satisfy the natural need to be the center of attention, for the audience watches the puppet rather than the child.[10]

Therefore, activities that can influence the child to identify with a puppet and thereby to act in an uninhibited manner may relieve the pressures that anxiety provokes.

Suggestions for using puppets in music:

Pantomime and sing nursery rhymes. Involve all the activities in the music program: singing, dancing (free movement), listening, creating, and playing to dramatize the lyrics of favorite songs.

Do you have other ideas in which puppets can be used advantageously in the school music program?

How to Make Paper Bag Puppets[11]

Two small or medium-sized paper bags (sacks) make one puppet:

1. Invert one bag so that the closed end is up. Draw a face for the puppet.
2. Use bits of yarn for hair and scraps of material for a hat; secure them in place with glue, staples, or by stitching with a needle and thread.
3. Stuff the bag with pieces of newspaper and close the open end of bag by tying it securely with string or yarn. Leave just enough room to insert your index (pointer) finger to manipulate this puppet head.
4. For the body of the puppet, invert the second bag so that the closed end is up. Punch a hole in center of the closed end and place your hand and arm up into the open end of the bag, inserting the pointer finger to make a hole in the closed end of bag and to go into the hole in the bag that is the puppet's head. Carefully measure and punch holes in the sides of the second bag for your thumb and third finger, which will serve as the arms of the puppet.

---

[10]Siegel, op. cit., p. 53. (This quote is from article by John E. Lent, "Helping Stutterers in the Classroom," in *The Exceptional Child: A Book of Readings,* by James F. Magary and John R. Eichorn (New York: Holt, 1962), pp. 327–29.

[11]Nan Comstock, ed., *McCall's Golden Do-It Book* (New York: Golden Press, 1969), pp. 122–123.

5. Using paints, crayons, and scraps of material or construction paper, fashion the dress or costume of the puppet for the second bag. Complete the puppet by adding shoes out of construction paper at the bottom of the second bag.

    d. Use classroom instruments as a casual but appropriate accompaniment to such songs as "Over the River and Through the Woods."

        Use: jingle bells, sleigh bells, coconut shells tapped together. Relate this old familiar song of going to Grandma's for Thanksgiving on the farm by horse and sleigh to our present modes of travel: bus, airplane, train, automobile, and even helicopter.

        Sing "Hickory, Dickory, Dock," or any familiar clock song, so that every child can tap rhythm sticks or pencils to imitate the ticking of a clock. Can you think of other such songs in which children can escape the pressures of individual performance? Group work or working with a partner enables the handicapped child to become less preoccupied with himself and more aware of others.

    e. Guide group discussion through questions pertaining to the music just heard or the song just sung: How did this music move? Fast? Slow? In between? Was this dancing music or marching music? Did the music remind you of something special happening? What made you think so? Was it a parade marching by? What makes you think the band was moving and not sitting still on the concert stage? Did the music remain loud throughout or were there times when it seemed far away or softer? (These questions could relate to any parade music or, specifically, to Ibert's "Parade," from *Divertissement*, from *Adventures in Music*, Grade 1, Volume I.)

This type of group discussion can be very rewarding for everyone in the class because one answer may trigger another question or answer. The skillful teacher will manipulate the discussion so that each child is involved and accepted for his or her contribution.

Points to remember:

The handicapped child cannot work under pressures of time. (Some *normal* children also become frustrated under tension.) Anxiety and tension can be reduced by including humorous songs and stories in the program so that "the teacher's warmth, good-naturedness and accepting attitude . . . can also promote 'groupness' inasmuch as the class as a whole shares the humorous situation."[12] A child's attention span is shortened when he is anxious; therefore, strive to keep activity enjoyable and, preferably, short in duration. This will depend, of course, on the nature of the activity and the age group involved.

[12] Siegel, op. cit., p. 54.

Intermediate grades respond enthusiastically to group discussion concerning listening activities when discussions include all class members. Intermediate grades also respond enthusiastically to any type of group activity that involves listening; playing classroom instruments; or rhythmic improvisation using drums, congas, bongos, claves, and other percussion instruments of their choice to accompany free creative movement. Participants interested in improvising dance movements often move within their own structure or design, which relates to a definite phrase length. Therefore, experiences in composition through improvisation will be in evidence through aural, visual, and physical responses to the music. Tape recording the sound can be exciting and is an aid in notating the score through symbols at first. If an improvised MELODY is added to the percussion score, the entire composition score can be notated on staff paper. When the class is divided into three or four groups with a leader for each group, a spirit of competition evolves that is rewarding for everyone.

Can you list other group experiences your class might find pleasurable that relate to music?

Difficulty in Paying Attention

There is a theory in education that if the child is totally involved in classroom activities the problems of daydreaming and other distractions that might arise will be eliminated.

Suggestions for minimizing distractions during the music period:

1. Reduce extraneous stimuli.
    Clear desks of paper, pencils, books, and in general, all material that could distract attention from the musical activity. (This pertains to the situation in which the music class is conducted in the regular classroom and not in a music room.)

2. Keep unstructured time to a minimum.
    Avoid such time-consuming tasks as copying words and music from a chalkboard. Distribute materials quickly and strive to have overhead projectors, film projectors, and all such equipment ready and set to go. Alternate performers or performing groups. Give each child or group of children an equal opportunity to recite or perform.

3. Ask prodding questions.
    "Would you rather use drums or bells in this part of the song? Why? Does this music make you want to dance or march? Why?"

4. Make certain all visual aids or stimuli can be viewed comfortably: charts, chalkboard, bulletin board, pictures, posters, and screens for projectors.

5. Employ a variety of teaching techniques.

Avoid lectures. A variety of musical activities should be included in each lesson if possible: singing, dancing (free creative movement), listening, creating, and playing.

6. Utilize specific listening training.

Play fragments of phrases of familiar tunes on melody bells for identification: Christmas songs such as "Jingle Bells"; folk songs such as "Shoo Fly, Don't Bother Me," "Happy Birthday to You"; nursery rhyme jingles with which the children are familiar, such as "Mary Had a Little Lamb"; and game songs that are familiar, such as "Did You Ever See a Lassie?"

Can you compile your own list of children's favorite songs to be identified in this manner?

Clap the RHYTHM of the MELODY of the preceding favorite "mystery" tunes for the children to identify; then, after the tune has been identified, invite the children to clap the RHYTHM of the entire MELODY while they sing along. For a more complex development, divide the class in two groups. Have group 1 clap a steady beat and have group 2 clap the RHYTHM of the MELODY. Have both groups sing in unison while they clap their assigned rhythms. (Refer to Chapter 7, RHYTHM, p. 161, for a sample lesson of this activity presented developmentally.)

Echo clap phrases or melody patterns in a new song. Have the children select an instrumental accompaniment to use as a narrator relates a fairy tale or favorite story in folklore. (Refer to Chapter 6, MELODY, p. 130, for an example of this activity.)

Dramatize poems to an instrumental accompaniment. Divide the class into groups of four or five members. Have each group choose a favorite poem to dramatize or pantomime to the accompaniment of classroom instruments. If pantomime is chosen by groups, the children must be certain to keep secret the name of the poem their group has chosen until their classmates have been given the opportunity to "guess and tell."

Introduce listening activities in music in which children are directed to identify loud or soft passages in the composition by raising hands and in which they are directed to identify when the TEMPO of music changes by keeping time with rhythm sticks or by tapping toes and clapping hands softly.

Refer to individual Chapters for compositions recommended for listening for the elements of music: MELODY, RHYTHM, HARMONY, FORM, DYNAMICS, TEMPO, and TONE COLOR.

■ *Listening Activities Recommended for the Intermediate Level:*

> Listen for and identify the elements of music in recommended recordings. Listen to current musical hits and identify such characteristics as a repeated rhythm pattern by, perhaps, drums and string bass (ostinato). Listen for repeated melody patterns that are very obvious; for differences in DYNAMICS; and for changes in TEMPO within a composition.
>
> Use tape recorders to play back musical activities in the classroom for evaluation by the class.

7. Plan interesting music activities.

> Relate materials to children's interest: sports, school assemblies and other programs, arts, and crafts.
>
> Can you add other activities to these that are of interest to your class and that can be related to music time?

8. Use a game format.

> The rules of the singing game must be well defined: "Here We Go Looby-Loo," "Here We Go 'Round the Mulberry Bush," "Go in and Out the Window," and "Turn the Glasses Over." The game of musical chairs can be fun, but it also can cause tension and frustration. The teacher must know and understand the emotional nature of her or his children before introducing this game. Various rules can be made for playing this game: "Listen for the tonal center (home tone) and plan to arrive at a chair when you think it will be heard."

9. Use the unit-method approach.

Traditionally, educators have suggested that at least some classroom teaching be adapted to the unit approach because the unit (1) grows out of life situations (thereby rendering school experiences more meaningful to the child); (2) can develop social skills as well as subject matter mastery; and (3) integrates the various subject areas instead of reinforcing artificial boundaries.

In addition, this method seems ideally suited to the education of the exceptional child in the regular classroom:

> 1. A wide range of abilities, interests and needs can be accommodated by a carefully chosen unit.
> 2. The unit method lends itself readily to individual remedial instruction periods.
> 3. It allows the child who is less capable academically to achieve status by performing some nonacademic duties.
> 4. It fosters goal-directed activities.
> 5. It provides for physical mobility.
> 6. It fosters learning by "doing."
> 7. It can be inherently interesting and motivating.
> 8. It can tend to create a feeling of solidarity and mutual acceptance among the handicapped child and his normal classmates.[13]

[13] Ibid., p. 63.

A unit for the primary level:

Title: Music of Today and Yesterday

Reference: Wheeler, Opal, and Sybil Deucher. *Mozart the Wonder Boy.* Philadelphia, Pa.: McGraw-Hill Book Company, 1943.

This unit was developed by grade 5 of the Pike Elementary School, Pike Metropolitan School District, Indianapolis, Indiana, under the guidance of their teacher, Mrs. Mary Lou Jones. The objective is to discover our rich heritage of music through related arts.

SOCIAL STUDIES

Compare and contrast the geographical characteristics of the United States of America to Austria.

Suggested questions for encouraging children to do research for themselves:

Where is Austria on the map? Is it far from America? Where is Salzburg in Austria, Mozart's home? When Mozart was six years old, he and his sister, Nannerl, were driven by horse and carriage to Munich, Germany, to perform in their first concert. Can you find Munich on the map? Is Germany mountainous? Can you point out the mountains on the map? Would it have been a long trip from Salzburg to Munich for young Mozart traveling by horse and carriage?

Many more questions can be structured that relate to social studies. Can you list your own questions to motivate children to want to explore and discover for themselves the interesting physical features of Austria's neighboring countries?

ENGLISH AND DRAMA

After having read a biography about Mozart, have all of the children in the class contribute to the content of a script for a play to be produced as a class activity. Puppets will represent the characters: Mozart, Nannerl, mother, father, and a current popular rock, folk, or jazz group. The members of the class will represent American children who are eager to visit Salzburg, Austria, Mozart's home.

The story line of the play focuses on those American children (including the popular musical group) preparing to leave America by airplane to visit Salzburg, the birthplace of Wolfgang Amadeus Mozart. Before leaving for Austria, the children are made aware of interesting anecdotes about Mozart as a child prodigy, and they are taught to identify aurally the music of Mozart through listening to short compositions played at the keyboard by a child, as well as through recorded selections. A demonstration of the minuet, the dance of that historical era, is performed by class members.

Before leaving for Salzburg, the timetable is moved back to 1700, to show that Mozart lived long ago and that seemingly by magic we, too, will be visiting

Salzburg in 1700. The timetable is constructed of a piece of cardboard approximately 36″ in diameter and is in the design of a clock, except that the numbers on the face of the clock represent centuries. The hands of time are movable and can be manipulated to point to the time that an historical event occurred.

Example:

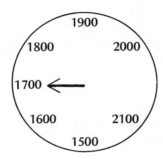

The children meet Mozart and his family (puppets) who graciously entertain them. The popular musical group from America performs their music, which seems quite loud and dissonant to the Austrian audience, who cover their ears to try to escape from sounds to which they are not accustomed. The American children realize that the musical sounds of the eighteenth century differ greatly from those of the twentieth century. After exploring and discovering for themselves the difference in sound, the children depart from Salzburg in 1700 and return to America in 2000. During the return trip to America, the entire class sings the Austrian hymn "Glorious Things of Thee Are Spoken" as a final tribute to *Mozart the Wonder Boy.*

ART

How to Make Puppets:

Puppets can be made from two Jello boxes.

1. Cover or paint both Jello boxes.

2. Insert a red felt strip for a tongue by gluing the strip on top of the thumb box.

3. Use scraps of cloth, crepe paper, and yarn to create a head and facial features, using the boxes as the base from which to work. Then, fashion the puppet's clothing, suspending it from the lower box. Refer to the illustration.

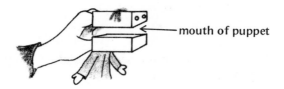

mouth of puppet

4. Puppets of the young Mozart, Nannerl, mother, and father and the music group are the principal characters. However, every child in the classroom should make a puppet to represent himself as an American child preparing to journey to Slazburg. The use of paper bag puppets (see p. 288) can serve equally as well as the Jello box puppets described above.

DANCE

These are the basic steps of the minuet: Take a partner and stand side by side. Join your inside hands. Starting on the outside foot—the foot farthest away from your partner—walk this rhythm pattern of walk, walk, walk, point. Always begin walking with the foot you have just pointed. Raise the foot slightly before taking the next step.[14]

Walk, Walk, Walk,   point

MUSIC

The prelude to the performance should be a recording of the *Jupiter Symphony*, fourth movement. The music of Mozart (some short compositions) should be performed at the keyboard by class members. Recorded compositions also should be played. The Austrian hymn "Glorious Things of Thee Are Spoken" should be sung by the entire class at the conclusion of the program.

A unit for the intermediate level:

Title: The Symphony Orchestra

This unit was developed for the intermediate grades at Pike Central Elementary School, Indianapolis, Indiana; therefore, the Indianapolis Symphony

---

[14] Edna Doll and Mary J. Nelson, *Rhythms Today!* (Morristown, N.J.: Silver Burdett, 1965), p. 97.

Orchestra was the performing group for relating the study of the instruments of the orchestra. However, any symphony orchestra in your locale could provide the center of interest for a comparable unit of study involving related arts.

SOCIAL STUDIES

Study the history of the geographical region in which the Indianapolis Symphony Orchestra was organized.

ART

Make and assemble a scale model of the orchestra; create wall murals pertaining to the symphony orchestra.

MANAGEMENT

Study the organization, management, and financial aspects of a symphony orchestra.

MUSIC

Do research of the musical sounds, design, and performing skills of the families of instruments from recordings, films, live demonstrations, charts, and so on.

Difficulty in Organizing

The minimally handicapped child with learning or behavioral problems who is enrolled in a regular classroom frequently presents a rather discouraging picture of disorganization.

The teacher, by understanding and accepting these children, by praising them for even small signs of growth in the area of organization and by striving to maintain a tension-free classroom climate, can successfully assist the child in diminishing his disorganization.[15]

Suggested activities for the music period:

Allow ample time for the children to choose or distribute classroom instruments and for them to collect the instruments at the end of the period. Encourage the children to keep their music books or materials at a specified location for easy accessibility and praise them for the slightest improvement they display in performing these tasks. Always avoid negative outbursts of disapproval when tasks are not performed satisfactorily. Rather, encourage the children to "do a better job next time" so that they can operate in a tension-free classroom.

[15] Ibid.

Difficulty in Copying Written Material

> Children presenting learning and/or behavior problems often encounter difficulty in writing. . . . Particularly troublesome to these children is the task of copying written material from the blackboard to their papers.[16]

Use any available duplicating method to avoid the need for copying musical notation, verse of songs, and any other musical data from the chalkboard.

Poor Coordination

"Most (if not all) minimally brain-injured children present some kind of coordination problems."[17]

General suggestions for improving coordination:

1. All experiences—physical education, arts and crafts, and/or academic subject areas—should move sequentially from the simple to the complex. The fundamental locomotor movements—crawling, walking, running, jumping, hopping, leaping, sliding and galloping—can be arranged sequentially. The musical activities of listening, singing, playing, dancing, and creating correlate with most areas of the curriculum and also should be approached sequentially. Art activities such as finger painting or using chalk to execute large arm movements to express the rhythmical movement of a recorded composition logically should precede work in a more limited area.

    A physical education activity might include a sequential performance of rolling a ball, bouncing a ball, and throwing a ball. Use bean bags and balloons to precede the use of hard balls, and use large balls (beach balls or playground balls) to precede small balls (tennis balls). These physical education activities can be performed while singing this song:

ROLL THAT RED BALL*

Illinois game song

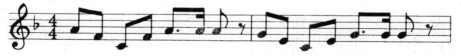

1. Roll that red ball down to town,   Roll that red ball down to town,

*Reprinted with permission from *Music for Young Americans* (Kindergarten), from the ABC MUSIC SERIES, 1963.

---

[16] Ibid., pp. 65–66.
[17] Ibid., p. 68.

Roll that red ball down to town So ear - ly in the morn - ing.

2. Bounce (etc.)
3. Throw (etc.)

In relating drama to social studies, have children pantomime pioneers "building a nation" through large body movements: felling trees, sawing logs, chopping wood, building houses, painting houses, planting corn, riding horseback, and climbing mountains.

Can you think of other activities in which pioneers helped each other?
In studying all the countries in the world, could the work habits of all peoples be represented through pantomime or dramatization? Could classroom instruments be used to imitate work sounds? Could recreational activities be interestingly pantomimed as well—ice skating, basketball, swimming, and so on? Could environmental sounds (the movement of the wind, trees, clouds and ocean waves) be interpreted by using colored nylon scarves in free rhythmic movement to appropriate sounds produced by classroom instruments?

Example:

OCEAN WAVES*

M. Lament

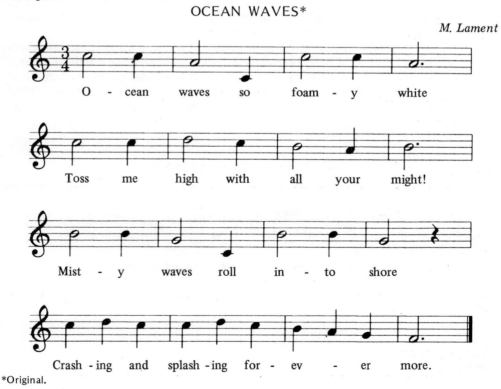

O - cean waves so foam - y white

Toss me high with all your might!

Mist - y waves roll in - to shore

Crash - ing and splash - ing for - ev - er more.

*Original.

■ *Suggested Instrumental Sounds to Accompany "Ocean Waves":*

    a.   "Swish" sand blocks and whisper "swish."

    b.   Elicit a soft resonance from finger cymbals.

    c.   Wearing a mitten or holding soft cloth, move your hand up and down the keyboard (glissando) or, holding rubber-headed mallets, perform the same movement on melody bells. (This provides the tonal effect of ocean waves rushing into shore.)

    2.   Children should pantomime the movement of animals—birds, bears, rabbits, and so on to dramatize the movement of trucks, airplanes, trains and buses.

    3.   Provide for visual perceptual training.

Example 1: Reading a symbolic musical score for rhythm instruments

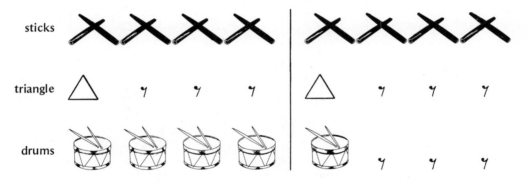

    Can you expand this brief illustration of symbolic score reading to create your own symbolic score to play as an appropriate accompaniment to any favorite song?

Example 2:

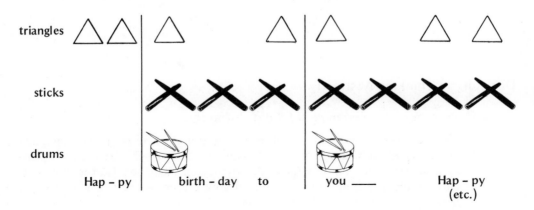

When your pupils can read this pictorial (symbolic) score satisfactorily, insert actual notation above the pictures. In that way, note reading is approached slowly in a simple-to-complex procedure.

4. Assisted by the children, make up symbolic scores for playing unconventional sounds. (Refer to Chapter 3, pp. 40–41 for sample scores of unconventional sounds.)
5. When singing cumulative songs, motivate the children to keep the song moving by using such visual aids as murals, charts, and posters that illustrate the words of the song.

Example:

Use pictures of farm animals as an aid to remembering verses of "Old MacDonald Had a Farm."

Verse 1:   Verse 2:

Verse 3:   Verse 4:

Difficulty in Thinking Abstractly

General suggestions to encourage thinking abstractly:

1. Use concrete materials. Concrete materials are experienced sensorially; hence, they are more "real" (meaningful) to children than a pure symbol or idea. They offer multisensory experiences; that is, children can touch and manipulate them. Using concrete materials motivates interest and increases attention span.

2. Use memory-promoting activities. Because the ability to conceptualize is usually impaired in handicapped children, activities that encourage memory are advised.[18]

■ *Suggested Musical Activities for the Primary Level:*

1. Identify contrasts in sound: bells jingle, but drums boom! The sound of the triangle is high, but the sound of the drum is low. Can you make up other activities that would promote noticing the differences in the sounds of musical instruments: melody, percussion, orchestral, band; differences in the singing voices of men, women, children; sounds of the environment; and so on?

2. Participate in memory games. These directions are for "Name the Missing Instrument."

    a. Children see and explore the sounds of five percussion instruments lying on a table.
    b. They close their eyes while one instrument is removed from the table.
    c. They open their eyes and try to identify the instrument that has been taken. (Repeat this game as often as desired, using different musical instruments and modifying the directions.)

For the "Name the Animals" game, follow these directions:

    a. Sing any cumulative song related to animals (or compose your own animal song such as "Barnyard Song" ("I Had a Cat") or "Old MacDonald Had a Farm."
    b. Without the help of any visual aids, ask the children to name the animals in the song in numerical order.

Can you make up other games that would be tension free but challenge children in primary grades?

3. Sort objects, pictures, classroom instruments, and so forth, by category. Let this lead to recalling a favorite song to be sung or music to be heard.

Example:

Pictures or charts can recall a familiar song:

"How Much Is That Doggie in the Window?"

---

[18] Ibid., pp. 78–79.

"Old MacDonald Had a Farm"

"My Hat, It Has Three Corners"

Vehicles of transportation, such as bus, train, airplane, and automobile suggest "When the Train Comes Along" and "The Bus" (refer to p. 306). Pictures that relate to safety, such as a policeman, traffic lights, traffic signs, and school patrol boys suggest songs to sing that are pertinent to safety rules. Refer to music textbooks available in your school. For example, see "Stop! Look! Listen!" Book I, *This Is Music* (Boston: Allyn), p. 77. 1967.

MY HAT*

German folk song

*Reprinted with permission from *Pocket Songs* Delaware(, Ohio: Cooperative Recreation Service, Inc., n.d.).

Suggestions for dramatizing the words of the song:

1. "My hat" (point to your head)
2. "three" (hold up three fingers)
3. "corners" (tip your "pretend" hat)

Charts of band instruments suggest a listening activity: any recording of marching band music, such as the compositions of John Philip Sousa.

4. Dramatize fairy tales (refer to Chapter 6, MELODY, pp. 130–131). The children can choose instruments whose sounds are appropriate to the characters in a story that is being told by a narrator. The story can be dramatized by members of the class.

Suggested listening activity:

Prokofiev: *Peter and the Wolf*

5. Make up musical riddles.

Riddle riddle riddle ree
    Tell me, can you answer me?
Tic, tac, toe, a–way we go
    I am high or I am low!

          (Ans.: Sharp sign #.)

Ping!   ping!
    I ring!   I sing!
Ping!   Ping!   ping! (Fade out.)
       (Ans.: The bell on the teacher's desk—finger cymbals.)

Kittle, kettle, riddle, reddle
    I can holler BOOM! BOOM! BOOM!
Kittle, kettle, riddle, reddle,
    I can whisper tum, tum, tum.

         (Ans.: Kettle drum.)

VER — — — — — ooo — — — — — oooooommmmm
   VER — — — — — ooo — — — — — oooooommmmm
I can harmonize and I can croon.
   VER — — — — ooo — — — — — oooooommmmm
   VER — — — — — ooo — — — — — oooooommmmm
I can even pluck a tune!

         (Ans.: Autoharp.)

6. Train the children to recognize absurdities.

■ *Suggested Musical Activities for the Primary Level:*

Sing songs and nursery rhymes with absurd lyrics:

Hey Diddle Diddle

Hey diddle diddle, the cat and the fiddle,
    The cow jumped over the moon.
The little dog laughed to see such sport,
    And the dish ran away with the spoon.

Suggested questioning techniques:

Who jumped over the moon? Could a cow jump over the moon? Where do cows live and what do they eat? Is there any other place in this song that the words seem silly? Where? What words? Why?

Baa, Baa, Black Sheep

Baa, baa, black sheep, have you an–y wool?
  "Yes, sir, yes, sir, three bags full:
One for my master and one for my dame,
  And one for the lit–tle boy that lives in the lame."

In this song, who is talking to the sheep? What is this person asking the sheep? Who answers the question? Is it likely that the question would be answered in this way? Why not?

Can you think of other songs that have silly words? Can you tell why you think the words are silly?

Camp songs: "She'll Be Comin' 'Round the Mountain," "I Went to the Animal Fair," and "Mr. Frog Went a-Courtin'"

Familiar songs: "Oh, Susannah" and "I Got Shoes"

7. Display pictures of items or objects with missing parts. After the children have identified the parts that are missing and have supplied them, conclude the activity by singing a familiar song to which the picture relates.

Example 1:

Suggested questioning techniques.

Boys and girls, why does this rabbit look so funny? Can you fill in the missing parts?

What song does this picture remind you of? ("Mister Rabbit.") Do you remember the words to the song? Can we all sing about Mr. Rabbit as someone offers to point to his ears, foot, coat, and tail? Why can't we see the bunny's tail?

MISTER RABBIT*

Southern folk song

1. "Mis - ter Rab-bit, Mis-ter Rab-bit, Your ears might-y long!"

"Yes in - deed, they're put on wrong."

Refrain:

Ev - 'ry lit - tle soul must shine, shine, shine.__

Ev - 'ry lit - tle soul must shine,__ shine, shine.

2. "Your foot's mighty red!"
   "Yes indeed, I'm almost dead."

3. "Your coat's mighty gray!"
   "Yes indeed, 'twas made that way."

4. "Your tail's mighty white!"
   "Yes indeed, I'm going out of sight."

*Public domain. From Making Music Your Own BK I. Courtesy of General Learning Corporation.

Example 2:

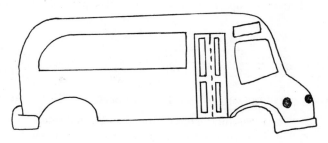

Suggested questioning techniques:

What does this picture look like? If you think it looks like the frame of a yellow school bus, what parts of the bus are missing?

(Ans.: wheels, driver, children, windows, and window wiper.)

Now that we've made our school bus complete, let's sing our song about "The Bus."

THE BUS*

Play song

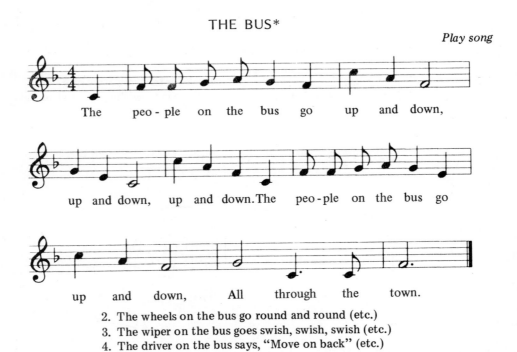

The peo-ple on the bus go up and down,

up and down, up and down. The peo-ple on the bus go

up and down, All through the town.

2. The wheels on the bus go round and round (etc.)
3. The wiper on the bus goes swish, swish, swish (etc.)
4. The driver on the bus says, "Move on back" (etc.)

*From *Singing On Our Way* of OUR SINGING WORLD series, © Copyright, 1959, 1957, 1949, by Ginn and Company. Used with permission.

Can we see the horn on the bus? No, but do we ever hear it? How does it sound? (Sing the song again, making the sound of the horn on the school bus.)

■ *Suggested Musical Activities for the Intermediate Level:*

a. Add bar lines at the proper places on this musical staff by grouping the quarter (♩) notes in sets of three.

Here is an illustration of how the problem was solved:

Continue by underlining the correct answer to the following questions:
What sign in this musical example tells you to group in sets of three?

(a) sharp (♯) sign (b) flat (♭) sign (c) <u>meter or time sign</u> (¾)

Which number of the time sign (top or bottom) tells you to group in sets of three?

(a) <u>top number</u> (b) bottom number

b. Add bar lines at the proper places on this musical staff by grouping the notation in sets of three.

Here is an illustration of how the problem was solved:

Continue to underline the correct answer to the following questions: (For the purpose of reinforcement use the same questions as in step a.)
What sign in this musical example tells you to group in sets of three?

(a) meter or time sign   (b) flat (♭) sign   (c) sharp (♯) sign

Which number of the time sign (top or bottom) tells you to group in sets of three?

(a) bottom number   (b) top number

(For the purpose of introducing new thought-provoking questions add the following, or similar, queries.)

This note ♩ is called a

(a) whole note   (b) quarter note   (c) half note

This sign 𝄽 is called a

(a) sharp   (b) rest   (c) flat

Note:

After sufficiently reviewing the classroom music lessons, structure similar problems, moving from the simple to the complex, to stimulate the recall of previous music lessons without causing frustration.

c.   Play the game "Jumbled Jingles."

Display the notated fragments of three familiar melodies:

Sing "Jingle Bells" and design the direction of the song using hand levels. Identify the staff on which a fragment of "Jingle Bells" is notated. (Staff 1.)

Can you think of other challenging musical activities to encourage abstract thinking in a tension-free environment?

Note:

Activities should be introduced developmentally.

8. Recognize which sounds are different and which sounds, words, and actions are alike.

   Examples:

   a. Sing different words to the tune of a familiar MELODY: "Merrily We Roll Along" uses same tune as "Mary Had a Little Lamb." Use these questioning techniques: What is the name of this song as you first learned it? ("Mary Had a Little Lamb.") What are the words to this song as you first learned it? Can we all sing it together? Can we sing and play the song together on melody bells? (Rotate the melody bells so that all the children will have an opportunity to play them if a set is not available to each child.)

   b. Play the game of "Detective."
      A blindfolded child searches for claves or castanets in a shoebox filled mostly with rhythm sticks. (Refer to p. 49 for illustrations of these instruments.) The child wins when he or she identifies the claves or castanets by touch and sound.

   Note:

      This game can be played using different combinations of instruments. Also, the game rules can be modified using the children's ideas.

■ *Suggested Musical Activities for the Intermediate Level:*

   a. Sing familiar songs or listen to recordings and identify whether the music moves in sets of 2s, 3s, or 4s by tapping along with the music and listening for the accented beat. How will you tap the accented beat, loudly or soft? How many weak beats follow the accented beat? If the accented beat is followed by two weak beats, how would you say the music moves? (In sets of 3s.)

   b. Divide the class into groups of eight and learn to perform square dances following specific directions for the familiar "Duck for the Oyster" or "Take a Little Peek" or a song of your own choice. Then, listening to a current popular recording, have everyone in class (teacher included) move independently to the sound of the music. How does this independent dancing differ from square dancing?

9. Strive to strengthen concepts.
   Suggested musical activities relating to the elements of music, including sample questioning techniques for exploring the concept, appear here.

Examples:

(1)   Element: MELODY

(For a more detailed analysis of concepts relating to the elements of music and their components, refer to the sample lessons in Chapters 6 through 10, including lessons for the intermediate level.)

Sing a new or familiar song. Sing the song again and design it in the air. How does the song move? Up? Down? Does it ever move straight ahead? On what words?

(2)   Element: RHYTHM

Choose a classroom percussion instrument and tap along as you listen to the music. Was your tapping jerky or steady? Was your tapping even or uneven? Were you tapping the steady beat of the music or the RHYTHM of the MELODY?

Divide the class into two groups. Have group 1 tap a steady beat and group 2 tap the RHYTHM of the MELODY. Repeat the activity with group 2 tapping the RHYTHM of the MELODY and group 1 tapping the steady beat.

(3)   Element: HARMONY

Sing "Are You Sleeping?" while strumming autoharps. Push down the C button for the entire song. Did you sing what was being played on the autoharp? If the MELODY you were singing was different from what was being played on the auto-harp, why did the performance sound good? Would you say all of the sounds fit together or blended well? In music, what do we call it when many different tones heard at the same time blend well together? (HARMONY.)

(4)   Element: FORM

Sing "Twinkle, Twinkle Little Star." Sing the song again and raise your hand if you hear a part that is repeated. Were there any parts of this song that were repeated? Which words were repeated? Were the words and the MELODY ever repeated?

Sing the song third time and raise your hand at the end of each section. How many sections or parts are there? (Three.) Which part is repeated? (Part 1.) Which part is different? (Part 2.) If you were to give these sections letter names, what would they be?

part 1 = A
part 2 = B
part 3 = A (because part 1 is repeated)

In music what do we call the plan, or design, of the music? (FORM.)

(5)   Element: DYNAMICS

Sing "Mister Rabbit" (p. 305.) Pretend that you are holding a bunny in your arms. How does it feel? Does a bunny's fur feel soft? How does a bunny hop? Lightly? Can you show me how a bunny hops by making your hands bounce on your knees? Does the bunny make a loud noise when he hops? Can you sing this song again softly?

(6) Element: TEMPO

How does a fire truck move when it is being driven to a fire? (Fast.) Choose classroom instruments that imitate the sound of fire trucks racing to a fire.

(Have five members of the class form a line, one behind the other, holding on to the shoulders of the child in front, while one child pretends to be a fire truck answering a fire call.) Move around the classroom to the accompaniment of the "sounds" of the fire truck. Will you move fast or slow? Can you think of animals that move slowly? Can you think of some animals that move fast? Can you name animals that can move fast and slowly? Take turns pretending that you are any animal of your choice. Move around the room as that animal moves in the jungle or forest while the rest of the class guesses which animal you are.

(7) Element: TONE COLOR

Sing "Listen to the Rain" (p. 82). Choose classroom instruments that, when played, imitate the sound of raindrops as they fall:

against a window pane =	triangle or finger cymbals
on the roof =	fingertips on a small drumhead or tambourine
on the porch =	hand on a large drumhead
on a rain barrel or an empty box =	hand on a large conga drum

In music, TONE COLOR can be described as the sounds heard from different instruments as well as the differences in the sounds of voices: man, woman, child, baby, and vocal groups.

Behavior Problems

■ *Suggested Activities for Maintaining Favorable Behavior on the Primary Level:*

1. The teacher should avoid too much talking, but, rather, should encourage children through questioning techniques and other guidance procedures, to make up their own rules for appropriate conduct when listening to music or singing a song; when distributing and collecting classroom instruments or song books and ideas, and when holding instruments before it is time to play them. To maintain discipline in the classroom, use a cue for attention: shake maracas or ring jingle bells.

2. Periodically, the children and the teacher should sit in a circle (even on the floor in a circle at times) for music time, rather than keep the conventional seating arrangement. Sitting in a circle projects a feeling of total involvement.

3. Attention wanes and behavior problems often begin when activities do not involve everyone. Use songs that attract attention and encourage involvement. Counting songs incorporate the independent use of classroom instruments which are played as specific numbers are sung: "One Little, Two Little, Three Little Indians"; "One, Two, Buckle My Shoe"; "There Was One, There Were Two, There Were Three Little Angels"; and "My Hat, It Has Three Corners."

Can you create your own ideas for finger plays or dramatizing the words of these songs to the accompaniment of classroom instruments?

Some song activities demand attention when they are performed.

Example:

Sing "Twinkle, Twinkle, Little Star."

a. Distribute triangles and finger cymbals at random.
b. Appoint a conductor to use a baton to cue the children to play the instruments one at a time.
c. Simultaneously, have the entire class sing "Twinkle, Twinkle Little Star." Rotate the instruments so that all the children have an opportunity to play.

Scale songs can be played on melody bells, resonator bells, and piano keyboard. (Refer to pp. 137–139 for examples of scale songs.)

THE ANGEL BAND*

South Carolina folk song

There was one, there were two, there were three lit - tle an - gels,
There were four, there were five, there were six lit - tle an - gels,
There were seven, there were eight, there were nine lit - tle an - gels.

Ten lit - tle___ an - gels in the band._____

Refrain:

Oh, was-n't that a band, Sun - day morn - ing, Sun - day

*"THE ANGEL BAND" from "36 South Carolina Spirituals" by Carl Diton copyright 1930, 1957 by G. Schirmer, Inc. Used by permission.

morn - ing, Sun - day morn - ing? Was-n't that a band,

Sun - day morn - ing, Sun - day morn - ing soon?____

THREE BLUE PIGEONS*

American folk song

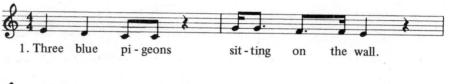

1. Three blue pi - geons sit - ting on the wall.

Three blue pi - geons sit - ting on the wall.

Spoken: One flew away. O-o-oh!

2. Two blue pigeons sitting on the wall.
   Two blue pigeons sitting on the wall.
   Spoken: Another flew away.
   O-O-o-o-oh!

3. One blue pigeon sitting on the wall.
   One blue pigeon sitting on the wall.
   Spoken: And the third flew away!
   O-o-o-o-o-o-oh!

4. No blue pigeons sitting on the wall.
   No blue pigeons sitting on the wall.
   Spoken: One flew back.
   Whee-ee-ee!

5. One blue pigeon sitting on the wall.
   One blue pigeon sitting on the wall.
   Spoken: Another flew back.
   Whee-ee-ee!

6. Two blue pigeons sitting on the wall.
   Two blue pigeons sitting on the wall.
   Spoken: And the third flew back!
   Whee-ee-ee-ee!

7. Three blue pigeons sitting on the wall.
   Three blue pigeons sitting on the wall.

*Public domain. Courtesy of General Learning Corporation.

    a. Have every child make a finger puppet by pasting a bird seal or a picture of a bird on three fingers:

b. Place three movable pigeons on a wall on a flannel board or chart.

c. On the words "one flew away," remove a pigeon from the chart. Make him fly away while the members of the class at their seats pretend that a bird finger puppet is flying away.

d. Make the pigeons "return home" when the appropriate words of the song are sung.

Some finger plays (songs and chants) demand attention when performing:

Examples:

"Put Your Finger in the Air"

"Eensy, Weensy Spider"

"My Hands"

Can you think of other finger plays that are fun to perform? Can you make up your own MELODY to the words?

■ *Suggested Musical Activities for Maintaining Favorable Behavior on the Intermediate Level:*

Use Latin-American instruments in the performance of such songs as "Yellow Bird," "Marianne," and "Jamaican Farewell." (Refer to Chapter 7, RHYTHM, p. 163, for a sample of simple-to-complex procedures for using these instruments.)

Songs of ethnic groups incorporate simple folk dancing and use classroom instruments for appropriate tonal effects.

Note:

Emphasize music activities that are easy but whose performance is effective for teaching. Most often, children are impatient and respond negatively to activities that are too challenging and that require concentrated attention for a long period of time. Proceed cautiously with developmental procedures.

Social Immaturity

All of the preceding suggestions for correlating a music education program to the needs of handicapped children in a regular classroom situation can promote growth in social maturation.

Siegel states that "Activities which stress listening, auditory memory, various language concepts, and correct articulation are recommended."[19] The following suggestions for musical activities support this statement.

1. Through guidance in listening activities, children can learn to discriminate among sounds of the environment, unconventional sounds, and sounds of classroom and orchestral instruments. Through listening, children can also become discriminative in identifying sounds that are loud and soft, fast and slow, like and unlike, and so forth. They will become more articulate in verbalizing ideas or concepts relating to these sounds.

Note:

To foster development in the art of communication, the teacher can encourage the child to express himself more clearly by using complete sentences rather than one-word answers. To promote this skill, the teacher can incorporate questioning techniques or activities (dramatics, oral reports, and oral descriptive analyses) that require verbal responses to which the child will react spontaneously. These activities can relate to all musical activities: singing, playing, listening, dancing (creative movement), and creating.

2. Auditory memory is encouraged through echo games.

    a. Imitate or echo clap the rhythmic patterns tapped on a drum or tom-tom by the teacher or a classmate.
    b. Repeat or echo sing short melody patterns intoned by the teacher and then try to identify the song. When successful, sing the entire song. Instead of always echo singing the melody patterns, try to play them on the melody bells.

3. Social skills can be developed through such musical activities as folk dancing, square dancing, the unit method of work, playing classroom instruments together, incorporating a "buddy" system in learning how

---

[19] Ibid., p. 98.

to play some classroom instruments (autoharp and piano—classroom keyboard experiences—melody bells, and bongos) and all instruments that are appropriate for promoting a one-to-one relationship or a group relationship.

"A mildly handicapped child in the regular classroom may need lots of experience socializing with one child before being ready for group socialization. The teacher can encourage such a one-to-one relationship by judicious seating and grouping—committee assignments during units of work, 'buddy' system, etc."[20]

SUMMARY

In conclusion, it seems appropriate to list the most important factors in learning as cited by Samuel A. Kirk:

1. Progress is from the known to the unknown, using concrete material to foster understanding of more abstract facts.
2. The child is helped to transfer known abilities from one situation to another, rather than being expected to make generalization spontaneously.
3. The teacher uses many repetitions in a variety of experiences.
4. Learning is stimulated through exciting situations.
5. Inhibitions are avoided by presenting one idea at a time and presenting learning situations by sequential steps.
6. Learning is reinforced through using a variety of sense modalities—visual, oral auditory, kinesthetic.[21]

However, Siegel notes that these principles should be regarded merely as guidelines and urges the teacher to be aware of when and how they should be modified to coincide with prevailing circumstances and situations. For example, learning is not necessarily stimulated through exciting situations, especially in the case of hyperactive children who have been stimulated or disturbed by a variety of activities or experiences prior to the learning situation.[22]

---

[20] Ibid., p. 102.
[21] Samuel A. Kirk, *Educating Exceptional Children* (Boston: Houghton, 1962), pp. 120–121.
[22] Siegel, op. cit., p. 83.

Bibliography

Books

"American Indian." *The World Book Encyclopedia.* Vol. 10, 1972.

Aronoff, Frances Webber. *Music and Young Children.* New York: Holt, Rinehart & Winston, Inc., 1969.

Barksdale, Lena, ed. "Counting-Out Rhyme." *In The Treasure Bag.* New York: Alfred A. Knopf, Inc., 1947.

Bergethon, Bjornar, and Eunice Boardman. *Musical Growth in the Elementary School.* 2nd ed. New York: Holt, Rinehart & Winston, Inc., 1970.

Birge, Edward. *History of Public School Music in the United States.* Boston: Oliver Ditson Company, 1928.

Bloom, Benjamin, ed. *Taxonomy of Educational Objectives: Cognitive Domain.* New York: David McKay Co., Inc., 1956.

Broudy, Harry S. "The Case for Aesthetic Education," *Documentary Report of the Tanglewood Symposium.* Ed. by Robert A. Choate. Washington, D.C.: Music Educators National Conference, 1968.

Bruner, Jerome. *The Process of Education.* Cambridge: Harvard University Press. 1960.

Burgess, Evangeline. *Values in Early Childhood Education.* Washington, D.C.: National Education Association, 1965.

Carpenter, Ethelouise. "Readiness Is Being." *Early Childhood—Crucial Years for Learning.* Ed. by Margaret Rasmussen. Washington, D.C.: Association for Childhood Education International, 1966.

Cartwright, Dorwin, and A. Zander. *Group Dynamics.* New York: Harper and Row, Publishers, 1953.

Comstock, Nan, ed. *McCall's Golden Do-It Book.* New York: Golden Press, 1969.

Conant, James B. *The Education of American Teachers.* New York: McGraw-Hill Book Company, 1963.

Cook, Lloyd Allen. *Intergroup Education.* New York: McGraw-Hill Book Company, 1954.

Cox, Artelia Moore. *Arts and Crafts Are More Than Fun in Special Education.* Danville, Ill.: The Interstate Printers and Publishers, Inc., 1970.

Dimondstein, Geraldine. *Children Dance in the Classroom.* New York: The Macmillan Company, 1971.

Doll, Edna, and Mary J. Nelson. *Rhythms Today!* Morristown, N. J.: Silver Burdett Company, 1965.

Gabriel, John. *Children Growing Up.* London: University of London Press Ltd., 1969.

Garretson, Robert L. *Music in Childhood Education.* New York: Appleton–Century–Crofts, 1966.

Gary, Charles (ed.). *The Study of Music in the Elementary School—A Conceptual Approach.* Washington, D.C.: Music Educators National Conference, 1967.

Grant, Parks. *Music for Elementary Teachers.* New York: Appleton–Century–Crofts, 1960.

Hartshorn, William C. "The Role of Listening." *Basic Concepts in Music Education.* Ed. by Nelson B. Henry. Chicago: University of Chicago Press, 1958.

Jordan, Thomas E. *The Exceptional Child.* Columbus, Ohio: Charles E. Merrill, Publishers, 1962.

Kirk, Samuel A. *Educating Exceptional Children.* Boston: Houghton Mifflin Company, 1962.

Krathwohl, David, et al. *Taxonomy of Educational Objectives: Affective Domain.* New York: David McKay Co., Inc., 1964.

Leeper, Sarah Hammond, et al. *Good Schools for Young Children.* 3rd ed. New York: The Macmillan Company, 1974.

Leonard, Charles, and Robert House. *Foundations of Music Education.* New York: McGraw-Hill Book Company, 1959.

McCall, Adeline. *This Is Music for Kindergarten and Nursery School.* Boston: Allyn & Bacon, Inc., 1966.

Mager, Robert. *Preparing Instructional Objectives.* Palo Alto, Calif.: Fearon Publishers, 1962.

Martin, Samuel, and Hugh Borton. "Japanese Literature." *The World Book Encyclopedia.* Vol. 11, 1972.

Marsh, Mary Val. *Explore and Discover Music.* New York: The Macmillan Company, 1970.

Mukerji, Rose. "Roots in Early Childhood for Continuous Learning." *Early Childhood—Crucial Years for Learning.* Ed. by Margaret Rasmussen. Washington, D.C.: Association for Childhood Education International, 1966.

Mursell, James J. *Education for Musical Growth.* Boston: Ginn and Company, 1948.

National Society for the Study of Education. "Basic Concepts in Music Education." Chicago: University of Chicago Press, 1958.

Nye, Robert, and Verna Nye. *Music in the Elementary School.* Englewood Cliffs, N. J.: Prentice-Hall, Inc., 1970.

Packman, Martin. "Jamaica." *The World Book Encyclopedia.* Vol. 11, 1972.

Piaget, Jean. *Judgment and Reasoning in the Child.* New York: Harcourt Brace Jovanovich, Inc., 1928.

Preston, Ralph C. *Teaching Social Studies in the Elementary School.* New York: Holt, Rinehart & Winston, Inc., 1958.

Raebeck, Lois, and Lawrence Wheeler. *New Approaches to Music in the Elementary School.* Dubuque, Ia.: William C. Brown Company, Publishers, 1969.

Siegel, Ernest. *Special Education in the Regular Classroom.* New York: The John Day Company, Inc., 1969.

Starkey, Otis P. "Caribbean Sea." *The World Book Encyclopedia.* Vol. 3, 1972.

Swanson, Bessie. *Music in the Education of Children.* Belmont, Calif.: Wadsworth Publishing Co., Inc., 1969.

Symonds, Percival M. *What Education Has To Learn from Psychology.* 3rd ed. New York: Teachers College Press, 1968.

Tannenbaum, Abraham J. ed. *Special Education and Programs for Disadvantaged Children and Youth.* Washington, D.C.: The Council For Exceptional Children, 1968.

Tellstrom, A. Theodore. *Music in American Education.* New York: Holt, Rinehart & Winston, Inc., 1971.

Wheeler, Lawrence, and Lois Raebeck. *Orff and Kodaly Adapted for the Elementary School.* Dubuque, Ia.: William C. Brown Company, Publishers, 1972.

Widmer, Emma Louise. *The Critical Years: Early Childhood at the Crossroads.* Scranton, Pa.: International Textbook Company, 1970.

Wilson, Knox. "Folklore in the United States." *The World Book Encyclopedia.* Vol. 7, 1972.

Woodruff, Asahel D. *Basic Concepts of Teaching.* San Francisco: Chandler Publishing Co., 1961.

Periodicals

Benn, Oleta. "The Place of Music in a Technological World." *Music Educators Journal,* XLV (Feb. 1959), 29-33.

Broudy, Harry S. "Educational Theory and the Music Curriculum." *Music Educators Journal,* LI (Nov.-Dec. 1964), 32-36; 140-144.

Educational Policies Commission. "The Role of the Fine Arts in Education." *Music Educators Journal,* LV (Oct. 1968), 27-31.

Kaplan, Max. "Music Education and National Goals." *Music Educators Journal,* XLIX (April-May, 1963), 33-36.

Michel, Donald E. "Filling a Special Need." *Music Educators Journal,* 58 (April 1972), 7.

MENC and American Association of School Administrators. "Music in the School Curriculum." *Perspectives in Music Education* (Washington, D.C.: 1966), 194-198.

Reimer, Bennet. "Developing Aesthetic Sensitivity." *Music Educators Journal,* LI (Jan. 1965), 33-36.

——. "What Music Cannot Do." *Music Educators Journal,* XLVI (Sept. 1959), 40-45.

Sand, Ole. "Schools for the Seventies." *Music Educators Journal,* LII (June-July 1966), 40-42; 122-128.

Schwardron, Abraham A. "Aesthetic Values and Music Education." *Perspectives in Music Education* (Washington, D.C., 1966), 185-194.

Taylor, Harold. "Music As a Source of Knowledge." *Music Educators Journal,* LI (Sept.-Oct. 1964), 35-38; 151-154.

Van Bodegraven, Paul. "Music Education in Transition." *Perspectives in Music Education* (Washington, D.C., 1966), 19-41.

Woodruff, Asahel D., et al. "How Music Concepts Are Developed—And How They Are Applied." *Music Educators Journal,* LVI (Feb. 1970), 51-58.

Article

Heimann, Hope M., et al. "Profile, The Child 3-5." *Music in Early Childhood Study.* Atlanta, Ga.: MENC National Commission on Instruction, 1972. (mimeographed).

Appendix

Publishers of Current Elementary Music Textbooks

Allyn and Bacon, Inc., 470 Atlantic Avenue, Boston, Massachusetts 02210

American Book Company, 430 West 33rd Street, New York, New York 10001

Follett Educational Corporation, 1010 W. Washington Boulevard, Chicago, Illinois 60607

Ginn and Company, 191 Spring Street, Lexington, Massachusetts 02173

Holt, Rinehart & Winston, Inc., 383 Madison Avenue, New York, New York 10017

Macmillan Publishing Company, c/o School Division, 866 Third Avenue, New York 10022

General Learning Corporation, Silver Burdett Publishing, 250 James Street, Morristown, New Jersey 07966.

Publishers of Choral Music

Educational Music Bureau, Inc., 434 South Wabash Avenue, Chicago, Illinois 60605 (dealers in choral music)

Neil A. Kjos Music Company, 525 Busse, Park Ridge, Illinois 60068

J. W. Pepper & Son, Inc., 231 North Third Street, Philadelphia, Pennsylvania 19106 (dealers in choral music)

Theodore Presser Company, Presser Place, Bryn Mawr, Pennsylvania 19010

G. Schirmer, Inc., 609 Fifth Avenue, New York, New York 10017

Schmitt, Hall & McCreary Company, 527 Park Avenue, Minneapolis, Minnesota 55415

Shawnee Press, Inc., Delaware Water Gap, Pennsylvania 18327

Willis Music Co., 440 Main Street, Cincinnati, Ohio 45202

Index of Musical Terms

DATE DUE

DEMCO, INC. 38-2931